John Macgregor

Through the Buffer State

A Record of Recent Travels through Borneo, Siam and Cambodia

John Macgregor

Through the Buffer State
A Record of Recent Travels through Borneo, Siam and Cambodia

ISBN/EAN: 9783744757584

Printed in Europe, USA, Canada, Australia, Japan

Cover: Foto ©Andreas Hilbeck / pixelio.de

More available books at **www.hansebooks.com**

THROUGH THE BUFFER STATE

A RECORD OF RECENT TRAVELS THROUGH

BORNEO, SIAM, AND CAMBODIA

BY

SURGEON-MAJOR JOHN MACGREGOR, M.D.
INDIAN MEDICAL SERVICE
AUTHOR OF
'THE GIRDLE OF THE GLOBE,' A DESCRIPTIVE POEM IN TEN CANTOS;
'TOIL AND TRAVEL,' A PROSE NARRATIVE, ETC.

'To me more dear, congenial to my heart,
One native charm than all the gloss of art'
GOLDSMITH

LONDON
F. V. WHITE & CO.
14 BEDFORD STREET, STRAND, W.C.
1896

All rights reserved

DEDICATED

TO HIS ROYAL HIGHNESS

PRINCE KROMMUN DAMRONG

MINISTER OF THE INTERIOR OF THE REMOTE KINGDOM

OF THE WHITE ELEPHANT

BY

JOHN MACGREGOR

PREFACE

JUST as this book is issuing from the press, the entanglements of the Buffer State are being amicably settled between Great Britain and France. And as the French have had it all their own way, it is to be hoped they will generously release the poor patriot, Phra Yott, who was sentenced, when I was travelling through the country, to twenty years of penal servitude for the fearful crime of defending his native land, and whose name is mentioned more than once in the following pages. Far be it from the purpose of this volume to suspect the prophetic foresight of the powers that be in coming to this agreement with France, but there is no doubt it has taken people of all political opinions by great surprise.

We have handed over to France the British province of MONGSIN, formerly belonging to Upper Burmah, and are withdrawing our outposts there. We have also agreed to France wresting from Siam the provinces of ANGKOR and BATTAMBONG, through both of which I travelled about the time of the Franco-Siamese crisis, and which are two of the most important provinces throughout all Siam. It is in the Province of Angkor that the wonderful but little known ruins of Angkor-Wát are situated; and they are described in detail in this volume. And not only this, but France has also acquired the town of CHANTABOON (as well as the surrounding province), near the Gulf of

Siam; and the town of Chantaboon is the most flourishing port in the country with the single exception of the capital town of Bangkok itself. (*Vide* map, page 54.) We can only hope that this so-called '*Rapprochement*' with France will lead to the good understanding which we would all wish to see between the two countries.

J. MACGREGOR.

London: *February* 3, 1896.

CONTENTS

CHAPTER I

The Pamirs and Persia—The Land of the White Elephant—The 'Rajah Brooke'—A Tumbling Sea—Infallible Cure for Sea-sickness—Arrival in Borneo—Reception at Kuching—The Rajah of Sarāwak—Courtship at Kuching—Collision of the 'Little 'Un'—Trip up the Sadong—Orang-outang and Long-nosed Monkeys 1

CHAPTER II

The Sago Palms—Trip to Interior—The Mines of Tegōra—Underground Caves—'For oh, it was so dark, so dark'—Subterranean Stream—A Tight-fitting Passage—Edible Birds'-nests—Their Peculiarity—The Birds that Build them—The *jam-jam* of John Chinaman 8

CHAPTER III

A Rough Climb—The Dyaks at Home—Their Village Golgothas—Their Head-hunting Sports—Same Suppressed by the First Rajah Brooke—Deafening Gongs—Dancing with the Dyaks—The Remote Missionary—Parting with Mr. D——The Battang Paths of Borneo—The Pitcher-plants and Traveller's Palms—Their Uselessness 16

CHAPTER IV

A Sloppy March—Bloodthirsty Leeches—An Awkward Tumble—A Planter on the Mountain Side—Abdoola the Laggard—Climbing Serappi—A Misleading Aneroid—Technicalities of Tea—Monkey-brand Coffee—Return to Kuching—Story of 'Dr. Meyer from Melbourne'—Farewell to Sarāwak . . 24

CHAPTER V

Remarks on Sarāwak—The Original Rajah Brooke—His Roving Disposition—His Hatred of John Company—The Projected 'Schooner'—Discouraged by his Father—His First Cruise—He tried again, and became a King!—His Father's Death—Remarks on the relative value of Wealth and Friendship—The Rajah's Character and Chequered Career—Murder of Muda Hassim—Ross, the King of the Cocos Islands . . 34

CHAPTER VI

Return to Singapore—The steamship 'Independent'—My German shipmates—Chinese Chow-Chow—Frightening evil spirits—Gregorivitch, the Russian officer—Arrival at Bangkok—Jackson the pilot—'Don't you smell it?'—Ocean-butterfly Fort—The 'John Baptist Say'—French and British men-o'-war at Bangkok—Chinese New Year—The British Flag—King Chulalongkorn—Description of Bangkok—My Dutch 'Casual'—Toasting the German Emperor—Visit to Koh-si-chang—Landing there of French troops—The Siamese Navy 46

CHAPTER VII

Captain Bertuzzi—Away for Phrabāt—The Menam River—Swarming with Fish—Arrival at Ayouthia—Chang the Chinaman—Tramp to Phrabāt—'Gie's Peebles for Pleesure'—The Din in the Distance—The Priests and the Players—Don't Sleep on the Outskirts—The Nose and the Conscience 66

CHAPTER VIII

Toilet *al fresco*—Chang with the Hare-lip—His Vanity—An Unsuspected Stranger—Comparisons of Languages—Buddhism a Religion of toleration—Visit to the Real Phrabāt or Sacred Footprint—Watching the Worshippers—History of Phrabāt—First discovered by a king—Defects of the Footprint—'A Blind Man's Blot'—Description of the Buddha—Judging his size by Inductive Philosophy 75

CHAPTER IX

Return from the Shrine—'My Father was an Englishman'—Lost sight of the Missionary—The Menam a Misnomer—The ex-tutor of the Crown Prince—Captain Bertuzzi Imprisoned—West and Vālloo—Search for Passports—The

Royal Palace—The Emerald Buddha—Prince Damrong—
White Elephants—Trial of Phra Yott—Short Cut to the
Millennium 87

CHAPTER X

Phra Yott continued—The charges against him—Their punishments—Siamese judges—Prince Bitchit—Phlegmacy of Asiatics—Its moral effects—Chewing the cud—Moors and Arabs
in Europe—The smoking lady 99

CHAPTER XI

My passports at last—Departure from Bangkok—Supplies left
behind—Landing at Paknām—Uncomfortable cabin—Disturbing influences—A welcome message—Reach Pechim—
Corporal of the Guard—Chowmuang of Pechim—Twenty
sons and thirty daughters—Prolific royalties—The strolling
players—Siamese superstitions 104

CHAPTER XII

'March, march, Ettrick and Teviotdale'—Bivouac in Open
Fields—The Läos Mountains—A Melting Atmosphere—Vil-
lage of Chandakān—Initiating Priests—Straggling Bullocks
—Country Waggons and Country Tracts—The Forbidding
Mudfish—Tactics of Tactoo—Its Geographical Distribution—
A new-born Baby—Vicarious Lying-in—A Dying Sufferer—
The Evils of Quackery 116

CHAPTER XIII

West and his ghost stories—Warlocks of Wattaná—Their *Aqua
fontana*—Siamese shanties—Dropsy and its diagnosis—
Love-making philtres—The prowling Pontianas—'Gog-og-
oo!'—Pontianas pursuing West—Arrival at Arrānh—Origin
of 'Farrang'—Crossing the watershed—A gay villager—A
modern distillery—The web and the weaver—A bantering
wife—The Lady of Läos 126

CHAPTER XIV

The parasitic parricide—Its mode of germination—Two-tree
Tank—Abandoned village—Foul-drinking water—Dissensions
in the camp—'Amn't I a man, too?'—A bump on the rump
—Välloo, the dark delinquent—Forest camp-fire—Välloo
vanishes—The Tragedy of an Omelette—Välloo recovered—
Helplessness of native coolies 136

CHAPTER XV

Arrival at Sisophon—The ancient Kingdom of Kumĕr—Sisophon a frontier garrison town—Scarcity of water—Where now the Pitcher-plants of Borneo?—Cocoanut milk as a substitute for water—Village of Penhom-Sok—Going astray—The young Chowmuang—China a paradox—Ceremony of Kohnchúk—Monster bird with four legs—A Chinaman and his wives—Milk at a discount—Reach Siäm-Réäp . . . 145

CHAPTER XVI

Ancient ruins of Angkor-Wát—March thereto—Don Quixote and Sancho Panza—A plague of Mosquitoes—The Moon being eaten by Rahú—Description of Rahú by Father Sangermano—His great size—Not big enough to swallow the Moon—A partial Eclipse—Invisible at Greenwich—Angkor-Wát relegated to Owls and Bats—Though I ate the Lotus I did not forget my Country! 156

CHAPTER XVII

Description of Angkor-Wát Ruins—Its Ancient Grandeur—Its Bas-reliefs—An old world Tug-of-war—An undeciphered Tablet—*Bomb-bomb*—Scattered Sculptures — Angkor-Thóm—Rozinante comes down—Angkor-Wát Built by Angels—Compared with Borobodo in Java—Borobodo a Buddhist Shrine—Overlapping of Symbolic Sculptures—The same of Religious Forms—The Theory of Evolution and Devolution—The Cannibal who first ate an Oyster—First View of Telé-Sáp—The 'Roderick Dhu' and the 'Lady of the Lake' . 163

CHAPTER XVIII

Mirage Village—Wife 'o'er the Border'—An afternoon Visit—Kampong-Khām—Native fishing-nets—A rough day's work—Tyndall and the sound of falling Waters—Relapsing into utter Barbarism—*Charab*, the Chatterer—Reach region of Modern Cambodia—Prĕäm-Préstong—Fishing *à la mode* with the Boat's Tiller—Trawling and other Methods—Pelicans and 'The Ancient Mariner'—*Charab*, the Jingo—Cast away at Night-time—Mode of Mooring Boats—It's all Specific Gravity 179

CHAPTER XIX

Landing at Chunnok-Tréän—Chinese praying paper—Why do devils wear shoes?—Outlets of Telé-Sáp—General remarks on ditto—Telé-Sáp's future prospects—The Giantess and the

Pig—A truant husband—Floating down the river—Reach Kampong-Chenáng—A French frontier village—Reception by the French—Where, where was Captain Bertuzzi now?—Mispronunciation—'Mussoo, Mussoo Docteur'—Steam launch 'Cambodge'—Arrival at Penhom-Penh—English the coming Volapuk—But Gaelic shall never die . . . 190

CHAPTER XX

Description of Penhom-Penh—What is a pagoda?—A work of merit—Promotion to Nirvana—Effects of pagodas on scenery—The great pagoda of Penhom-Penh—French Governor of the Kingdom of Cambodia—Atenuse, my *secrétaire peculier*—Royal palace of Penhom-Penh—*Kohn-Chuk* again—King Norōdom the Second—His habits of life—Unable to visit him—Luang-Prabang—View of the Buffer State . 202

CHAPTER XXI

Farewell to Penhom-Penh—In England they drink scandal and tea—In France, coffee and brandy—The 'Nam-vian'—The Irrawaddy and the Mekong compared—Shallow coast of Cochin-China—Reach Saigon—The Café Anglais—Noor Khan the Mohammedan—The steamship 'Schwalbe'—Commercial interests of Great Britain and France in Siam—Progressive character of the Siamese—What to do with the servants—Vālloo turns trump—Becomes a Frenchman—A peculiar advocate—The town of Saigon—British bunkum . 208

CHAPTER XXII

Vālloo converted against his will—Bite of a mad dog—Vālloo again in trouble—Could not possibly part with Vālloo, my Arab steed—Cape St. James and Poulo-Condor—The s.s. 'Tibre'—Her French captain—'Oh, yes, yes'—Indian conjurers—Robbery of my gold watch—Conjurers confined in cells—The Baron and his jewels—The guilty thief—Sentenced to two years' imprisonment—Vālloo becomes the Old Man of the Sea 217

CHAPTER XXIII

The country mouse—Saigon and Singapore contrasted—Singapore the City of Rickshaws—Steam no match to two-legged ponies—Mrs. Bumble and the Rickshaws—Reasonable inquiries—The fate of Captain Bertuzzi and of Phra Yott—The French and Chantaboon—His Highness the Sultan of

Johore—An 'At Home' with His Highness—The recent breach of promise case—General opinions—The sighing Penelope and lost Ulysses—Parting with *Jimmy*—His varied accomplishments—Thoughts of becoming a Mahdi . . 225

CHAPTER XXIV

Old Malacca—Its change of hands—St. Xavier's curse—The town's decay and its cause—Malacca the 'Blighted City'—Malacca and Madras compared—Its equable climate—Its shallow anchorage—Ancient and modern Argosies—Cities struggling for existence 235

CHAPTER XXV

Untravelled travellers—Uncomfortable passages—Malacca Resthouse—Ancient Cathedral—'Upper Crust Club'—Mount Ophir—Its Scripture basis—Khlang and Qualo-Lumpor—The coffee and tin industries—The future of John Chinaman 239

CHAPTER XXVI

The Orang-Bukits—A primitive people—Their poisoned darts—The effects of clairvoyance—Their Æolian harps—Loathsome leprosy—Visit to general hospital—Foundering of steamship 'Setthi'—Saved by the bite of a mad dog—The durian and mangosteen 248

CHAPTER XXVII

Mandalay revisited—Scenes of lang syne—Changes of Mandalay and surroundings—'Britannia: a Dream'—The vile Kabyoo—The wounded Corydon—Two golden rules—Married on a wooden leg—The Woundouk of Bhamó—A real ruby ring—The Burmese crown jewels—Travelling hints on Burmah—Stranded on the Irrawaddy—Mr. Streeter and the Burmah Ruby Mines 256

CHAPTER XXVIII

Benefits of travel—Bacon's opinion—Advice of the Author—Reading compared with observation—The Indo-Chinese race—Original divisions of mankind—Presumable origin of the Indo-Chinese—Religious tenets—The Mohammedan Malays—Habits of the Indo-Chinese—Their social system—Minor differences among themselves—The barber in Eastern nations—'The Maid of Mandalay'—First fiddle to *Mandalay Herald* 270

CHAPTER XXIX

Calcutta the mother of thieves—Trip to Darjeeling—A lost cashbox—Predicaments of penury—From blunder to blunder—My last rupee—My own master again—Recovery of cashbox, broken and robbed—Advice to intending travellers—The value of money—Lord Love *versus* Lord Lucre—Mount Everest in clouds—Beauty of Darjeeling scenery—Philosophical conclusions of 'Through the Buffer State'   . 283

LIST OF ILLUSTRATIONS

H.R.H. Prince Krommun Damrong	*Frontispiece*
Two Blithe Dyaks	*To face p.* 22
Map of Southern Siam	,, 54
Corporals of the Guard	,, 110
Parasitic Parricides	, 136
Ground Sketch of Angkor-Wát Ruins	164
Lake Dwelling on Telé-Sáp	*To face p.* 180
The 'Lady of the Lake'	,, 198
Válloo, the Dark Delinquent	,, 224
H.H. the Late Sultan of Johore	,, 230
Láös Tribesman	,, 272
The Maid of Mandalay	,, 282

THROUGH THE BUFFER STATE

CHAPTER I

> Stand, stranger, stand and say whence come,
>   And whither duly bound;
> And whence the pass by which you roam
>   On this forbidden ground.
>
> I come from out the stormy North,
>   And go where Fate may guide;
> My only passport is the blade
>   That hangeth by my side.
>
> *The Old Crusader.*

The Pamirs and Persia—The Land of the White Elephant—The 'Rajah Brooke'—A Tumbling Sea—Infallible Cure for Sea-sickness—Arrival in Borneo—Reception at Kuching—The Rajah of Sarāwak—Courtship at Kuching—Collision of the 'Little 'Un'—Trip up the Sadong—Orang-outang and Long-nosed Monkeys.

WOULD it be the Pamirs, or would it be Persia? was the question as my leave was at last becoming due. In Persia there were ancient ruins and hoary old tales. In the Pamirs there were neither ruins nor tales; but there were plenty of hoary old mountains, covered with eternal snow, and promising to make tales in the future, when the Muscovites will make that wonderful march of theirs through their frowning passes; though what they will do after that need not be dwelt upon in this faithful record.

And so I sometimes pictured myself groping among the ruins of Babylon, and sometimes climbing the Karakoram range, till at last I found myself free, and at that very time quite a different kind of country began suddenly to attract public attention. This country was none else than *the*

Land of the White Elephant. If it did not possess the winning attractions of massive mountains and mouldering ruins (some of which it really did, as the reader will see) it at any rate possessed the charming attraction of novelty to a greater extent than either of the others. For both the Pamirs and Persia had of late years been extensively travelled over by various travellers, with their henchmen behind them, whereas I was going as a wayward wanderer without any protection at all.

And so I was off as fast as the train could carry me. After the various tossings and tumblings incidental to a sea voyage, and passing Christmas at sea, we duly arrived in the pretty port of Singapore, where I intended to make arrangements for my future journey. While casually glancing over the advertisements of one of the local newspapers there, I noticed among others the sailing advertisement of a ship called the 'Rajah Brooke,' and wondered where she would be trading to. Though my real destination was Siam, yet I had long wished to pay a flying visit to Borneo, and this ship, I thought, would be trading to the very portion of Borneo which I particularly wished to visit. I found that my surmise was correct, and I shall therefore describe my short visit to Sarāwak or Rajah Brooke's Territory before proceeding to describe my more extended journey through the wilds of Siam.

The name of Rajah Brooke is vaguely known to some people as a bygone restless rover, who founded a little kingdom somewhere in the Eastern seas; but the name of his particular territory is comparatively unknown. I naturally thought that a ship bearing his name was not unlikely to be trading to the possessions of the late rajah.

Only the large regular ocean liners go to the wharves at Singapore, on account of the heavy dues. The smaller steamers, and almost all the sailing ships, lie in the harbour outside, some of them at considerable distances away from the shore; and among them all was the 'Rajah Brooke.' When I went out in the harbour to see her in a Chinese surf-boat, she looked a smart little craft of some five or six hundred tons, and one of the cleanest vessels of her kind in the whole of the Singapore Bay. The captain was on board too, and hoped I should go with the ship to visit Sarāwak or Rajah Brooke's Territory. Three evenings afterwards I was on board the 'Rajah Brooke' as she was steaming out of harbour bound for that interesting country.

The ship had very little cargo on board. It was also the north-east monsoon season in the China Sea, which is the stormy season in that locality, instead of the south-west monsoon, which is the stormy season in India and surrounding regions. The 'Rajah Brooke' therefore tossed about quite to the satisfaction of the captain, who, I think, said he had never been sea-sick; yet not at all to the satisfaction of a mere land-lubber like the writer, or of the only other European passenger on board the ship. The latter happened to be an up-country official of the very land I was going to visit; and though the trip was altogether too boisterous for making much of his acquaintance on the voyage, yet I afterwards found him a very hospitable and obliging friend.

The captain was quite sympathetic. But sympathy is mostly thrown away on nauseous passengers during their first forty-eight hours on a stormy sea. The greatest kindness is to be let alone, and I think it is a very good precept to follow in the great majority of cases, though of course there are exceptions, as to every other precept under the sun. The best thing to do, in short, is to do nothing at all. Father Time, and that beautiful recuperative power of Nature, are by far the best physicians, and will generally put everything right in the end. If not, I, as a physician myself, will recommend one infallible cure, namely—Go ashore and stay there.

In due time we were sailing up the river, already forgetting the discomforts of the passage, during which I was thrown out of my bunk two or three times. And after twisting away for some twenty-five or thirty miles, between muddy banks fringed with luxurious verdure, we were at last blowing our horn to announce to the inhabitants of Kuching, the capital town of Sarāwak, that the gallant 'Rajah Brooke' was coming, as she usually did twice every month.

The arrival of the 'Rajah Brooke' is quite a red-letter day in the calendar of Kuching, and every European and *quasi*-European in the place, wend their way down to the wharf to give her a welcome. Not that she ever carries many European passengers, for the place is too far out of the way for the ordinary tourist; and so the stragglers that find their way to Sarāwak are few and far between. But the people go to see the 'Rajah Brooke' in her own proper person, as well as to see her popular captain, who, I found, was known over here under the pet nickname of 'The Greek.' Then as Christmas comes but once a year, so the 'Rajah Brooke' comes but twice a month; and her visits are therefore rare enough to impart a tinge of novelty to her repeated arrivals. She also carries news from various quarters of the world to this remote region, as well, no doubt, as a lot of Singapore gossip through the genial captain; and so when to all this is added the freshening *stinga* which everybody drinks to the health of everybody else on the quarter-deck. it is no cause for wonder that the repeated appearances of the 'Rajah Brooke' are looked upon as a genuine source of joy to this lonely community.

There are about a dozen Europeans in Kuching, almost all of them being officials in the Sarāwak Service, and I had the pleasure of making the acquaintance of at least three-fourths of them before I landed from the ship. There is a small resthouse recently erected in the town, to accommodate up-country officials when visiting the capital. But there is no provision whatever for the weary wanderer, for the very plausible reason that there be no weary wanderers to require the same. I was prepared, however, for this contingency, as I had my tent with me, ready to be pitched whenever or wherever required. But there was no occasion for it this time, as among the passengers that came on board the 'Rajah Brooke' was the amiable Dr. F——, the Principal Medical Officer of the Sarāwak State, and he at once took me in hand in this strange land of exile.

The original Rajah Brooke himself is as dead as Queen Anne; and the present Rajah, who is a nephew of the original one, was in England at the time of my visit, being represented at Kuching by one of the Residents, of whom there are some half a dozen, scattered here and there throughout the Sarāwak Territory. Like his uncle, the present Rajah is very fond of the natives, over whom he is practically the king. And the Dyaks in return regard the Rajah with great veneration, though perhaps not quite with as much as his uncle before him. The Rajah therefore is quite careful of his dusky subjects, to whom he behaves in an old patriarchal manner.

But the people of Kuching, whether Dyaks, Chinese, or Malays, are said to be very fond of gallantries in the dark, like many other people beside them, and are greatly given over to the habit of 'meet me when the sun goes down.' Moreover, they are said to make the chief portion of their courting in small boats, which go under the name of *sampāns* all over the Malayan Archipelago. These small boats flit about the harbour in the dark, at the will of the afflicted ones. It is therefore the concern of the Rajah that no harm will happen to them. For that purpose, there is, I believe, a standing order of the port of Kuching that no steamer is to move in or out of harbour in the murky hours between shadow and shine, for fear of injuring these frail craft, with their interesting and sometimes frail occupants.

This rule was set aside on one occasion during my visit, and not at all with the happiest results. Up the Sadong river, some sixty or seventy miles round the coast from Kuching, there are flourishing coal mines from which the Rajah receives a considerable portion of his revenues; and the Sadong district too is one of the few places in Sarāwak—indeed, one of the few places in the world—where lives the celebrated manlike ape known as the *Orang-outang*.

The Resident, who was acting for the Rajah at this time, took into his head to visit the Sadong district, and further, decided to start at the very murky hour of three o'clock on the Sabbath morning. Dr. F—— was going on the same trip in his own professional line, and I was very pleased to accompany him as his guest, as I hoped to be able to see not only the coal mines, but also our elder brother of the orang-outang in his native wilds, for the very meaning of the word 'orang-outang' in the Malay language is the 'Man of the Wood.'

The little ship in which we intended to sail was called the 'Adeh,' which, being translated from the same language, means the 'Minor' or the 'Little 'Un,' and she was at the time lying out in the middle of the stream. The Doctor and I went on board the 'Adeh' about midnight, and the Resident followed soon after. It was a dark, rainy night, and after a while I laid myself down on a bench under the awning and beside one of the paddle-boxes, so as to be able to watch the little ship manœuvring out of harbour, when she started later on. With the exception of native craft, there were only two other ships in the port at the time, the 'Rajah Brooke' moored to the wharf, and the 'Aline' moored in the river a little lower down. The latter is a pretty little ship of three or four hundred tons, and combines in her own person both the flagship and the yacht of the Rajah, as she is the only armed vessel in the country.

The hour arrived in due course, and we were shortly afterwards, as I thought, going full-speed down the river, when I was suddenly startled with a great crash beside me, for the 'Little 'Un' had fallen foul of the 'Aline,' the fluke of one of whose anchors caught in one of the paddle-boxes of our ship, and was fast tearing it to pieces at my very elbow. 'Stop her,' I heard some gruff voice shout out in the dark, and the 'Little 'Un' stopped. We had now got clear of the 'Aline,' and soon discovered that the anchor of the latter had not only torn away the woodwork of the paddle-box, but had also twisted two or three of the iron bars of the paddle wheels, and that we could not proceed any further. 'Drop your anchor,' shouted the same gruff voice again in the dark, and we dropped our anchor accordingly.

Captain M——, a brawny Scotsman, is at one and the same time master-mariner, chief engineer, and top-sawyer-in-general on board the 'Little 'Un,' and he began to work in real earnest to put matters right again. It was no fault of his that we had fouled the 'Aline,' for wasn't the vessel being piloted at the time by the far-famed and skilful Cadia, who had passed all his life in these quarters ever since he was caught as a boy in a pirate prow that had fared rather badly in a conflict with the late Rajah? Nor was it the fault of Cadia either. It was the fault of the thick dark night and the swift-flowing current. But M——, who worked with wonderful energy, managed to replace the twisted rods by spare ones on board, and we were nearly ready to start at daybreak. And thus we paid for the forbidden fruit of sailing out of Kuching at three o'clock on the Sabbath morning against the orders of the port, though, luckily for all, there were no love-making *sampāns* sunk, nor anybody injured in any way.

In the afternoon we reached our destination up the Sadong river. It rained incessantly all that evening, all that night, and all the next morning. And so I succeeded in seeing neither the coal mines, which I did not particularly care to see, nor yet the orang-outangs, which I wished to see very much.

It would have been very interesting to watch a group of these 'elder brothers' discussing their dinner of fruit on the top of the tall branches, for this peculiar manlike ape is very confined in his geographical distribution, as he is only to be found in certain portions of Borneo, and to a very limited extent in the island of Sumatra, from which he is said to be rapidly dying out. He has not yet been interviewed by the wonderful Professor Garner, as his brother, the gorilla of Africa, has been. But his time is no doubt coming, and I hope the learned professor will be able to understand his language thoroughly, though some captious critics declare that he cannot talk to his favourite gorilla yet, let alone an orang-outang, whose language must be much more refined and complicated.

Besides the orang-outang, there are various other monkeys in Borneo, notably the Long-nosed Monkey (*Nasalis Larvatus*), which is entirely confined to this island, and which, though not so high in the scale as the orang-outang, is even more striking in his own way. For whereas almost all monkeys are wanting in nose (though not in 'cheek'), the only specimen I saw of this monkey possessed a long fleshy humanlike nose, that would do credit to the most nosey old Jew.

CHAPTER II

> For oh, it was so dark, so dark,
>   That grim and gruesome lair;
> With ne'er a gleam of light to mark
>   The wild beasts crouching there.
> *The Robbers' Retreat.*

The Sago Palms—Trip to Interior—The Mines of Tegōra—Underground Caves—'For oh, it was so dark, so dark'—Subterranean Stream—A Tight-fitting Passage—Edible Birds'-nests—Their Peculiarity—The Birds that Build them—The *jam-jam* of John Chinaman.

AND so we turned back again without being able to accomplish anything except seeing a goodly portion of the country, and having an accident to make things look a little more lively. The trip also brought me in contact for the first time with sago in its native form; for more than half the sago of the world comes from Borneo alone. Does the reader know what sago is? I confess I didn't exactly; and I afterwards asked others, who ought to know as well as myself, and they were fully as ignorant, if not more so. Had I been asked I might probably have made some random reference to the sago palm; but I might have felt puzzled as to what part of it constituted sago. Is it the root or is it the fruit? It is neither root nor yet the fruit, but the pith of the stem, or what practically constitutes the counterpart of the runt of the common or garden cabbage.

These sago palms take seven or eight years to come to maturity, and are watched at that time for their forthcoming virgin blossom. At its very first indication the palms are cut down near the ground, when by far the greater portion of the stem is found to consist of a crude semi-transparent and semi-solid substance, from which the sago of commerce is in due course prepared.

When in Sarāwak, I was fortunate in being able to see more of the country than I could at first have reasonably expected during my short stay in the island. A day or two after my return to Kuching, I was able to start on a fresh journey. Among the principal productions of the province may be specially mentioned that of mercury and antimony, while small quantities of gold are also extracted by Chinamen by the process of washing. The old Borneo Company have the monopoly of both the antimony and mercurial mines. The Borneo manager of this company, whose ordinary residence is at Kuching, took an opportunity at this time of making one of his periodical visits of inspection to these mines, and kindly invited me to go with him. After steaming up the river in a small launch some fifty or sixty miles from the sea, we arrived at Būsau, and had afterwards to travel nearly twenty miles through a forest country, and over a very difficult and slippery pathway, on which I had my first experience of the *battang* roads of Borneo, of which I shall speak later on.

Before nightfall we reached the Tegōra mountains in which the mercurial mines are placed, and put up with the young engineer in charge of the mines. Though a fairly abundant metal, mercury is not at all a very widely distributed one, and these Tegōra mines have been among the most productive anywhere. The very richest of all are in Spain and Austria; and from them is obtained almost all the mercury of commerce in Europe, while the Tegōra mines of Borneo supply most of the needs of the Far East through the Hong Kong market.

The metal exists here both in the pure or virgin state, in the form of minute silvery globules, which may be seen oozing here and there through the rock, or making its presence known in red patches of cinnabar on the broken rock surface. The place where the metal abounds is very steep, and is so honey-combed by the mines, that it is by no means an easy task to inspect them thoroughly, as we did the next morning. The principal quarry pierces through the mountain from one side to the other, in a very irregular and breakneck fashion. After inspecting the mines and watching the Chinamen blasting the rocks with dynamite, we returned to Būsau, where the antimony mines are situated. And there my companion parted with me, and kept on to Kuching back again, while I remained with the official in charge of the foundries here for further information.

The engineer of the Tegōra mines, who had entertained us the previous night, came to see his friend of Busau the next day, and on the following one the three of us paid a visit to Mr. D——, my *quondam* shipmate on the 'Rajah Brooke,' who was living only four or five miles away from us.

Borneo abounds greatly in what is known as 'edible birds'-nests,' of which I had often heard, though I had never seen any of them. And some of the caves, in which the birds build these peculiar nests, were within two or three miles of Mr. D——'s residence. None of my companions, though residents of Borneo, had ever taken the trouble of visiting any of these caves, thus proving what I had often noticed before, namely, that people take very little interest in interesting matters, when they have the misfortune of being placed, as it were, under their very noses. But I prevailed on two of them to come and visit these caves with me. For D——, who previously knew of my intentions, had already made the Dyaks prepare the necessary arrangements. But Mr. M—— would not take the trouble on any account, and as matters turned out, he was quite right in his decision.

After a walk of two or three miles through most bewildering jungle, we at last reached the ridge of hills in which the caves were, and there we found our friends the Dyaks waiting our arrival. We had a good hard climb before we reached the entrance to the caves, which were situated, as usual, in limestone mountains.

I fancy that all large underground caves are to be found in limestone formations only, and I had previously visited perhaps the two largest and most famous of them all, namely, the Jenōlan Caves of Australia and the Mammoth Caves of Kentucky, in the United States. I need not dwell upon why it is so, as that would lead me into a labyrinth of geological detail, like the caves themselves.

Another peculiarity of these caves is that there is generally a stream of water running through them somewhere or other. Such is the case with the Jenōlan Caves and with the Mammoth Caves; and such also was the case with the caves we were now visiting. The Dyaks, the aborigines of this portion of Borneo, are themselves quite familiar with such caves, as the robbing of the birds'-nests forms a great portion of their livelihood, and a great portion of their daily toil during a certain season of the year. Besides, the taxes derived from the sale of these nests form a perceptible and integral part of the yearly revenues of the Saräwak State Territory.

On this occasion the Dyaks were amply provided with torches, each consisting of a number of strips of resinous wood, held together in conical bundles by means of thongs made of bark. The burning ends of these torches are the wide ones, and the Dyaks regulate the amount of light by these strings of bark, so as to economise the torches when detained in the caves.

When but little light is required, they slip the rings of bark towards the wide burning ends of the torches, and by thus pressing the strips of wood together, they lessen the supply of air and of light accordingly. When the amount of light requires to be increased, they slip the rings back, the burning ends open up from one another, the torches are rapidly swung round the head two or three times through the air, and forthwith begin to burn brightly. The simple Dyaks, of course, know nothing of the reason why, yet they practise this method as if they were quite familiar with the scientific laws of combustion.

We groped and groped with these torches through many a devious and tedious passage under the ground, and sometimes waded considerably more than knee-deep in the lukewarm water of the stream. When we had thus groped and groped for nearly three-quarters of an hour we were at last within reasonable limits of the birds'-nests that we went so far to see. And then we reached a narrow, irregular, up-and-down passage, with a deep pool of water at the bottom of it, and how to get through it became the question of the day.

The Dyaks, though hardy and lithe enough, are considerably smaller than the average of Europeans, and they were also familiar with these caves. So they got through this passage without serious difficulty. My two young companions were also more than usually slender and graceful, and they too forced themselves through this passage, though not without a great expenditure of sighings and squeezings. Though of only ordinary size myself, they were both much slimmer than I was at that time, and it was rather puzzling for me how I was ever to wriggle myself through this nasty underground passage.

But the eye of the needle, through which the other two

Europeans had already passed, would never be abandoned by me, at any rate, without a very serious effort. And so I made the effort, and did get through at last, after a vast amount of toil and trouble. The passage itself was perhaps twelve or fifteen feet from top to bottom, and when I reached the middle of it I thought I was safely anchored there, without the possibility of going either up or down. But I finally reached the top, and when I did so I found a couple of buttons torn off the breast of my braw tight-fitting kakee coat, so very tight indeed was the constriction through which I had just forced my way, and how to get down through it again on our return was a riddle I did not at all care to think about.

And so we reached the locality where the birds'-nests really were. The Dyaks had previously prepared for our visit at the request of Mr. D——, and had erected tall primitive scaffoldings of bamboos to reach the different galleries and crevices of the caves. And then they began to climb them and grope along, torch in hand, to get at the nests they were searching for, much to the disturbance of the poor little birds, that objected to the rude intruders with noisy declamation.

They managed to get only a fair number of nests, as this was the very fag end of the nesting season, and this cave was also the very last one to be searched during that period, and known to the Dyaks themselves under the name of the New Cave, as it had only lately been discovered, or, at any rate, exploited for birds'-nests.

Needless to say that it had never been visited by the pale-faced European before, and probably never will be again. The floor of the caves at this particular spot was covered with birds' guano, probably for several feet deep. But they said that the guano from these caves throughout Borneo is not very valuable, as it rapidly loses its ammonia and other active properties on exposure to air, though it is difficult to understand why it should be so with this more than with other guano from various quarters of the globe.

After waiting for a long time watching these climbers over our heads, visible only now and again through the glare of the torches, we thought at last it was high time for us to be retracing our footsteps. We would have been getting anxious about the fate of the torches by this time too, and fearing we might be left where Moses was when the light went out. But the Dyaks themselves showed no uneasiness on that account, and of course they knew their own business.

And then rose the unpleasant question of how we were to return, and how to get through that horrible passage again. It was a tight enough fit to get up through it, but to get down through it was far worse. For every one, who has ever climbed rocks in his youth, will easily remember how much more easy it is to climb up than to 'climb down' on these occasions. No wonder, then, that it occurred to me that Mr. M——, who stayed at home, was a much wiser man than I was after all, for he could never have managed to force his portly and well-favoured figure through that constricted communication. But if we were all equally wise, would wisdom be so highly valued?

Observing our dilemma on the return journey, the Dyaks, who knew the ramifications of the cave, brought us through a looped passage, by means of which we could avoid the narrow straits referred to. This was a longer way, and required a good deal of creeping and horizontal squeezing, but was not altogether such a tight fit as the previous one. In fine, we were all very glad at last to emerge from these dark and straggling caves, and to reach open daylight once again, after enduring for several hours this sort of underground burial.

There were but few stalactites in the cave, and the best thing of that sort that we came across was in the shape of a pillar of limestone, about the size and shape of the pillar in the Jenōlan caves that is known as 'Lot's Wife.' This, I need scarcely say, was a stalagmite, rising from the floor of the cave, and not a stalactite, hanging from the roof.

The birds that build the peculiar nests that we went to see are a species of swallow, of a glossy black colour, with the usual pointed wings, and characteristically forked tails. They are of much about the same size as the common swallow of northern climates, and are probably permanent residents of these regions, instead of being migratory birds like our swallows. In the Eastern Hemisphere they are mostly confined to the Malayan Archipelago and neighbourhood; and abound especially in Borneo and Java, which may be called their native habitat.

The peculiarity about the 'edible birds'-nests' is the

fact that they are mostly constructed of a glairy viscous substance, which is either a secretion of the bird itself, or consists, as some maintain, of partially macerated food from the crops of the birds, and poured out at a certain stage of maceration. And thus the nests consist of shallow cup-shaped cavities, truncated, as it were, at the side where they are attached to the rocks, exactly like brackets to the wall of a room ; and consisting of an elastic, semi-transparent, and gelatinous material.

There is always a certain amount of down mixed up in the substance of the nests, and their commercial value is in inverse proportion to the quantity of this downy adulteration. The very best nests have a minimum of down, and are on that account known as 'white nests.' Those we were able to obtain were only of a medium quality, with a fourth or fifth part cut off, as it were, where they were glued to the rocks. The nests are also best when occupied by eggs only, for later on, when the brood becomes hatched, the edible walls of the nests become hard, sapless, and much less valuable as a table delicacy.

The Dyaks take away these nests two or three times during the nesting season, and then let the birds alone to bring forth their brood in peace and quietness. The nests first built are the best ones, and every succeeding lot deteriorates by a greater admixture of downy feathers. As this then was the very end of the nesting season, the nests could scarcely be expected to be of the very best quality. There were but few eggs among them, and I was only able to procure one of them unbroken, which I brought with me, and which afterwards went bad, so that I had to throw it away. It was rather smaller than the egg of a lark, and of a pale pinkish colour. It may be remarked that it is not the eggs which are relished so much as a delicacy, but the substance of the nests themselves. The eggs in any individual nest are said never to number more than two or three, so that the birds probably breed several times during the nesting season.

When we returned to Mr. D——'s bungalow, late in the evening, we found that the Dyaks had taken there not less than three nests, with the young birds still alive in each of them, and with only one bird in each nest. All the young birds were pretty full-grown : and one of them, as he sat contentedly in his nest, with his bill resting on the edge of it, looked nearly as large as one of the parent birds. And what struck me as rather curious was that all the birds—including the big one, which I am sure could fly—had their legs glued to the floor of the nests, so that they could not tumble off even if they tried. The young birds were sure to die, poor things, and I thought how nicely they would look stuffed *in situ*; but they were all left on a table in the verandah during the night, forgetful that there were cats in Borneo as everywhere else, and so, when we got up in the early morning, there were the nests, but where were the younglings?

These birds break their trammels, no doubt, when they are strong enough to take to flight properly. There are, of course, various birds that build their nests in lofty situations, but I am not aware of any others whose young are glued down in this way till they are able to take care of themselves; and I therefore submit this remark, to be confirmed or disproved by future observers.

These strange birds'-nests are considered the real *jam-jam* by the wealthy Chinese over the Far East, who pay a high price for them, too, especially the 'white' variety already spoken of. They literally hold the first place among delicacies to the Chinese palate; while next to them, and before any other tit-bits, come the fins of sharks and sun-dried cuttle-fish! It is therefore no great wonder that we esteem the heathen Chinese as a little 'peculiar.'

Europeans seldom eat these nests, except for mere curiosity; and it was for this sake of novelty that we got some of them prepared the morning I left Kuching for Singapore, and in real orthodox Chinese fashion; for John Chinaman seasons the bird's-nest soup with sugar, while Europeans prefer to season it with salt, in the way that some of the Gentiles prefer porridge. Mine was seasoned with sugar; for when a person is inquiring into John Chinaman's delicacies he should of course do so in John Chinaman's own recognised way, and prepared in this way the bird's-nest soup is decidedly toothsome. It is of a mucilaginous consistency, and the small glairy fragments of nest scattered here and there throughout it impart to it a flavour like that of turtle soup, so much in favour at Lord Mayors' dinners.

CHAPTER III

> We started on a wild-goose chase,
> On a wild-goose chase at a merry, merry pace;
>   But ere the race was ended,
> The hunters broke the sporting rules,
> And some of the very best John Bulls
> Had urgent need to go to Poole's [1]
>   To get their breeches mended.
>
> *The Wild-goose Chase.*

A Rough Climb—The Dyaks at Home—Their Village Golgothas—Their Head-hunting Sports—Same Suppressed by the First Rajah Brooke—Deafening Gongs—Dancing with the Dyaks—The Remote Missionary—Parting with Mr. D——The Battang Paths of Borneo—The Pitcher-plants and Traveller's Palms—Their Uselessness.

ONE of the things that I particularly wished to do was to spend a night in one of the primitive Dyak villages, away entirely from the trammels of civilisation; and my *quondam* shipmate, Mr. D——, was able to gratify this curiosity, as he was going on duty in the direction of one of the said hamlets. So the next morning we left his bungalow at Bhāku, called again at Būsau on our way, and after paddling up the river for a mile or so, we broke off overland in the requisite direction, with some Dyak youths to show us the way, and to carry whatever necessaries we required to bring with us.

The village of Singhi is situated on several eminences, scattered here and there on the spur of a mountain, the highest eminence of which is quite a thousand feet or more above the general level of the plain below; so that the

---

[1] Poole is the fashionable West-end London tailor, especially for riding breeches; and I hope he will feel duly grateful to the author of the 'Wild-goose Chase' (whoever he may be) for this honourable mention of his name.

village was by no means an easy task to get at. The path was extremely steep, and sometimes consisted of the roots or trunks of trees, notched here and there to give some sort of precarious foothold to the climber.

In choosing a few articles of wear and tear for this inland journey, I unfortunately by mistake picked out of my kit a couple of kakee riding-breeches, very tight at the knee, and I had every reason to regret the mistake before the journey was ended; for I had already burst one of them during my scrambles over the rocks of the Tegōra mines, and the other was sorely put to the test in my efforts to reach the very steep hill-village of Singhi. However, by dint of perseverance, and after a great deal of puffing and panting, we duly arrived at the *Barook*, or head-house of the village at last.

It must not be supposed that this *Barook*, which is to be found in every village, is really the house of the headman, or *Orang-kaya* of the same; oh, no. It is rather the house where the Dyaks keep the heads of their decapitated victims, and the general rendezvous of the male population, where they used to hold their councils of war, as well as their general palaver, or *bitchāra*, as they call it in that country. Not long ago a Dyak who had not killed somebody and possessed himself of his skull, was held but of small account by the fair sex of his tribe. It is said that it did not matter materially whose it was, though preferably, no doubt, an enemy's. But lacking that, the skull of a friend, or even of one's great—great grandmother-in-law would serve the purpose. The lovelorn swain must, at any rate, have a single skull to present to his fair one, and if he had several, so much the more merrily was he welcome to her bosom.

In the time of the first Rajah Brooke, head-hunting, as they called it, was abolished in the province of Sarāwak. And it is very amusing to read in his 'Life' of the repeated applications of the Dyaks to him, to be allowed to take a few heads—only a few—as if they were children asking to be allowed to play with toys.

But the Rajah was always obdurate, and his usual reply to them is equally amusing; they would not be allowed, he would say, to indulge in the fine game of head-hunting within his dominions, but they were at perfect liberty to take a voyage over to Singapore, and chop off the heads of the people there, knowing full well that this arduous undertaking was not within the sphere of practical possibilities. And when on the pleasant topic of head-hunting, it must not be supposed that it was only the Dyaks alone who indulged in this pretty pastime. For even Jehu, King of Israel, got not less than seventy skulls of the sons of Ahab sent to him for a present in baskets!

Yet though the practice of head-hunting has been abolished some time ago, there were sundry skulls still preserved in this headhouse, some of them suspended on strings, while others were carelessly lying about here and there in out of the way corners. And with these savage emblems of victory, the villagers would not part on any account whatsoever. The headhouse, where we passed the night, consisted of only one large capacious room, with a fireplace for cooking in the middle of it, and with a floor consisting of split bamboos. The floor was raised several feet above the ground, as is usually the case in these swampy and sultry climes; while the ground of the empty space below was covered with all sorts of filthy abominations, among which pigs wallowed with grunts of great satisfaction, as everything valuable (to a pig) is always dropped down through the chinks of the floor into this cesspool receptacle.

There, in that headhouse, Mr. D—— and myself remained during the rest of that day and the succeeding night. When the Dyak villagers came to know that pale-faced white people had come among them, they flocked round in great numbers, and began to beat the gongs in the headhouse with much vigour. And what a beating of gongs it was! There were six of them of different sizes, and therefore of different pitch and tone, hanging in a certain place, and all of them being beaten by young lads armed with sticks for that purpose. It was a deafening sound, of which they never seemed to tire, and which anybody but themselves would very soon get heartily sick of. For the most confirmed neurotic that was ever startled by the skirl of the bagpipes, would consider them but the quiet music of the spheres, when compared with this dreadful beating of gongs, and the squealing of pigs below, coming in as interludes of the drama.

After a long while the din abated a bit, and the two of us had our frugal repast, squatting cross-legged on the bamboo floor, and surrounded by quite a crowd of curious onlookers. Thereafter the *bitchāra* again commenced, when everyone seemed so very wise and so very voluble in expressing his own very wise and profound opinions, and never listening to his neighbour's.

The Dyaks are quite a lively and loquacious people, and apparently very fond of gossip and conversation. Mr. D——, who understood their language, and whom they seemed to treat like an elder brother, had endless questions to answer: and the genial manner of the Dyaks towards him, though they had never seen him before, was very interesting to observe. For the Dyaks, besides being naturally a genial race, do not look upon themselves as a conquered people. They invited, they say, the Rajah themselves at first, and chose him to be their ruler of their own freewill and accord—which, I believe, is really the case so far as the Dyaks themselves were concerned.

When the *bitchāra* had gone on long enough we were anxious to see some of their native dances. But they were very shy to begin. Even the *Orang-kaya*, or headman of the village, encouraged them both by precept and example by dancing himself, but without much success. There was one young lad who appeared eager enough to get some one to dance with him, and rather than see him disappointed I went to dance with him myself. But a little jumping about barefooted on the rickety bamboo floor goes a long way; and I was not dancing very long when one of the bamboos suddenly twisted, and I sprained my right ankle in consequence. 'Served him right for dancing with the Dyaks,' some uncharitable reader will probably say. And I can only say in reply that it is a poor heart that never rejoices, and that I only indulged in this very wicked (?) pastime for the sake of encouraging the Dyaks to dance, and not from any personal predilection to high jinks myself.

Then a graceful young Dyak, who seemed rather bashful at first, took up my place, and the pair of them kept on dancing for a long time, writhing and twisting themselves in a very odd way. For this was a war-dance, if you please, and each of the combatants was armed with a *kris*, or sword of the period, to show off his agility and prowess. But even at their best these dances of Eastern lands look very feeble to one who has roamed o'er the mountains afar, and after seeing a good many of them in various lands, I really think a good Highland fling is worth the whole pack of them put together. Truth to tell, the Asiatic does not possess enough agility, nor yet enough sensibility of the poetry of motion, to make a very graceful dancer, and these turnings and twistings of theirs are vain and unprofitable as the very merest of chandelier crawls.

It was getting very late at night, but still that endless *bitchāra* went on, and everybody began to get very friendly with everybody else under the mild influence of some little *ginevre* that we had brought them. Two of them huddled themselves quite close to where we two were squatting down, with their eyes blinking, yet earnestly discussing what was to be done on the morrow, as my companion and I were then going to part, and one of them, they said, was to accompany each of us on our way. Indeed, watching these amusing people it was hard to conceive that they would be guilty of cruelty and bloodshed. Yet such are the effects of traditions and customs over the human heart that, taken from any given standpoint, it is difficult to judge fairly of the various practices prevalent among the different races of mankind.

By three o'clock in the morning most of our visitors had gone home, but enough of them still remained to keep up that palaver of theirs, of which we were by this time getting heartily tired. We laid down at last, but could scarcely sleep a wink with that incessant jargon going on around us. For it must be as hard for a Dyak to hold his tongue as it is said to be for a woman by those who are too fond of talking themselves.

During the course of the evening we got an invitation that rather surprised us; for it was from an Italian missionary who was living on a spur of the mountain lower down, and of whom my companion knew nothing, as he had only been lately appointed to that district, and had never been at Singhi before.

Some nine or ten years ago, when stationed at Bhamó, on the interior borders between Burma and China, another missionary took people by even greater surprise. There was a standing order that none were to go outside the stockade of that far-away corner without being armed and in parties only, as the surrounding country was at the time in a very disturbed state. But one fine evening, as the people were listening to the band immediately outside the stockade, who suddenly turned up but a missionary from China, unarmed, unfriended, and alone, while he was also dressed in the orthodox garb of the heathen Chinee, including even the ridiculous pigtail. He had crossed from China over the intervening Kachin mountains, and had been detained for some time by one of the *Sawbwas* or Chiefs of that country, but there he was, safe and sound at last. As I happened to be writing to one of the Anglo-Indian papers at that time I made honourable mention of this soldier of peace in one of my letters. Though he did not really know who had written about him he suspected me, and was very angry, as he said I had praised him too much! Wherever one goes throughout the dark corners of the earth, if he happens to meet any European at all, he is almost sure to be a missionary of some denomination or another, and a later experience of my own on this same trip will be faithfully recorded hereafter.

We were not able to accept of the missionary's kind invitation to put us up that night, for we were already settled down in this veritable Golgotha, or place of skulls; and in fact we really had gone to the village for the very purpose of doing so. But we would call, we said, in the early morning, which we did. And when we did call we found him living on a lower spur of the mountain than where we had passed the previous night. He could speak English fairly well, and though an Italian by birth, he was then engaged in connection with a French mission, the name of which I quite forget.

He did not seem to suffer from any persecutions from the simple Dyaks because of his religious opinions. For the Dyaks, poor bodies, have scarcely any religion at all of their own, and though good enough at the *bitchāra*, or gossip-talk, they can scarcely be counted among profound philosophers. He was not able, however, to enlighten many of the parents, but had some twenty children in school with him, whom he boarded, clothed and fed, and whom he hoped to bring up in the true Catholic faith.

His great trouble, he said, was about funds (a not very rare kind of trouble with the great majority of people), for the parents thought they were obliging him greatly by allowing him to teach their dusky urchins, and so they not infrequently asked boons and favours for themselves on the strength of this obligation. We had some coffee with him that he grew in his own garden, and after the usual dose of palaver we took our way.

Here also Mr. D—— and myself had to separate, as he was turning back again to his lonely bachelor's home, while I went forward on my journey. Our blithe young Dyaks of the previous night were there ready for us in the morning, as fresh as paint; and two of them accompanied me as guides and to carry what little luggage I happened to have with me. The path before us was said to be extremely difficult, if not entirely impassable, at this rainy season of the year. However, though the tramp in front of us was not very promising, 'where there's a will there's a way.' The ankle that I had sprained the previous night gave me not a little concern, as it began to pain me going down the mountain side. But after I got down to the swampy plain, and warmed to the work, it did not give me half the trouble I anticipated.

Yet this road was hard to travel, and it leads me therefore to make a few remarks on what are known as the *battang paths* of Borneo. These at best are of the most primitive kind, twisting through dense primeval forest, or stretching over swampy marshes and bogs of every description. When these bogs are too boggy even for the Dyaks, they cut down some large bamboos or more substantial trees, and stretch them end to end across the morasses. These are the *battangs*, from which the paths derive their name. They are frequently so covered with mud and water that they cannot be seen, and are, moreover, so slippery that it requires quite an education to become an expert bog-trotter among the *battang* paths of Borneo.

I proved but a poor apprentice on these paths, as I was continually slipping off the *battangs* into the deep, deep mud beside them; while the little Dyaks, though carrying my luggage, kept their foothold with wonderful tenacity. But besides their life-long familiarity with these paths, it must be said in addition that they were barefooted, as well as,

TWO BLITHE DYAKS.
(Armed with a "Kris," or Malay Sword.)

perhaps, that in their case, as in the case of others, Providence tempers the wind to the shorn lamb.

On this road might also be seen some fine specimens of the pitcher-plants of Borneo, whose flowers, so to speak, sometimes grow to the capacity of a pint or even a quart measure. They are invariably full of water and entirely useless and out of place in a country like Borneo, where it always rains except when it snows, the latter of which, of course, it never does. In such a place therefore these pitcher-plants are quite superfluous in the economy of Nature. For though it is quite possible for a man to starve in Borneo, yet it requires a great stretch of the imagination to fancy a man dying from thirst in this very rainy island.

Another plant, the Traveller's Palm, is equally abundant in Borneo, and equally useless. This palm, at a height of fifteen or twenty feet from the ground, begins to spread out its long fleshy leaves in two opposite sides of the stem. And as the lower leaves are gradually larger and larger than the upper ones, their disposition imparts to the plant the appearance of a perfect fan, with a long handle comprised of the stem of the palm. The leaf-stalks of these leaves, especially the lower ones, grasp the greater portion of the circumference of the stem where they join it, and are necessarily gouged out for that purpose. The hollow thus formed is always full of water in Borneo, as it is always raining there; and I one time broke off one of these leaf-stalks that contained in its hollow a bottle or two of water, or perhaps even more. But *cui bono?*

For these palms are only found in very moist climates, where water is always plentiful. And besides, if the water contained in the hollow of these leaf-stalks were urgently required, how was the traveller to get at it?—as he could seldom reach the very lowest of the stalks without artificial means. Nevertheless, they might possibly be useful in the scorching deserts of Africa or Arabia, where, alas! they are not found. And as the watery fluid is not a secretion of the plants themselves, but purely accidental, they could not thrive anywhere but in moist climates, as would be the case also with the pitcher-plants just mentioned.

CHAPTER IV

> Before we climbed the mountains, the mountains, the mountains,
> Before we climbed the mountains, they looked so proud and tall
> But by the time we scaled them, we scaled them, we scaled them,
> By the time we scaled them the mists had veiled them all.
> *Fitful Gleams.*

A Sloppy March—Bloodthirsty Leeches—An Awkward Tumble—A Planter on the Mountain Side—Abdoola the Laggard—Climbing Serappi—A Misleading Aneroid—Technicalities of Tea—Monkey-brand Coffee—Return to Kuching—Story of 'Dr. Meyer from Melbourne'—Farewell to Sarāwak.

But let us return to our *battangs*. Well, whenever I did return, I found it so hard to stick to them that I gave them up at last as a bad job, and had consequently to wade, sometimes nearly to the waist, in mud and water. Our progress was therefore necessarily slow. But at last we thought it high time for us to be approaching our destination, as we were now beginning to climb the hills again; and the end of our journey this time was to be the bungalow of a coffee planter whom I met at Kuching, and whom I promised to visit on my random journey.

I had brought no servants with me from India, as I knew they would only be a burden to themselves and to me in these countries, by reason of their ignorance of the languages and other causes. But I had reason to regret this decision before I returned to that country again—as my carelessness in personally looking after my property resulted to me in serious loss, which will be duly related later on. For this excursion, however, I was provided with a Malay servant, who spoke a few words of broken English, and whose name was Abdoola.

Abdoola was not very strong, I thought, and appeared to feel the journey much more than the Dyaks, though they were carrying burdens, while Abdoola had nothing to carry except my coat, which I found uncomfortably warm for me.

But the roving and seafaring Malays are really most at home in boats and ships, and are almost out of their element on an inland journey like this one. Each of the two Dyaks carried a fairly heavy portmanteau, hanging down his back from a strip of bark passing round the top of his forehead, for this is the way that the Dyaks invariably carry burdens since the time of the Flood. Arrived at last near the trunk of a large tree, that was lying along our path, I asked Abdoola how long we were likely to take yet. He consulted the Dyaks and replied that we should only take half an hour. 'Well, Abdoola,' cried I, 'if we'll only take half an hour more, we'll sit down and have a smoke.' And suiting the action to the word, we flopped down on the dead trunk beside us. While in the act of admiring my mud-covered boots, I noticed peculiar little worms wriggling through my stockings round my ankles, and taking off my boots hurriedly, I found my legs covered with leeches sucking away in great style. I had caught them when tramping through the swamps, and had not felt their bites during the exercise of walking, for the bites of leeches are not very painful at any time.

The half hour of which Abdoolah told me stretched out to nearly two hours. The mountain side here began to be covered with a taller and more open forest, and with much less of the tangled undergrowth so common in countries like Borneo. Further up still, a number of large trees had been cut down, whose decaying trunks were lying about in every direction across gulleys and streams. There was another path, the Dyaks said, but they had chosen the shorter, though much more difficult one. It would probably have been better for us to have taken the long road under the circumstances, as it was surer and more easy, even if slower and longer. Over and across these trunks of trees, then, we had to make our way as best we could, and I frequently nearly tumbled off them, as they were extremely slippery on account of the rain, and the decaying vegetable mould with which they were covered.

When passing across a hollow on one of these trunks I at last did tumble off, and fell into a heap of black rubbish some five or six feet below. I might have been badly hurt by the fall, if there had been stumps of trees under me. But fortunately there were none, and no harm was done, except that I got covered nearly all over with the mould that had already fallen from the rotting trunk. Soon after we stopped, as we had now reached the lower boundary of the plantation, where the coolies were gathering the coffee beans into a shed, and I could not help reflecting how foolish it was for me to be undergoing these physical fatigues, without any necessity whatever. But this much must be said in favour of travel, namely, that in the great majority of cases, the stings of travel are known but by their wings, while the pleasures thereof remain longer behind.

We reached our destination at last. When we got quite close to the bungalow, I looked out for my friend Abdoola, as I had got very dirty with the fall, and Abdoola was carrying my coat, which had not been soiled at the time. But Abdoola was not to be found. Nobody travelling through Borneo can be expected to look much of a masher, when he is on the tramp. But I had got so very dirty that I wanted my coat badly to improve matters a bit, before intruding myself on my host, who was a perfect stranger. So there we sat waiting for Abdoola's arrival. He at last turned up panting away, and with such a rueful countenance that I am sure he will not go to climb hills again in a hurry. He also looked very wrathful, as if we had left him behind us on purpose, whereas he had really fallen back from sheer fatigue, and nobody else noticed the fact till I required the coat he was carrying.

On that mountain side, then, I stayed with Mr. G—— for the next few days. I had no intention of climbing mountains on this journey for the sheer sake of climbing them alone, as I already had my share of that kind of fun. But I was now at Serappi, a spur of the Mattang, the highest mountain in this part of Borneo, and reported to be 4,500 feet in height, or about the same height as Ben Nevis. The top of it also was said to look into the Dutch portion of Borneo, as well as on the range of mountains that separate Dutch Borneo from the Sarāwak possessions. And so, as I happened to be there, I wanted to climb this mountain, and have a peep into the territories of our Netherland neighbours.

Mr. G—— had an aneroid which had not been used for some time, and which marked his bungalow at Mattang at 1,200 feet high. So there would only be 3,000 odd feet to climb, and I would like to take the aneroid to test it. A climb of only 3,000 feet may seem a mere nothing, but it is often a much harder task than is generally supposed by those who have never tried it, who, I presume, comprise the great majority of the interesting human race.

Up we went, then, myself and two Madrassees (or Klings, as they call them in this country) that Mr. G—— kindly lent me from the estate. He would have come up himself, but was at that time very busy; besides which he was far too heavy for a mountain climber, and was familiarly known among his friends in Sarāwak under the synonym of 'The Strong Man,' for everybody in Sarāwak appeared to have some good-natured nickname or other. On the lower slopes of the mountain there was a sort of pathway, cut there by the late Rajah, but in several places higher up the tall grass sometimes closed over our heads as we made our way through it. The ascent also was steep enough in some places, and sometimes passing over precipices, which would look dizzy enough but for the abundant vegetation that helped to cover their nakedness.

However, we reached the top of Serappi, and looked at the aneroid to see how high it was. To my surprise, the aneroid only marked it 2,600 feet. It is next to impossible to calculate the heights of mountains by the mere amount of personal fatigue incurred in climbing them, or by the length of time taken up on the journey. But, having started in the early morning from an elevation of 1,200 feet, it was hard to believe that we had only ascended 1,400 feet more. I tapped and tapped the case of that aneroid, and again and again laid it down to settle quietly. But there the indicator pointed, and would not budge. For the barometer stood at 26·92, and pointed to a height in the margin nearly represented by 2,600 feet. The thermometer was up to 93° Fahr. when we reached the top, but soon after went down to 86°, which in very truth may be considered a very high temperature on the top of a mountain.

It might be doubtful whether the mountain was really 4,500 feet high, but it was simply impossible that it was only 2,600 feet. Not long before this I had climbed the mountain in the pretty little island of Penang, which is said to be 2,500 feet, and I was certain, at any rate, that the top of Serappi was much higher from Mr. G——'s bungalow than the top of Penang Hill from the Waterfall Gardens. There, then, we waited for more than an hour to see if the aneroid would correct itself. But we might have waited as long as we liked, and be none the wiser, so far as that aneroid was concerned.

The view from the top was also by no means satisfactory. Mountains are very funny in their way. They are, I think, too much like Asiatic beauties, in being so fond of hiding themselves behind the veils of mists and clouds. And, indeed, it is very disappointing, after taking the very fatiguing trouble of climbing a mountain, to find that all these pains and penalties have been undertaken for nothing. And Serappi was no great exception to the rule on this day. Sometimes, however, the mists would roll asunder in great crumpled white fleeces, and would then reveal glimpses of the hilly range separating Dutch Borneo from the Sarāwak State, while at other times were revealed glimpses of the sea in the opposite direction, as well as of Kuching in the distance down below. The mountain itself was thickly covered with forest to the very top, and with numerous ferns, while occasionally we came across violets of sorts, and even with orchids, of the most delicate tints and shades.

After having luncheon on the top of the mountain we had to come down again, like the French king of old, and feeling very much puzzled about the aneroid, not knowing what was wrong with it, if it was wrong at all. Then we watched it at the bungalow itself, and found that the very same elevation that marked 1,200 feet in the morning, now marked only something under 1,100 feet on my return in the evening. There could be only one conclusion then, namely, that the aneroid was out of order for some reason or another. Aneroids, indeed, are not always the infallible indicators of heights that some people imagine, even when they are supposed to be in good enough order, as the experiences of Mr. Whymper have amply shown on the Andes. For he found that the different aneroids were so liable to vary, that he had to take the mean readings of three or four of them, in order to arrive at the proper conclusions with reference to heights.

Soon after our return I found that I had again been

attacked with those horrid leeches, as I had been in the swamps a day or two previously. There is something so bracy and breezy about mountains that the very mention of them inspires one with energy, and one would scarcely expect to be attacked by leeches on them. But on this, as on many other mountains, there are swampy patches here and there over which we had to cross. And, besides, these leeches live among the branches and leaves of trees, quite independent of the swampy regions. They are not exactly the leeches of the physician, so familiar to us, but I should think they are quite as sanguinary in their disposition. And, if they are found to be equally useful, there is an inexhaustible store of them to be found in Borneo and the islands round about.

They will tell you in Sarāwak that these leeches *see you coming*, but, whether they do so or not, they at any rate seem to *hear* you, judging from Dr. Russell Wallace's experience of them in another locality, and recorded by him in his interesting book, 'The Malayan Archipelago,' written nearly thirty years ago. This is what he says in one particular place :—

'We passed through extensive forests, along paths often to one's knees in mud, and were much annoyed by the leeches, for which this district is famous. These little creatures infest the leaves and herbage by the side of the paths, and when a stranger comes along they stretch themselves out at full length, and if they touch any part of his dress or body quit their leaf and adhere to it. They then creep to his feet, legs, or any other part of his body, and suck their fill, the first puncture being rarely felt during the excitement of walking. On bathing in the evening we generally found half a dozen or a dozen on each of us, most frequently on our legs, but frequently on our bodies; and I had one who sucked his fill from the side of my neck, but who luckily missed the jugular vein. There are many species of these forest leeches. All are small, but some are beautifully marked with stripes of light yellow. They probably attach themselves to deer and other animals which frequent the paths, and have thus acquired the singular habit of stretching themselves out at the sound (*sic*) of a footstep or of rustling foliage.'

The above remarks might appear to be an exaggerated 'traveller's tale,' but they are really the remarks of a wide traveller and a distinguished man of science. At any rate these little creatures left their marks on my legs for weeks afterwards; for when leeches are rubbed off, instead of being allowed to gorge themselves and drop off, they leave their so-called 'teeth' in the wounds, which are liable on that account to inflame and fester.

The rest of the time I stayed with Mr. G—— I generally spent doing nothing, but occasionally pottering about the plantation to improve my knowledge, not only of coffee, but of tea also, for he happened to be growing both of these useful commodities; so that I am now quite a past-master in the mysteries of *Orange Pekoe*, *Souchong*, *Conjou*, and *Bohea*, though I shall not disturb the equanimity of the reader by inflicting their description upon him.

The inquiring mind, however, may be enlightened on what is known among planters as *Monkey coffee*. Most of the coffee has hitherto been grown on the mountain sides of tropical climates like India, Brazil, and Ceylon, as it was not known till lately that it would condescend to grow on the mere plains at all. The vicinity of these coffee plantations, then, is generally covered with virgin forests, the very home and dwelling-place of grinning monkeys of various kinds. Monkeys are notorious for having a sweet tooth, and great delicacy of taste also; and it is needless further to say that they are therefore very fond of coffee berries. The coffee berries, too, when they are first ripe enough to be plucked, are fine and fair to look upon, and quite calculated to win the affections of both men and monkeys.

Perhaps Jacko does not care so much for their good looks as for their good quality, and in his own 'cute, thievish fashion he generally feeds on the very best coffee berries of the gardens that his honour frequents. But he only swallows the pulp round the seeds, while the seeds themselves are rejected. Hence certain places that Mister Jacko frequents are sometimes literally strewn with these choice seeds, which are by far the best of the best possible quality, as Jacko is a great connoisseur in his choice of berries. I accidentally came across this valuable piece of information, which I now offer to the reader gratis. For at the time I was staying with Mr. G—— one of his native gaffers had gathered bags of these much-prized seeds, and concealed them for his own evil purposes; and as freely I have received the information, even so do I now offer it for the reader's enlightenment. And if this straggling book will at all serve its purpose, and go through at least fifty editions, I shall expect by-and-by to see on every post and pillar a famous advertisement, in glaring red letters, recommending everyone to 'Ask for the Monkey Brand.' The reader is probably already familiar with the 'Monkey Brand' of soap that 'won't wash clothes,' but perhaps he has never before heard of the 'Monkey Brand' of coffee 'that cheers but does not inebriate.' Mr. G—— is the only planter in the whole of the Sarāwak possessions, and as he is an excellent host and a very amiable person (forbye being a brither Scot !), I am sure I wish him every success in his undertaking.

But it was now getting high time to say good-bye both to Mattang and Sarāwak. From our lofty eyrie on the side of the mountain, we could see through our glasses the 'Rajah Brooke' lying again at Kuching, and the burly 'Greek' walking up and down the quarter-deck, ready for sailing on her usual voyage to Singapore ; and so, on a fine warm, sultry, and very rainy morning, I started back to return to Kuching. There is quite a network of small sluggish streams in this portion of Borneo, as the littoral of the island is mostly composed of alluvial *débris* washed down from the mountains during the lapse of ages. One of these streams came within a mile or two of Mr. G——'s residence, and there in a creek was the brand-new boat that was going to bring me back again.

The crew consisted of three Malays (by far the most amphibious race in the East), and of one African Somali, another race with whom I had been fairly well acquainted some years before. And the poor Somali, with his coal-black skin, looked very disconsolate and out of place among these Bornean brownies. Mr. G—— had only quite recently settled down at Mattang, and the boat, as I said, was fresh and new ; for it was while finishing it off at Kuching, before bringing it home, that I happened to have the pleasure of meeting him for the first time. And the trip that she was now taking, to convey me to Kuching, was her veritable maiden voyage. I can only hope, then, that the 'Mermaid,' as I called her, will live for a long time, and will make many and many a voyage yet, with more valuable cargo.

On reaching Kuching I found that the 'Rajah Brooke' was sailing the next day for Singapore, and with her I said farewell to Borneo. Just before leaving Kuching I was told a funny story that was held back from me while I was still living there. As already remarked, the stragglers that visit remote Borneo are not very many. But about two years before this time one of these rare birds did manage to visit the island and passed himself off as 'Dr. Meyer from Melbourne.' In this way he imposed on Dr. F——, who took him into his house with the same feeling of brotherhood as he showed myself on the present occasion.

'Dr. Meyer from Melbourne' was the best of good company, had gone through a lot of adventures, and quite charmed the unsuspicious people of Kuching with his winning ways and pleasing manners. He was an adept at whist, and sang like a mavis. In short, he could show a wrinkle or two to the most accomplished of the Kuching community. Besides, he was delightfully communicative of his private affairs, was a millionaire in fact (for all Australians are millionaires), and was also engaged to an American heiress—for all American maidens are heiresses, of course!

In this way he passed a fortnight at Kuching in a very pleasant manner, nobody suspecting or caring to question whence he came or whither he was going. But at all events he was going to send bales of all sorts of valuable materials to Kuching, when he returned to civilisation back again, including a Persian carpet for Dr. F——'s sitting-room. And so the time glided away, and 'Dr. Meyer from Melbourne' at last took his departure. He was not long gone, however, when his friends here saw in the newspapers the hue and cry being raised after a notorious swindler, one of whose many *aliases* was 'Dr. Meyer.' He was evidently a man who had played many parts, and had quite easily gulled the simple people he was living with.

Nobody knew what eventually became of him, or whether he was caught or not. But it was generally believed that he went to Sarāwak to escape the clutches of the law, and that he probably hoped to escape into the interior, perhaps into Dutch territory. On reaching Kuching, however, he found himself in a *cul-de-sac*, from which there was no practicable outlet, save returning by the way he came, which he finally did. So all the valuable presents never arrived, and neither a Persian carpet nor a Persian cat ever reached the Doctor, who was so kind to him during his stay. Yet all the people at Kuching were very pleased that he behaved himself so decently when living with them. They prided themselves greatly on this, and perhaps ascribed the fact to their own very exemplary precept and example in reforming the unreformed. But perhaps 'Dr. Meyer' thought otherwise. He probably thought that the amount of swindling he could do in Kuching would not be worth the trouble, and he wisely let it alone. Was this then another 'Dr. Meyer from Melbourne,' and was Dr. F—— to be again imposed upon ? Let us hope not.

CHAPTER V

> He lived and died misunderstood,
>   Yet true as he was brave,
> And now in silent solitude
>   He moulders in the grave;
> E'en so shall moulder in the dust
> The noblest hearts—for so they must.
>
> The Hero's Epitaph.

Remarks on Sarāwak—The Original Rajah Brooke—His Roving Disposition—His Hatred of John Company—The Projected 'Schooner'—Discouraged by his Father—His First Cruise—He tried again, and became a King!—His Father's Death—Remarks on the relative value of Wealth and Friendship—The Rajah's Character and Chequered Career—Murder of Muda Hassim—Ross, the King of the Cocos Islands.

HAVING thus briefly recorded my own short journey through Sarāwak, it may not be out of place to refer in general terms to this interesting country, and its still more interesting founder. Sarāwak, then, is on the north-west coast of Borneo, between four and five hundred miles almost due east of Singapore, and is nearly as large as England in superficial area. The island of Borneo itself, of which Sarāwak forms only a part, is said to be the largest island in the world, with the exception of the island-continent of Australia; but some maintain that the island of New Guinea is as large, if not even larger.

The remote interior of both these tropical islands is very little known, and this remark is borne out by the fact, if fact it is, that the highest mountain in the world, Mount Hercules, has quite recently been discovered in New Guinea, and is 32,000 feet high, against the 29,000 odd feet of Mount Everest in the Himalayas, which has hitherto been considered the loftiest peak on this puny globe of ours. Mountains are prominent and obtrusive objects, are they not? And that the highest mountain in the world should remain undiscovered till this late day of the nineteenth century must surprise not a few people, and goes far to show how much New Guinea has yet to be explored. I have seen this statement made on several occasions in Anglo-Indian and other papers lately. I do not know who discovered Mount Hercules with its matchless 32,000 feet. But be that as it may, one thing remains certain, and that is that nobody will ever be able to climb it, as the highest point yet reached by man is only twenty-two thousand feet.[1]

Fifty years ago Sarāwak formed a part and province of the then extensive territory of the Sultan of Brunei, a town and state of that name to the north-east of Sarāwak, and from which the whole of the great island of Borneo is evidently called, the word 'Borneo' being in fact a corruption of the word 'Brunei.' This old state of Brunei has become extremely contracted of late years, partly by the encroachment of Sarāwak on the one hand, and partly by that of North Borneo on the other. A chain of mountains, culminating in Kinnabaloo, 14,000 feet, runs through a great portion of Borneo, and separates for the most part Dutch Borneo from the Sarāwak State, as well as from Brunei and North Borneo, all of which territories are placed in the north and north-east of the great island.

By far the greater portion of Borneo, by no means excluding Sarāwak, is covered with dense jungle and impenetrable virgin forest; and the climate of it is so rainy, every day and Sunday, that instead of the island being called by the corrupt name of Borneo, it ought really to be called Daily-drizzle Island. During my own short stay in that region, I scarcely ever saw the sun all the time, and

[1] After writing the above statement I happened to come across Sir William MacGregor, the present Governor of British New Guinea. He knew of the rumour, and said it sprang from a romance written some years ago by some Captain Lawson. I afterwards took the trouble of hunting out the very book in the library of the British Museum, and have now much pleasure in nailing this lie to the counter, as lies are so easily set agoing, and so hard to stop again. Brave old Mount Everest! You still hold your own, and will probably do so till the great day when the elements will burn with fervent heat, and the islands will flee away—and the *mountains* will not be found any more. *Vide* 'Wanderings in New Guinea,' by Captain J. A. Lawson, page 153, where the following statement is made :—' I calculated that it was 30,000 feet high; it proved to be 32,783 feet above the sea level, or 30,901 feet above the surrounding country.' The above sentence then is the nonsense from which the error has sprung, and the press marks of this book in the British Museum are 10,491. ee. I.

when going about anywhere, I generally got drenched to the skin. A small official print, the 'Sarāwak Gazette,' is published monthly at the capital town of Kuching. And as I was travelling there at the beginning of the year, I came across the annual number of this Gazette, in which were given the statistics of the previous one. And the following table, copied from that paper, will show the reader a bird's-eye view of the monthly rainfall, as well as of the total rainfall for the year in question, which was said to be about an average one.

Month	Ins.	Month	Ins.
January	27·71	July	14·73
February	9·88	August	7·91
March	10·82	September	7·82
April	12·11	October	16·75
May	10·34	November	19·70
June	12·06	December	25·63

Total rainfall for the year = 175·46 inches.

The reader will the more easily appreciate these figures when I remind him that the average yearly rainfall of rainy Great Britain is only between 30 and 35 inches.

This great and incessant moisture, in the presence of such heat and profuse vegetation, leads to a considerable prevalence of miasmatic fevers, as well as of *Beri-beri*, a somewhat curious ailment which is rather common in this country. This disease of *Beri-beri*, which is rare in Hindustan, appears to prevail under the climatic conditions that obtain in Borneo, namely, heat and moisture, in the presence of profuse vegetation; and its real nature, like that of many more common complaints, has hitherto been but little understood.

The population of the Sarāwak State is said to be considerably under half a million; so that the country is apparently very sparsely inhabited. Indeed, nothing seems to retard the growth of population more than thick jungles and impenetrable forests, wherever on the earth's surface they are to be found. For the bleak moors of the North and even the barren *steppes* of Central Asia produce a much more numerous and a far manlier race than these luxurious and evergreen climates.

This population of Sarāwak consists mostly of Dyaks, the native aborigines of the country. But there is also a considerable sprinkling of Malays and Chinese, the last of whom rebelled once against the first Rajah, burnt his house, killed a lot of people, including a few Europeans, and very nearly took away the Rajah's own life. But the Rajah was one too many for them, and finally brought them into subjection. It is not, however, in them that the traveller to Sarāwak is most interested; for he can see plenty Pigtails all over the East, without going to Sarāwak for that purpose. His interest will naturally be more in the Dyaks, the original people of the place, and the very particular concern of both the late and the present Rajahs.

The Dyaks are short in stature, but a well-knit and brown little people, scarcely to be distinguished from the Malays, who live among them along the coast, and to whom they must be very nearly allied in racial descent, as I shall mention more fully in a future chapter.

Their habits of head-hunting have already been alluded to, and are happily now but mere memories of the past, at least as far as the Dyaks of Sarāwak are concerned, who live a happy, peaceful, lazy life, under their beloved sovereign, His Highness Rajah Brooke the Second. They did not appear to me to be at all so primitive or savage as the conceptions I had previously formed by reading about them. And to the stranger they look frank, genial, and intelligent enough.

Yet they have scarcely any religion of their own, but, like the Red Indians of America, they believe in some 'Great Spirit' they call *Jiwati*, who is a tremendous big bogey in his way. Their lingual vocabulary is also said to be extremely limited, with individual words having very many, and entirely different kinds, of meanings—just the same as among ourselves.

But what is rather amusing among them is that a father is called after his son, instead of a son being called after his father, thus being a living and breathing example of a child being the father of the man, which people generally consider as a mere poetic flight of fancy. For whenever a man has got his firstborn son and gives him a name, he himself is no longer known by his previous appellation, but by that which he has given to his child, who repeats the same process when it comes to his turn to have a child of his own.

Deer are rather numerous in Borneo. And so another funny custom the Dyaks have consists in the fact that if the cry of a deer is heard roundabout on the night of a marriage, the marriage therewith and thereby becomes null and void; because they think the children, I presume, of such a union would be as timid in danger as that very timid animal. And we all know that various primitive races prize the flesh, and especially the heart, of ferocious animals, like the lion and tiger, under the false impression that, by eating their flesh, they become brave like these animals.

I have heard of various other customs noted among them, but most of them, I think, will be found on closer scrutiny to be customs common to the Dyaks and to other tribes, in the same state of civilisation, separated sometimes from one another far and wide over the world. But the best trait in the character of the Dyaks, as recorded by those who know them best, is that they are punctiliously truthful, honest, and of a naturally kind and affectionate disposition, in spite of all their ancient love of head-hunting, which seemed to come to them as a sort of second nature.

How the original Rajah Brooke came into the possession of Sarāwak has been the cause of much vehement and angry discussion, which frequently led to such damaging accusations against him as must often have embittered the Rajah's life. And, moreover, his position in Sarāwak was so unique that a few words about the same may not seem out of place here.

The original Rajah Brooke was the son of an Anglo-Indian, who must frequently have shaken the Pagoda tree to some effect in those days of fat rajahs, and when the rupee was worth two and sixpence instead of the inglorious shilling it is only worth now. He was half Scotch, half English by blood, and his interesting though chequered career does infinite credit to both sides of the Border, if even for nothing else than his splendid tenacity of purpose, through good and evil report, of which he had more than the usual share.

He was of an adventurous disposition from his early youth, and began life in the Honourable East India Company, or John Company, as it was more colloquially called at the time. He was wounded in some action or other, and returned home to recruit his health. He does not seem ever to have taken kindly to soldiering, as his restless spirit could but ill brook the dull routine of regimental life. And he was not therefore in any great hurry to return to India. He arrived, however, at last in 'The Land of Regrets,' but found, probably not to his regret, that he would be over five years absent before he could take up his appointment in the north of India. This was the extreme limit of absence from duty on any plea whatsoever, and I think that most people will agree that the terms were liberal enough in every conscience.

But he had no love for the service, and he therefore threw up his commission and sailed for England from Madras *viâ* China, which must be acknowledged to be a very roundabout way of doing business when in a hurry. A letter from him to one of his sisters at this time, and quoted by Miss Jacob in her book, 'The Rajah of Sarāwak,' reveals his inward feelings at this period of his life :—

'How delightful the thought,' he writes, 'of once more meeting you, my dear sister, and meeting you free from the shackles which have bound me! I toss my cap into the air, and my commission into the sea, and bid farewell to John Company and his evil ways. I am like a horse that has got a heavy clog off his neck, and feels himself at liberty to gallop or feed wherever his inclinations may prompt. Come what may, I am clear of that creature in Leadenhall Street. Here goes a puff of my cigar, and with it I blow the Company to the Devil or anywhere else, so they trouble me no further.'

He saw something of the Malayan Archipelago on this voyage to and from China, and after reaching home he resolved to make this the scene of his future labours, though he would no doubt be equally willing to meet with adventures anywhere else, so long as John Company troubled him no further. His mind got completely taken up with the project of a 'schooner,' with which he was going to do wonders, and roam among these tropical islands, to the advantage of the world in general, and of the barbarous natives of the islands in particular. But there was one serious obstacle in his way; and that was an obstacle that has curbed the career of many an aspiring youth before him, and will no doubt do so after him also. In short, he had no money.

His father had plenty, but, then, he was not dead yet. And consequently the son could not freely get at the hoard. In the book above referred to there is an amusing quotation from a letter of his, on this all-absorbing subject :—

'I feel existence a load that I would fain be quit of, were it not for some affections and future prospects. I do what I can to interest myself in what is going on around me, and keep my mind fixed upon the "Schooner plan," to which I have dedicated myself blindly. Often and often I say to myself, "Can I not bear the tedium of life till this time arrives (*sic*), when I shall be able to give scope to my spirit of adventure?" Sometimes this will keep me going, at others I droop and give all up in despair.'

In the book from which this is a quotation, there is nothing that comes out more prominently than the Rajah's domestic affections. Yet here he is at the age of thirty, secretly, and no doubt unconsciously, longing for his father's death, in order to be able to give scope to his spirit of adventure, as he himself tersely puts it. And though he would certainly be shocked if anybody told him so, yet there is no doubt that he was yearning and longing to come into what he considered his own, for he was the only surviving son, though there were two or three daughters.

Before leaving India on the journey I am now humbly trying to describe, I knew a young official who had recently applied for leave home, on the plea that an aunt of his, who was making him her heir, was going through the process of slow dying, and he was, he said, anxious to soothe her passage down the stream of Avernus. For some reason or other the leave was not granted at that time, and he was still remaining when I returned to India back again. 'Hallo,' I said to him, 'you here still? Hasn't your aunt died yet?' 'No, and it's very strange,' he replied, 'for two other aunts have died since'—but apparently not the one that was to leave the money, which I think was rather a pity.

When one calmly reflects how often people long for other people's death for the sake of their filthy lucre, he is compelled to acknowledge what a mighty god Mammon is in this mercenary world. And I have, therefore, sometimes thought that, from a worldly point of view, another verse might be almost added to the Sermon on the Mount, namely, 'Blessed are they who die poor, for they leave no legacy, and their friends will mourn for them.'

The Rajah's father was not at all in favour of what he considered his son's whimsical views of life, and regretted that he had now no fixed aim or profession. But as Delilah wearied out Samson, even so did the future Rajah Brooke weary out his father, though the latter confessed that he felt 'very much in the dark as to the nature of the proposed scheme.' And so the son was at last able to fit out his precious 'schooner' of 290 tons, and loading her with whatever he thought necessary to soothe the savage breast, he gaily sailed away in search of gold and fresh adventures. But like many another great enterprise, his first effort was a complete failure. He reached the enchanted regions right enough, but things went against him, and he had to come back again, without his darling 'schooner,' and a much poorer, but by no means a wiser man.

Rajah Brooke, however, was not a man easily subdued. What he lost in purse he gained in experience, which is by far the best practical way of learning anything. And during the voyage he became familiar with some places, as well as with the ways and manners of the primitive natives.

At last his father died, just to oblige him, and he then came into his own in peace and quietness. He was left a fair fortune, which would have kept him comfortably at home all his days, rocking in a cradle and sucking his thumbs, if inclined in that way. And most people, I think, would prefer to settle down comfortably, whether to suck their thumbs or not, rather than run after vain adventures in far away lands; for Rajah Brooke was at this time over forty years of age. Nor can it be denied that, though his life would have been less romantic, it would have been far more happy, for the Rajah actually died a poorer man as regards actual money than he was when he started again on this project; while during the whole of the rest of his life he was a veritable shuttle-cock in the hands of Mrs. Grundy.

No sooner did he come into his own than his love of adventure revived anew, if it really ever did flag for a moment. He bought another 'schooner,' and again sailed away in search of fresh fame and fortune. On this journey he reached Sarāwak in Borneo, and he remained in connection with this territory during the rest of his life, though he actually died at home.

In a cursory description like this, it is not intended to follow out the whole of his chequered career. Many maintained that he was an unmitigated pirate, while others as strenuously maintained that he was a devout philanthropist. He certainly led to the violent death of many seafaring natives in these regions, whom he and his friends called pirates, and whom his enemies called by a different name. His detractors pointed out that at the very best he was but a pirate punishing pirates, on the principle of a thief catching a thief, and that therefore hanging was far too good a punishment for him.

If these charges were true, then Rajah Brooke would certainly be one of the most dangerous and insidious pirates, and a scourge to humanity. Yet it is hard to conceive of him as a bloodthirsty pirate, as he was too romantic and Quixotic in his ideas to hurt the weak, and would much more probably be found fighting windmills in their defence.

That he was a bit of an adventurer there is no doubt, in the best sense of that much abused term. He would put matters to the touch, as it were, and stand by the issue. This is not an ignoble quality, and it is the truest definition of adventure. Chinese Gordon, it is said, used to maintain that Great Britain was created by her adventurers, of which he was himself, in this respect, no mean example. Small blame to Rajah Brooke, then, if he was an adventurer of this better sort.

How many young people, both before and after him, have gone to the gorgeous East in search of fame and fortune? And how many of them, alas! have had to turn back with enlarged livers and their tails between their legs? The process of this disillusionment is steadily going on before our very eyes at the present moment, and will go on for ever as long as Fortune will be such a shy maid and Fame so skittish. Nay more, Brooke had to turn back twice in the draggle-tail condition mentioned. But he tried yet again and became—a king!

It cannot be denied, however, that he got his first footing in Sarāwak by means of the strong hand. He had rendered some service to Rajah Muda Hassim, the Governor of Sarāwak, and uncle to the then reigning Sultan of Brunei, to whom Sarāwak then belonged. And the said Rajah had been making fair promises to Brooke, which he was in no great hurry to redeem. But the question came to a pitch at last, and this is the way in which Brooke himself writes upon the subject: 'Repairing on board the yacht, I mustered my people, and explained my intentions and mode of operation; and having loaded the vessel's guns, and brought her broadside to bear, I proceeded on shore with a detachment fully armed, and taking up a position at the entrance to the Rajah's (Muda Hassim's) palace, demanded and obtained an immediate audience.'

And thus without any bloodshed the future Rajah Brooke took possession of Sarāwak on the 24th day of September, 1841. The aboriginal Dyaks were at the time in rebellion against the Malay Sultan of Brunei; and his uncle, Muda Hassim, the Governor of the Sarāwak province, was unable to bring them into subjection again. It was under these favourable auspices that the roving James Brooke arrived on the scene with his inevitable *schooner*, went to the front inland, near the village of Singhi already mentioned, and in a pitched battle, in which one man was killed, he brought the Dyaks into a more amenable frame of mind.

These were the services rendered by Brooke, and in a good-hearted mood Muda Hassim promised Brooke the Governorship of Sarāwak, which at that time comprised a comparatively smaller extent of country than it does now, lying for the most part along the course of the Sarāwak river, of which the native village of Kuching formed the principal township, as it does to this day. But on further consideration Muda Hassim, as I said, was not in any violent hurry to redeem his promise, till Brooke at last, as he says himself, brought the schooner's broadside to bear.

But then and afterwards Muda Hassim and his brother Muda Mahomed were Brooke's firm friends. They finally both returned to Brunei, leaving Brooke in possession at Sarāwak. And there their friendly proclivities towards the white stranger eventually resulted in the cruel murder of the two of them, at the instigation of their nephew, the

Sultan of Brunei, who was probably more of a far-seeing politician than either of his victims.

But Brooke could not help some people getting attached to him, for it was his fate in life to make some very fond of him, while others hated him like poison. This quality in a man may, I think, be esteemed more or less of a distinction in itself, for your mere milk-and-water wee bodies are incapable of kindling either frantic love or frowning hatred.

Thus his life was by no means a happy one, for he was much traduced by some of the public press, and often found himself the subject of heated discussions. But he stuck to his colours till the very last. And whatever other people thought of him, the simple-minded Dyaks adored him. They looked upon him as a great deliverer from the oppression of the Sultans of Brunei. And now that he is dead they declare that his great spirit resides in a mountain not far from Kuching, ever watchful of the welfare of his dear little brownies. Though so venturesome a soul, he appears never to have been a man of strong physique, or to have enjoyed robust health either in Saráwak, or during his visits home. He died at last in England at the age of sixty-five, a poorer man in mere worldly wealth than when first he went to Saráwak. *Sic transit gloria mundi!*

The only other British subject that offers any favourable parallel to Rajah Brooke by becoming a little king in a foreign land was a man named Ross, a native of Shetland, who became ruler of the Cocos Islands to the south-west of the island of Java. Ross was an able-bodied seaman, whose ship was wrecked among these islands, and some of the crew were drowned. The survivors chose Ross as their leader in contending against the natives. This they successfully did, till one occasion when Ross and some others were on the war-path. On their return they found that their home-staying friends had rebelled, and had chosen another leader. Ross with his few friends attacked them at once, routed the rebels, and became king of the Cocos Islands, where his descendants rule to this day. The protection of the British flag (for which, by the way, the late Rajah Brooke was so very anxious) has lately been accorded both to Saráwak and the Cocos Islands. But while thus becoming an integral portion of the great British Empire, they have reserved to themselves a measure of Home Rule liberty, which ought to be satisfactory to all the parties concerned.

The original Rajah Brooke never married ; and though he died a poor man as regards mere cash, yet he left a fine heritage to his nephew, Mr. Charles Johnson, who assumed the name of Brooke, and is now designated His Highness Sir Charles Brooke, of Sarāwak, and second of that ilk. He was in England during the time of my visit, but when he is in Sarāwak he is monarch of all he surveys. He entirely follows in the footsteps of his uncle, the Great Rajah, and is said to be very particular about his insignia of office, the gold umbrella, to be held over him as he crosses the little river of Kuching from his residence, the *Estana*, to the Hall of Judgment, for the Rajah is a veritable Moses in this respect, without even having a priest of Midian to help him. The province has grown apace since the original concession was made, and the revenue has increased considerably, though not perhaps at the rapid pace that the eager old Rajah at one time anticipated.

The country is kept in order by a small police force, mostly of Indian Sikhs, scattered here and there over the land. And there are also four companies of native Dyak troops, known as the Sarāwak Rangers, commanded by Major D——, a retired British officer, who takes the greatest interest in his lively little levy. This little corps has everything complete, from the commanding officer down to the drummer boy, and even a national anthem that goes under the very melodious and patriotic name of ' *Rix-rax !* ' whatever that may mean.

CHAPTER VI

> On a tossing ship and a tumbling sea,
> We stemmed the waves frae our ain countree,
> Not knowing, alas! if we e'er again
> Should live to return on that sounding main.
> *The Exile's Lament.*

Return to Singapore—The steamship 'Independent'—My German shipmates—Chinese Chow-Chow—Frightening evil spirits—Gregorivitch, the Russian officer—Arrival at Bangkok—Jackson the pilot—'Don't you smell it?'—Ocean-butterfly Fort—The 'John Baptist Say'—French and British men-o'-war at Bangkok—Chinese New Year—The British Flag—King Chulalongkorn—Description of Bangkok—My Dutch 'Casual'—Toasting the German Emperor—Visit to Koh-si-chang—Landing there of French troops—The Siamese Navy.

But here we are of an early morning going into the bay of Singapore back again. I did not wish to go ashore there, as I was anxious to get as soon as possible up to Bangkok, the capital town of the Buffer State of Siam, from which this volume receives its name, and which was then, and is now, very much in evidence before the public, as the possible cause of a war between Great Britain and France. I also wanted to be in Bangkok during the Chinese New Year there, for the Celestials form the most important section of the population of Bangkok, and are said to observe this festival better than in China itself, on the principle that the further we roam the dearer is home. And, indeed, true to this principle, the Scotch festival of St. Andrew is far better observed in remote Calcutta than it is in Edinburgh.

When the 'Rajah Brooke' dropped anchor in the harbour of Singapore, there were several ships flying the Blue Peter, as an indication that they were sailing that day; and the gallant captain (the Greek) was good enough to place one of his boats and crew at my disposal, to find out if any of these ships were bound for the port of Bangkok. I went on board a steamer called the 'Labelle,' but neither a belle nor a beauty was she. The captain of the ship was on shore, and the two or three Europeans I met on board did not at all encourage me to proceed to Bangkok with the 'Labelle.' She was only a coalship, they said, and carried no passengers; which one could easily believe from looking at the ship's iron decks, covered with the coal dust which they were just shipping, as well as the smudgy faces of the speakers themselves. One of them casually remarked that further out in the harbour there was a German ship that was going to Bangkok, that she was faster than the 'Labelle,' and that she was leaving at once, while the 'Labelle' would not go till the next day or the day after.

On going on board this ship, the German captain of her, too, was on shore, but the mate said that the captain would make no objection to giving me a passage; and within a couple of hours thereafter I was on board the 'Independent' with all my property. The captain of the ship had come on board by this time, spoke English fluently, and had no objection whatever to my taking a passage. But there was someone else on board who required to be consulted. This was the Chinese supercargo or *compradore* of the ship. The 'Independent,' like the 'Labelle,' was entirely a cargo boat, and was chartered by Chinese merchants for a certain period, so that the captain sailed the ship wherever these good people desired. The Chinese supercargo tried to make out that it was a great favour to give me a passage; and when he discovered that I had no ticket or papers from shore, he shook his head sadly. How could he give me a passage without some papers from shore, and how could he know that I was not a fugitive from justice—another 'Dr. Meyer from Melbourne,' in fact? But though the heathen Chinee may be very fond of justice, there is another little talisman that he is fonder of still, and that is the almighty Mexican dollar, which is the current coin in the Straits Settlements.

After satisfying himself about the justice portion of the business, and also about the dollars, the heathen Chinee was good enough not to offer any further difficulty. Like the 'Labelle,' the 'Independent' had no cabins for passengers, but I had to pay Johnnie almost the same fare as for a passage in a first-class ocean greyhound. However, when a thing has to be done, there is no use haggling about it, especially with a Chinaman, when he knows that he is master of the situation. Fortunately there was a small house over the stern of the ship, which we may conveniently call the round-house or wheel-house, and which, besides the reserve wheel, contained two small compartments, separated from one another by a thin partition. The captain's proper cabin was amidships, but in one of these two compartments he had an extra bed; while in the adjoining one the captain, first mate, and chief engineer messed together. The captain then put the small compartment with the bed in it at my disposal, and I was also made welcome to mess with the three of themselves.

The ship was not able to sail till daybreak the next morning. She was entirely on water-ballast, without any cargo whatever, and was going to Bangkok for orders. We got strong head winds against us in the Gulf of Siam, and the light ship tossed about very much, but I was getting too used to tossing by this time to be entirely upset by the process. Through our unexpected delay that night at Singapore, and because of the strong winds blowing against us in the Gulf of Siam, we were later than we expected in arriving at the bar across the mouth of the river Menam, on which Bangkok is situated, twenty-five miles farther up. The passage was too rough to be called pleasant; but my foreign shipmates were very obliging, and helped to make up by their kindness for what I lost in mere material comfort. There were only seven Europeans among them all, the rest being Asiatics, mostly Chinamen. All the Germans spoke English, and said that they had learnt English at school, and that they had often sailed in English vessels with English crews. They even gave their orders in English when directing the Chinese to do anything, and their very compasses were of British manufacture.

As we were approaching the land one afternoon, I saw a group of Chinese eating their *chow-chow* with their chopsticks on one of the ship's hatchways, and I tried to get a snap shot at them with my kodak in their interesting entertainment. But immediately they saw my designs upon them they dispersed at once, and were not at all disposed to figure among my collection of 'strange animals that I have seen.' The captain, however, induced them to endure the operation, and I took what I hoped would turn out a good photograph of themselves and their chopsticks. Soon afterwards I took a photo of my three messmates, but I found that before taking the second one, I had not turned the spool round, and therefore, the two photos would be impressed on the same sensitive film. So the photos had to be taken again, much against the inclination of the Chinese, though they did not make any outward disturbance about it.

It is funny to note the objection of some primitive people to their portraits being taken. They sometimes fancy that if you possess their portrait or shadow, you become possessed of the power to injure them at your pleasure. Many well authenticated cases have been recorded about this superstition, which in reality underlies the idea of 'burning in effigy,' a species of diablerie still existing among ourselves. One of the saddest and strangest of these stories connected with portraits is that recorded of a Redskin chief, named Mahtochuga, as related in Sir John Lubbock's 'Origin of Civilisation.' The portrait of this chief was taken in profile by an Englishman, and it therefore depicted but half of the face sideways. His rude followers were wild about this, saying that their chief Mahtochuga was never afraid of looking any one *full* in the face; while his rival chief and enemy Shonka ('The Dog') said that the photographer knew very well that Mahtochuga was a coward, or half a man, and so took the portrait in this way. This led to a fight between Mahtochuga and Shonka, in which the innocent Mahtochuga was killed, while in revenge his followers killed both Shonka and his brother —all on account of that paltry profile photograph. Indeed, the susceptibilities of savages are often so strange and ridiculous, that it is not always easy for the traveller to avoid treading unintentionally on their tender corns.

The kodak, I am sorry to say, turned out a great failure, apparently from the film being too old, a fact which I had no means of knowing at the time. If I were taking photographs in beaten tracks, this would have mattered little, but I had taken such trouble to procure interesting ones, in out of the way places, that their want of success was a great disappointment for me.

The captain and chief engineer of the ship were really Danes by blood, as they belonged to the province of Schleswig-Holstein that has only lately been ceded from Denmark to Germany. They were, therefore, in sentiment more Danish than German; for it is far easier to attach countries than to win the hearts of the inhabitants. The chief engineer sailed under the very Scotch name of Ross. One day I alluded to his name, and said that he must be descended from some Scotchman who settled in Denmark some time or other. But to my surprise he did not rise to my flattering suggestion, but remarked that the Rosses in Scotland must be descended from those of Denmark. I leave this weighty question to some Rosses that I know, and hope they will be able to decide which of the Rosses had a boat of their own at the time of the Flood, the Danish ones or the Scotch ones, though I have a shrewd opinion of what their decision will be.

And this reminds me of another little story. That's the mischief of stories. They hang by one another's noses and tails like a string of Arabian camels. Some years ago I was sailing across the Pacific from Japan to America, and among the passengers was not only Miss Nellie Bly, the famous American racer, but also a Russian admiral and his aide-de-camp, who was a lieutenant in the Russian Navy, and whose name was Gregorivitch, which was exactly my own name, the 'vitch' at the end of his name corresponding precisely with the 'mac' at the beginning of mine. By the unchivalrous laws of my country, my name, for nearly two hundred years, could not be borne under the extreme penalty of death; and many bearing it wandered and died in foreign lands, rather than forsake the same. Could this then be a Muscovite descendant of the ancient clan Clan-Alpine? The aide-de-camp spoke English very well, and I asked him one day, for amusement. But he claimed no descent from the Land o' Brown Heath!

We were later in arriving at Bangkok than we at first expected, on account of the high winds against us on the voyage. But we were at last making land at eight or nine o'clock at night, and carefully on the look-out for the lightship off the mouth of the river. This was also the Chinese New Year's Eve, and as the ship was so light, we hoped to be able to get across the bar, and proceed to Bangkok without delay; a programme that would have suited me well enough, as I should be in Bangkok to see the Chinese jinks in celebration of that event, and which I rather wished to witness. We made out the lightship in due course, and sailing slowly up to it, we blew the ship's horn with a great flourish.

But for a long time there was no sign of recognition whatever from the lightship, so that we had to drop our anchor. It was only then that we could see a boat putting off from the lightship, and steering our way. This was one of the pilot boats, and the captain called the pilot by the name of Jackson. It was too late to take the ship up that night, he shouted, but he would be on board by daybreak in the morning. I felt rather annoyed at this, as I had lost the Chinese New Year at Bangkok in spite of all my energy, and for this I blamed the laziness of the pilot in taking such a long time in coming out to the ship. He did not come on board at all, and was just leaving the ship's side back again. 'Hullo, Jackson!' I shouted to him from the bridge. 'You have been rather sleepy to-night on account of the Chinese New Year.' 'Who's that?' replied Jackson, in a gruff, angry voice. 'Oh, never mind,' I said, 'it is only an old shipmate.' 'All right, then,' rejoined Jackson, 'I'll see you to-morrow morning;' and therewith the oars of the boat splashed in the sea, and Jackson headed for the lightship, while we turned in to sleep till the morrow, for my good intentions had failed this time again, as they had frequently done before.

In the very early morning there was Jackson before me on the bridge, but unfortunately he could not recognise in me the long lost shipmate that he expected. I excused myself for coming on to the bridge, but as I was a stranger, and wanted to watch the steamer going up, &c., &c.—but Jackson did not mind in the least. On the contrary, he became quite genial and talkative, for as a matter of fact he had little to do, and would probably find his way up to Bangkok with his eyes closed. For except at the bars at the mouth of the river, the Menam, or 'Mother of Waters,' though twisting about a good deal, is quite easily navigated up to Bangkok, there being scarcely any shoals on the way, and the banks being abrupt and uniform. So the pilot could afford to speak or listen at his pleasure; for Jackson is not only the oldest pilot, but probably also the oldest European resident in this remote land, and knew everything about everything and everybody else up here. He had been originally a sea captain, and was one of the first small batch of three or four European pilots, established and licensed to navigate the Menam thirty-eight long years before that date. The others had all died off, and Jackson alone was left behind, like Ossian after his brave comrades; and though he was now the oldest of the pilot service, over seventy years of age, and with a game leg, he still retained his youthful ways, with plenty of grit and game in the old salt still. He was very entertaining, and occasionally spoke in a slow *sotto voce* tone of voice that reminded one of Byron's Lambro—'the mildest mannered man that ever scuttled ship or cut a throat.'

But far be so base an imputation from my friend Jackson, whom I had the pleasure of meeting several times afterwards at the Oriental Hotel, at which I was staying. It was he who told me of the peculiar bar at the mouth of the Menam river—that there is never more than thirteen or fourteen feet of water over it at the highest floods, and not more than three or four feet at the lowest ebb-tides; and that the tides are so very erratic in their disposition, that no reliable tide-tables can be previously made for the high and low-water tides on this peculiar river.

When we started in the morning there was not a breath of wind blowing, and the ship was going dead slow at first. But shortly after, or about 6.30 A.M., the land breeze reached us, and I never felt a land or sea breeze before that announced its coming more abrupt and unmistakable. Jackson sniffed the breeze as the war-horse sniffs the battle. 'Don't you smell it?' ejaculated Jackson, 'it smells so fresh and cool.' It was certainly slightly cool, but to me it smelt neither fresh nor pure, but as if it were blowing across the very sink of iniquity. And though Jackson's nose had got used to it during thirty-eight long years, that's what it really was, as anybody should be able to understand who knew the lie of this country. The land about Bangkok for miles and miles is simply reticu-

lated with a net-work of foul canals and klongs that flow
up and down slowly with the tide. When the tide is out,
the exhalations from these klongs do not at all consist of
otto of roses ; and when the land breeze from over these
klongs suddenly blows with a whiff across the purer sea
air, it is not so fresh as Jackson fancied ; at least I
thought so, very decidedly, and some of my readers may
yet get the opportunity of judging for themselves.

After crossing the bar of the river, we passed to our
left a fortified island called Phi-sua-Smud, which in English means the Ocean-butterfly Fort ; (*Phi* = fort ; *sua* =
a butterfly ; and *Smud*=ocean). This is a strange name
for a stronghold, because butterflies, even the social ones,
are more noted for their charms of colour than for their
courage in danger ; and as for the ocean-butterfly, why, I
never heard of it before. 'Never-give-in Fort,' though
not so melodious, would be a much better name ; but alas !
it would not be a true one here, as this same Ocean-butterfly Fort had been smashed up by the French men-o'-war only a short time before. It was this same Jackson,
too, who had piloted the French ships on that occasion,
when they forced the Menam and steamed up to Bangkok,
an act that caused no little commotion at the time, and
was supposed to have brought Great Britain within
reasonable prospects of a war with France.

Jackson at that time was piloting to Bangkok a small
steamer of 150 tons, called the 'John Baptist Say,' which
was the only ship then regularly trading between Bangkok
and Saigon, the capital town of French Indo-China. The
French gunboats put some officers on board the 'John
Baptist,' and then followed in her wake in the dark, while
the Ocean-butterfly Fort opened fire on them. The French
gunboats coming on behind were more the object of the
Fort than the humble 'John Baptist,' as Jackson said
that he could hear the cannon balls whizzing over his head,
'but,' said he, 'not a bl—— one of them hit me'—as if it
would only be a mere scratch if they did. But though not
one of them hit Jackson himself, yet the 'John Baptist'
got her baptism of fire on this occasion ; for one of these
despised cannon balls hit her between wind and water,
and she began to sink so rapidly that Jackson had to
run her ashore, and was there and then made a prisoner

by the Siamese, along with everybody else on board the vessel.

They afterwards raised the 'John Baptist Say' (to give her full name), and we passed her further up the river, covered all over with mud, and looking very sorry for herself. But with this exception the Ocean-butterfly Fort does not appear to have done any great execution, for shortly afterwards some shots from the French gunboats caught hold of its corrugated-iron roofing, and tore it away in such a manner that it fell down on the men working the guns below, and killed several of them on the spot. So the Ocean-butterfly Fort was silenced, and the French gunboats proceeded up to Bangkok without any further molestation—and so did we on this more peaceful journey.

An incident that caused quite a flutter in the newspapers took place at this time. One of the French men-o'-war was said to have fired across the bows of H.M.S. 'Swift,' and to have ordered her out of the harbour. But what really occurred was that the French senior commander intimated to the British ship, for her own information, that he was going to open fire on the Fort if necessary. It appears true, however, that some French gunboat did fire across the bows of the 'Swift,' apparently by mistake. For after the French ships reached Bangkok, the captain of the gunboat in question said that in the dark he did not know he was firing across a British ship at all, and expressed his regret for the accident. This is what I was told in Bangkok itself from people who ought to know, and I believe it is the true version of the story.

The event, however, took place quite shortly after another unfortunate accident had occurred in West Africa. It will be remembered that, on that occasion, a native war party under French officers opened fire by mistake, and in the dark too, on a small native party under British officers. The unfortunate attack was repulsed, and several officers and men were killed on both sides, including the young French commander, who only lived long enough to explain his fatal error, as he had mistaken this party for a party of native rebels that he was in pursuit of. That these unfortunate accidents should happen about the same time

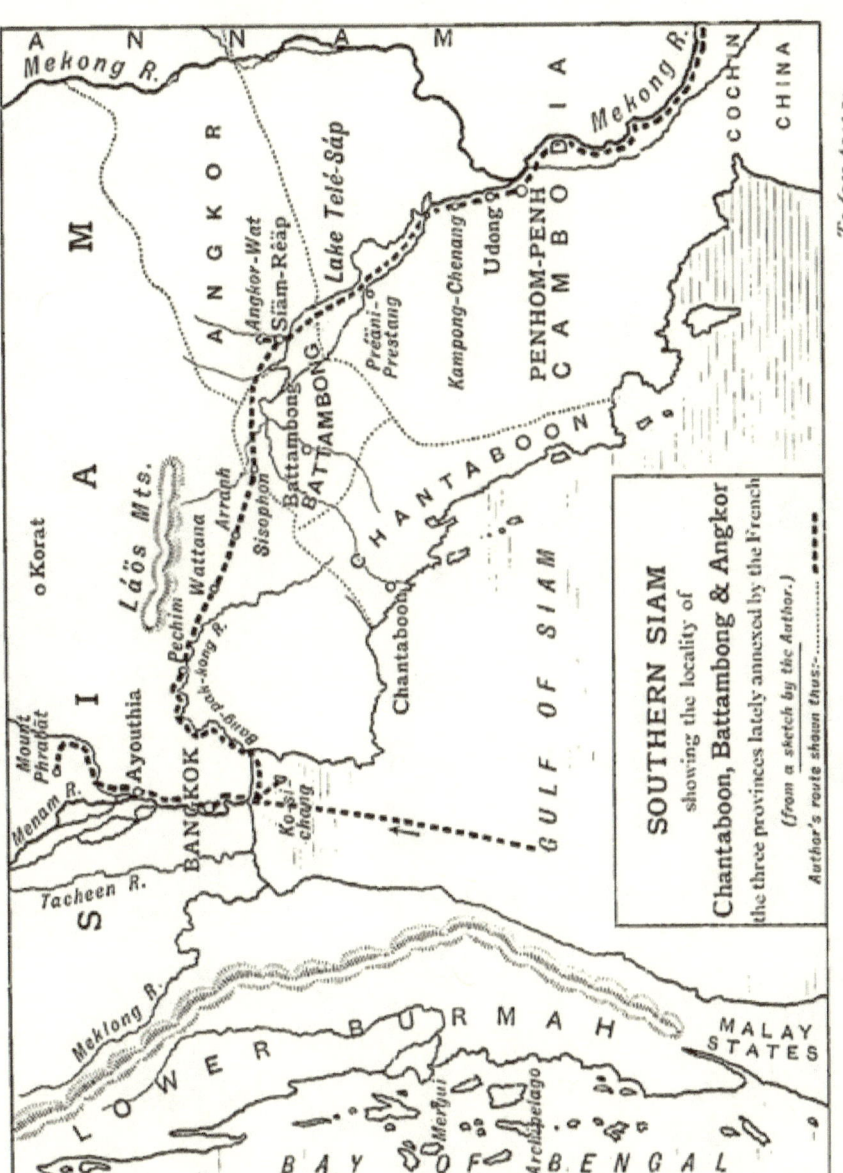

tended to aggravate the importance of them in the eyes of the public, and led some people to believe that they were intended as a challenge by France, whereas they were merely hapless accidents.

But when dwelling upon these warlike topics, we must not forget about the Chinese New Year. The 'Independent' did not go up all the way to the city of Bangkok that morning, but old Jackson took me in his pilot boat, and landed me safely at the Oriental Hotel, which I made my head-quarters during my stay there. There were only two men-o'-war in the river at this time, namely, one British gunboat called the 'Linnet,' and one French gunboat called the 'Aspic.' The French ship was anchored near the middle of the stream, opposite the French Legation; and the 'Linnet' occupied a similar position, a cable's length higher up, and opposite the British Legation. Both ships were within a few hundred yards from the landing place of the hotel, which is situated on the riverside a little below the French Legation.

Shortly after our arrival Jackson and I went to sit in the verandah among a lot of people gathered there, and consisting mostly of ships' officers of various nations. Suddenly they all got up to watch a steam-tug that was passing the landing-place. She was going up the river, and tugging after her quite a string of unwieldy rice-boats, by no means an uncommon sight at Bangkok. But what roused the curiosity of the onlookers was that this tug, as well as the string of rice-boats, were all gaily decorated with British flags, as they proceeded on their way. How the Chinese got a hold of so many of these flags nobody knew, but they were evidently meant as a demonstration. And when on the subject of flags, I think there is no flag in the world so fine as the British flag. That little Jack in the corner gives an air of sauciness to it that is quite beyond compare.

"'Tis only a flimsy fabric, 'tis only a tattered rag,
But the angels' eyes grow brighter at the sight of the British flag.'

Now this was the Chinese New Year's Day, and I had lost the Chinese New Year's Eve, with all its feasts and its lanterns, by our delay in the river during the previous night; and it appears that some of the Chinese in a merry mood, after last night's orgies, took it into their heads to make this great display of British flags from mere cussedness, and from nothing else. It was currently reported at the time that France was going to annex Siam, or at any rate as much of it as she could, and the demonstration was evidently intended to convey the impression that, if there was to be a partition, it was the British flag and not the French, that these holiday-makers preferred to follow. Thus the procession of tug and rice-boats with their borrowed or stolen flags proceeded past the British and French gunboats, much to the amusement of the spectators on shore, and probably viewed with different kinds of feeling by the onlookers from the two French and English ships. Not that the Chinaman loves us, for that he doesn't. But he has got a keen appreciation of the almighty dollar; and as he is a shrewd and mercenary kind of animal, he prefers our free-trade system to the protective system of France. That's it, and nothing more.

The king is dead—long live the king! Well, the king of Siam was reported to be dead that very morning. But as this curious king has been reported to be dead so often of late, he must possess the nine lives of a cat and one life more, and there may, therefore, be some prospect of his recovery.

He was certainly keeping himself very secluded at this time, and no European physician was allowed to see him at all, though at one time I had some hope of being able to visit the king on the plea of consultation with somebody else. He was rather unfortunate in his medical attendance then, as he had just lost Dr. Gowan, whom he is said to have trusted more than anybody else, and in more ways than in mere medicine alone. King Chulalongkorn, therefore, had no adviser at all, and hence the constant rumours about his death, which was supposed to be kept secret for political purposes. These rumours crop up at the very present time. And I hope the evil prophets will be encouraged, for it may safely be prophesied of these false prophets that if they only keep prophesying long enough, their predictions will eventually become true, as the poor king is bound to die some time or other, like everybody else.

That night I met a roving Dutchman at the dinner table, and we both went out afterwards to see what could be seen of the remnants of the Chinese New Year feast. People said it was dangerous to be running about the Chinese quarters at night, and at such a season. But it wasn't; and we drove through the town, as well as the walled city, right into the palace gates four or five miles away. That's all, however, we had for our labour; for the festivities, whatever they were, had taken place the previous night, their New Year's Eve, and were all over by this time.

On these gay occasions the Chinese expose in their houses, and sometimes on tables in the streets, great displays of meats and drinks, which they devoutly offer to the shades of their relatives and ancestors who have joined the majority. The latter obligingly descend from the realms above, and silently partake of the spiritual portion of the sacred offerings, while they leave the mere material and grosser parts untouched, and without any marks of their finger ends or chopsticks whatever. It is not easy to conceive of much spirituality contained in a dead leg of mutton, or more particularly of pork, of which Chinamen are so passionately fond. But opinions differ vastly in matters spiritual as well as in matters carnal, and at any rate this custom pleases Johnnie, as well as the shades of his ancestors, and is therefore satisfactory to all concerned. Besides, Johnnie's offerings are in the morning as he left them at night, and he eats the material portion himself, or distributes them among his poor neighbours, none of whom ever misses the spiritual essence of these dainty viands.

Occasionally, however, a stealthy pariah or village cur comes silently on the scene, and runs away with the leg of mutton. But that's another story; and, curiously enough, although Buddhists believe in transmigration, Chinamen never suspect that these poor dogs may possess the very souls of the ancestors to whom the offerings are being made, otherwise they would not beat them so mercilessly. Strange though this superstition may seem to us, yet it is one of the widest prevalence throughout the world.

All that we could see of the feast consisted of gaily dressed Chinamen squatting here and there by the sides of the bazaars, and steadily indulging in their pet passion of gambling, to which no other nation is so addicted. Fireworks were also popping off here and there with great briskness, for this is the favourite way, all over the East, for scaring evil spirits, who appear to be particularly afraid of detonating crackers and squibs of every kind. Before going to Singapore, the last voyage of the 'Independent' was from Hong Kong to Bangkok, and more than half the value of her cargo was composed of these rockets and cracking substances in general—all of them for this coming event, the Chinese New Year in Bangkok and surrounding country, which, unfortunately, are being quite overrun by these almond-eyed intruders.

We can't quite know why evil spirits should be so frightfully afraid of fire and sound, as they are presumably quite accustomed to them, but that they are so is a very common opinion throughout most of Asia, an amusing example of which appeared not long ago in one of the Anglo-Indian papers. Many of the more primitive natives of India attribute childlessness in married women to the machinations of jealous evil spirits; while the best way to frighten them off, and become as fruitful as Rachel, is to *set a house on fire!* The spirits are awfully afraid of the heat and the crackling and the terrible blaze. It is not at all necessary, as one would think, that it should be your own house you should set on fire. Oh, dear, no! Your neighbour's house will do even better, and in the case alluded to, the woman yearning for offspring set fire to a house actually on the other side of her village. I have not yet heard of the physiological effect of this smart manœuvre, but she was imprisoned by mere matter-of-fact British law for committing a very serious misdemeanour. But whether evil spirits are afraid of noise or not, men certainly are, and hence the yell recommended in charging an enemy, in the hope of demoralising him. Why, the very walls of Jericho, once upon a time, fell down to the blowing of rams' horns.

But, though I lost the Chinese New Year, I was yet in ample time for a still more interesting festival. For on the 20th of that same month there was to be a full moon, and on that same full moon was to occur the yearly devotion and homage paid by pious Buddhists at Buddha's sacred footprint on the holy hill known as Mount Phrabāt. This place is some one hundred and fifty miles from the sea by the river route, and thither Siamese pilgrims from all parts of the country foregather in their thousands at this particular period.

On my 'ticket-of-leave' from India only Borneo and Bangkok were recorded, but this was only because I was afraid I should not be able to get any further. Yet I devoutly hoped, if I reached the latter place, that I should be able to 'jockey the ghost,' and smuggle myself into the interior in some way or another.

One great difficulty was to procure servants, and though I was willing to content myself with only an interpreter and a cook, yet I found it very hard to secure either of these useful functionaries.

And so, when looking out for servants, and waiting to witness the great pilgrimage to Mount Phrabāt, I made use of my time by prowling promiscuously about this curious city. Bangkok is popularly known as the 'Venice of the East,' though Venice would certainly object to being called the 'Bangkok of the West.' Europeans imagine that all that is romantic and old is to be found in the 'gorgeous East.' This is quite a mistake, for though a certain amount of narcotic glamour and mystery is no doubt associated with the sultry Orient, yet, for right down romance, give me the 'breezy West' instead of it. It is to a great extent the imagination of the West, and the exaggerations of mere travellers' tales, that have invested the East with by far the greater portion of its glamour, especially because it was at one time considered so mysterious and so far away. And when reading such curious travellers' tales as those of Sir John Mandeville and others, one wonders at the fertile humbugging imaginations that these early travellers were blest with, and how easily they imposed on the ignorant community. At any rate, Bangkok in respect of romance contrasts unfavourably with its western equivalent, for here there is no St. Mark's, no Bridge of Sighs, nor memories of either Doge or Bucentaur, with all their historical and romantic associations. Bangkok, in short, is almost completely wanting in history; and what is anything without that?

There are certainly plenty of canals, and plenty of gondolas and gondoliers after their own fashion. The ground on which the town is situated is quite closely intersected by these canals running in various directions, and greatly facilitating the means of communication. Small puffing steam launches, and these native craft form quite a feature of the city, and to a great extent supply the place of wheeled carriages in less watery localities. The immediate banks of the river are thickly packed with the usual wooden houses for miles and miles, while a great many of these houses are floating on the water, and so movable from place to place, that their inhabitants may aptly be compared to the tortoise that carries his home upon its back. And it is somewhat amusing to see some of the smallest of these houses actually bobbing up and down from the wash from the launches steaming alongside of them. These floating houses are the very mart of Bangkok, and the river itself may be looked upon as the High Street of the city.

On land there is only one street worthy of the name, and this long street leads from near the Palace enclosure, for at least three or four miles, to the southern outskirts of the city, and running all through its course nearly parallel with the river and only a few hundred yards away from it. The rest of the streets, especially outside the walled city, consists for the most part of comparatively short offshoots, passing here and there; for the city, though said to contain 500,000 inhabitants, has no great inland depth in it, but is spread in a straggling way along the banks of the river, especially the left bank, on which by far the greater portion of the town is situated. This inland portion, comparatively narrow though it is, is much divided by intercommunicating canals, which, as already said, serve the purpose of both streets and drains in less amphibious cities.

The tide flushes these canals, or klongs, as they are called, twice every twenty-four hours; but yet they appear stagnant and muddy enough to look upon, as the water is generally rendered impure by natural as well as unnatural causes. These repeated flushings of the canals by the tide, however, conduce greatly to the salubrity of the city of Bangkok. Like most Eastern capital towns there is a walled city, occupying but a portion of the whole area, and in the centre of this walled city is the Palace of the King. When Mandalay was taken in 1885, the Burmans looked upon the Golden Palace of King Theebaw as the hub or physical centre of the universe. But though they were wrong, it had as much right to be considered the centre of the universe as any place else. Some people call London the hub of the universe, which shows what meagre conception such silly people must have of the immensity of the universe; for, granted that the universe has no bounds (and man is incapable of conceiving that it has), then it naturally follows that there can be no centre where there is no circumference.

One day my Dutch 'casual,' as I called him, and myself went down to Paknām at the mouth of the river, this being the only piece of railway, twenty-five miles long, in the whole kingdom of Siam: though they are at present proceeding with more extensive speculations of that same kind. This short railway is so narrow, that it is really more of a steam tramway than anything else; and here the cars run up and down to Paknām three times a day. We went down particularly to see if we could manage to visit the Phi-sua-Smud, or Ocean-butterfly Fort, which had been so much damaged quite recently by the French men-o'-war.

When we arrived at Paknām, we found the primitive little station arrayed in all the glory of bunting and Chinese lanterns of every description, and with a long table and chairs arranged on the platform. Apparently there was some great banquet to take place, and, seeing these decorations being superintended by a couple of Germans, we inquired what the business was all about. There are a goodly number of Germans in Bangkok, and all over the Further East, for that matter; and these preparations, they said, were being made to celebrate the birthday of the German Emperor, and the feast was to come off that same night. The day was not exactly the Emperor's birthday, but the celebration had been postponed till this date on account of the recent death of some valued member of the German community at Bangkok. Immediately behind the middle chair, which was the place of honour, the German flag was hanging gaily from the wall, with the British flag to its right and the American flag to its left, which were rather pleasant to look on, though these flags formed but a small part of the entire decorations.

We did our best to get a boat to row us o'er the ferry to the Ocean-butterfly Fort, which was on a small island near the opposite side of the mouth of the river, but we could not succeed. It was a very hot, sultry day, as most days must be at Paknām, and we had to turn back thoroughly roasted with the blazing sun, and at war with all humanity. We could not get back to Bangkok till four or five in the evening, and had therefore to wait at the station till then, without any comfort whatever.

Need it be said that we were as thirsty as thirsty could be, and that we wanted a drink badly? We went into what we supposed to be the station-master's house, but could not get anybody to hear us, however loudly we bawled; for the people, including the Germans, as it happened, were soundly enjoying their afternoon sleep.

By the time we returned to the station platform again, who did we see but the Chinese waiter who used to attend on us at the hotel, and who was in charge of the German creature-comforts, which had all been supplied by the Oriental Hotel, where we were staying. We conjured this heathen Chinee to give us a drink out of the Teutons' abundance, and as we drank it to the health of the German Emperor, we found it very soothing, for the weather was uncommonly hot and stuffy, and we had been a long time going about in the blazing sun. The Germans at last woke from their slumbers, like giants refreshed, and we told them of the liberties we had taken with their supplies under the pressure of necessity. And thus it was that we tapped the German feast and drank to the health of the German Emperor on that occasion, even before any of his own subjects at Bangkok, however much they might drink at the feast that was coming off in a few hours later on.

My 'casual' was going to Singapore, and, so as not to be idle, I went with him as far as the island of Koh-si-chang, about thirty miles from the mouth of the Menam river. This island is only a few miles from the mainland of Siam, and is rather important, as it really constitutes the seaport of the city of Bangkok itself. It cannot be more than a couple of miles long, nor more than a mile or two broad, and is hilly in physical features, being mostly composed of lime-rock formation. At the north end of it is an elevated prominence, which has lately been converted into a signal station, with the pretentious name of Phra-chula-chom-pla, opened in 1891, and already fissured at the top; while some four or five miles directly north of the island is Tenfoot Lighthouse, a melancholy and lonely-looking rock, with a light said to be raised only ten feet above high-water mark, and hence its name.

There is a fairly good harbour in the island of Koh-sichang, formed partly by the said island, and partly by a couple of smaller islands between it and the mainland. For the greater part of the year, all ships trading with Bangkok take in and discharge here; for as the bar across the mouth of the Menam only admits of thirteen or fourteen feet draught at the most, by far the greater part of the imports and exports has to be transhipped at Koh-sichang. Consequently several ships may be seen in the harbour, working their cargo, and surrounded by quite a number of handsome lighters, built of pure teak wood, which carry the bulk of cargoes between Bangkok and Koh-sichang.

The Siamese custom-house officer, who boarded the ship and spoke good English, was good enough to take us ashore in his boat, as my 'casual' went ashore with me for a visit, before his ship proceeded on her way. This Siamese was quite an authority on the recent occupation of the island by the French, who took down the Siamese flag, and hoisted their own tricolor instead of it; and then in a few weeks abandoned the island altogether. Our informant was probably the principal Siamese resident on the island, and the look of terror with which he described the way in which the French seamen took possession of the island, and made himself a prisoner, had something very seriocomic about it. But after landing and making him and others prisoners, the French appear to have treated their prisoners kindly enough; and if it is true that imitation is the sincerest form of flattery, this man must have thought a lot of the French invaders, judging from the corrugated eyebrows, and the shrugging of shoulders, with which he explained what occurred on that important occasion.

The day after arrival, we climbed to the flagstaff on Phra-chula-chom-pla peak, and were told that the ascent is nearly 700 feet, and consists of 980 steps of concrete; though why they did not make the full thousand of it, I don't know. We asked the keeper if any strangers ever paid him a visit on his lofty domicile. 'Never any,' he said, for probably the sailors, by whom the harbour is mostly frequented, are fonder of climbing masts than of climbing mountains. Nor was he yet provided with the usual 'Visitors' Book,' with which such places are generally supplied; and I therefore sent him one from Singapore, when I arrived there months later on. From the top of this hill, whose long Siamese name we need not repeat again, there is an excellent view of the surrounding sea, the harbour, and the hilly mainland of Siam; but though the scenery is pleasing and varied, it is nothing particularly grand.

On the south-east end of the island there is a short promontory jutting out for a little distance into the sea. On this pretty situation, Chulalongkorn, King of Siam and of all the White Elephants, had just been building a royal palace for the enjoyment of himself and his numberless wives. The spot was very well chosen, and the palace, which was mostly constructed of teak wood, was about three-quarters finished, when, alas! the ferocious Frenchmen came, and threw everything topsy-turvy; the builders ceased work, and ran away for fear of the enemy. And it was then stoutly maintained by those who knew best, that the promising building would never again be resumed, nor brought nearer completion. In truth, Asiatic potentates have often an unfortunate knack of taking buildings in hand like this one, and then of leaving them half finished, as if they get tired of them, the same as children do of toys.

Besides all this there is every reason to abandon the unfortunate project, according to the opinion of some superstitious cronies; for is there not an ancient Siamese prophecy, that when the King of Siam goes to live within sight of the sea, then his glory and his sceptre will rapidly depart, and Siam will no longer exist as an independent kingdom? For the purpose of fulfilment of this sad prophecy, Bangkok itself is already dangerously near the fickle element, as it is considerably within twenty miles of the sea as the crow flies. This prophecy, of course, like others of its kind, is mere rubbish and idle superstition. But how often has this same superstition, by its own very folly, brought about the fulfilment of its dreaded prognostications? Ayouthia, about one hundred miles up the river, was the ancient capital of Siam, but it is now in ruins; for the city was captured by the Burmese in 1767, and it was since then that Bangkok became the capital of the kingdom; so that, as already stated, it is a city almost altogether devoid of any eventful history. But this far and no further, so says the augury, for only another step, oh king, towards that beautiful and treacherous domain, and, Ichabod—thy glory has departed! I hope not, however; and I only mention the silly tale as the tale was told to me.

Finally, this pretty little island of Koh-si-chang is a sort of watering-place for the jaded people of Bangkok, but not nearly so much as one would expect, judging from its pretty situation. But the island labours under the awkward drawback of having no springs of fresh water, so that it has to depend on rain-water stored in iron tanks, or on water imported all the way from the mainland. And so much does the little community on the island feel the want of a reliable supply of fresh water in the island itself, that a party had lately been exploiting in search of the precious thirst-quencher, but without success, though in one or two instances they bored artesian wells down to a depth of nearly 200 feet. The Siamese navy for some reason or other is nearly altogether officered by Danes, taken out of the merchant services. One of these Danes was superintendent of the searching party at Koh-si-chang, but apparently without his divining-rod; for on one occasion, when making experiments with explosives, he blew off three or four of his fingers and seriously injured one of his eyes. He was a fellow passenger on the small tug that brought me to Bangkok back again. Having incidentally mentioned the Siamese navy, I may here remark in passing that the whole of the fleet may generally be seen a few miles up the river, above the European gunboats, and opposite the royal palace enclosure, one side of which sweeps along the river's bank. The navy, all told, consists of eight or nine ships, mostly wooden, and of various sizes; and none of them, I suspect, is very formidable to a formidable enemy.

CHAPTER VII

> Hark, don't you hear it, away, afar?
> Hurrah, hurrah, 'tis the din of war;
> 'Tis the din of war?—'tis only the hum
> Of heathen idolaters beating a drum!
> The Tinkettle Hero.

Captain Bertuzzi—Away for Phrabāt—The Menam River—Swarming with Fish—Arrival at Ayouthia—Chang the Chinaman—Tramp to Phrabāt—'Gie's Peebles for Pleesure'—The Din in the Distance—The Priests and the Players—Don't Sleep on the Outskirts—The Nose and the Conscience.

AND thus I returned to Bangkok before the noon of a certain day, preparatory to my going to witness the pilgrimage to Mount Phrabāt, for which I had been waiting all this time. But still no servants appeared ready to undergo the task of crossing the interior with me. Before going to Koh-si-chang, there was some probability of quite a suitable companion going with me, who knew Siamese thoroughly, and this was none else than the ex-tutor to the Crown Prince of Siam, who had just lost his appointment by Court intrigue, and was anxious to see something more of the interior of this comparatively unknown country, before returning again to his native land.

I was too late for the usual breakfast hour at the hotel, but just as I was going into the dining-room to have a late breakfast, I was told that somebody wished to see me. And this person was Captain L. Bertuzzi, who was very anxious to go with me across the country. He was an Italian by birth and a rover by profession, had been a sea captain, a coffee planter, and several other things besides; and from the fluent way in which he spoke English, it was evident enough that he had been a good deal among Englishmen. He also professed to speak French, German and Siamese, and was really, I thought, the very one I wanted.

The hotel had one capital new launch, among others, which I was bringing up the river with me so far as it could go in the direction of Phrabāt; and she was at this time putting up steam for starting immediately after breakfast. And so I took Captain Bertuzzi to have breakfast with me, and to talk the matter over, as there was none else in the dining-room. I was dressed in knickerbockers, and felt in very good humour, as I was now at last going to start for Phrabāt. In the middle of our rapid conversation the stranger broke forth with, 'I suppose you're a Scotchman?' 'Yes,' I replied, 'but how did you know?' An Englishman would probably know at once, but he, a mere foreigner, how could *he* know? I naturally expected it was from my name or speech, but it was from neither. It was only because I had 'dark hair and grey eyes!'—a personal distinction which I never knew before to be confined to the stormy North.

Yet, however complimentary, I could not engage him on the spot, because I was leaving the arrangement with the hotel manager, and because the previous proposals with the ex-tutor to the Crown Prince were still hanging fire; so, as I was just starting for Phrabāt, I left him to make any further agreement with the manager of the hotel. Immediately after he had gone away, one of the visitors of the hotel came up, and asked if I knew anything about my proposed companion across the wilds of Siam. Of course I knew nothing about him, except that he appeared a very smart, intelligent person. He then told me that this same Captain L. Bertuzzi was at this very time being watched by the police for murdering a native at Chantaboon, a town something like a hundred miles further south, and at present occupied by French troops; and, moreover, that he was trying to go with me to escape secretly out of the country. This revelation put me on my guard, and the hotel manager was told on no account to engage Bertuzzi, whether innocent or guilty, as he might either get arrested on the way, or might lead to serious trouble among the natives of the wild interior.

I proceeded about noon to the holy Mount Phrabāt in a capital new steam launch, with a crew of four natives, and a temporary Chinese cook. She steered very well, and as the little wheel that guided her was placed quite near the stem, I passed most of the day in holding her on her course myself, blowing the whistle to warn the native craft out of the way, as if I had been on the river as long as pilot Jackson himself. But when the sun set and the moon rose, I did not find the task such an easy one, as moonlight, I found, was very deceptive in judging distances. And so after going dangerously near a collision once or twice, I resigned my temporary command to the proper authority.

We proceeded gaily in the silvery moonlight, for it was only one day short of the full moon at which I hoped to be at Phrabāt. This river, the Menam, is swarming with fish of various kinds, which the launch kept continually disturbing out of their early slumbers, to make them suddenly jump out of the water. Several times they nearly jumped into the launch, and we sometimes tried to catch them in their jumps, but were not smart enough to do so. At length one of them nearly jumped into my lap. Later on at night, and when I had fallen asleep, three more of them performed the same feat of jumping on board, so swarming is this river with the beautiful finny tribes. I had travelled over the Irrawaddy through Burmah for over a thousand miles from the sea, and sailed over some portions of it five or six times, at different seasons of the year, but never saw anything like the same display of fishes as on the Menam; nor anything else on fresh water, except perhaps on Lake Telé-Sáp, which I shall describe when I reach so far. I noticed also that the banks of the Menam, for a long distance above Bangkok, are more thickly inhabited than the banks of the Irrawaddy above Rangoon. We reached Ayouthia about midnight, and here I expected to pick up a Chinaman who spoke English, and who was to accompany me to Phrabāt in the capacity of interpreter.

Ayouthia, as mentioned before, was the previous capital of Siam, but was destroyed and sacked by the Burmese in 1767. Indo-Chinese countries are rather fond of changing their capital towns, without any very evident reason. Kings are often very vain people, especially Asiatic ones; and they sometimes fancy they are not grand enough, unless they start a town on their own account. Thus there are half a dozen places which at one time or another were the capitals of Burmah. Penhom-penh has only recently become the capital of Cambodia. Tokio is only the capital of Japan for less than twenty-five years, and even Pekin has not always been the capital of China. But Ayouthia was not abandoned by the whim of potentates, but by the inexorable decree of fate.

After picking up the interpreter at Ayouthia we went on, and reached Tarua in the early morning. This was the place where had congregated all the boats of all the pilgrims who had come to Phrabāt by water; and there was such a crowd of them that it was not an altogether easy matter to effect a landing. The holy Mount Phrabāt itself was nearly twenty miles inland from this place on the river's bank. There were no riding elephants procurable, but by a stroke of good luck we were able to get two carts, with two buffaloes in each of them, and for which fancy prices were demanded at this particularly busy season, especially that I was a *Farrang*, or European foreigner, with nothing to do but to throw away money. It was useless to cavil at this, as we need not travel so far east as Phrabāt to find that supply and demand are the great and glorious twin gods of commerce. The owners of the buffaloes would not start in the heat of the sun, as these water buffaloes, strange to say, cannot stand the sun at all.

Bullocks in this respect are far superior, but the fact is that these extremely lazy and ugly water-buffaloes have a good deal of the hippopotamus about them, and are never so happy as when wallowing in the mire of lakes and rivers, with only the tips of their noses above the water. Besides, this was a frightfully hot day, as I knew to my cost, confined as I was to my small launch, with her awnings almost touching the top of my head whenever I stood up. The owners were induced to start at last—much earlier than they would have started of their own accord—and, oh, how slowly they did travel! The water-buffalo, wherever you see him in the East, is positively the laziest beast in the world, in addition to that other 'illigant' accomplishment of being about the ugliest. We stopped two or three times on the way to rest these brutes, that could scarcely at any time be said to be in motion. Then the drivers would take large mouthfuls of water and squirt it repeatedly over the buffaloes, after the manner of an ether spray, in order to cool these animals. The day faded, and Diana rose again, a clear silvery goddess, sailing her circuit without a speck or stain throughout the whole of the pure pale sky.

The buffaloes went so slowly, and the carts jostled so much, that I could not endure to remain in my hooded crib for long at a time; and when the moon at last rose, and the heat fell down a bit, I walked most of the way like a true palmer, with neither sock nor shoon. One of my boots was hurting me, and the track at this time was so dry and travelled over by so many thousand barefooted pilgrims, that it really felt rather soothing to my toes. An attack of fever and ague was naturally expected to follow this indiscretion; but, like many another bogey of which people are afraid, it never made its appearance. The road, or rather the broad pathway, leads at first through cultivated fields, near Tarua, and then through forests, often in the form of an avenue bordered on either side by various kinds of trees, among which long and graceful feathery bamboos were a prominent feature, sometimes forming almost an arch across the path.

Mount Phrabāt, though a very interesting place, and probably quite under a hundred and fifty miles' travel from the sea, has been but seldom visited by Europeans. During my stay at Bangkok I experienced what I had sometimes experienced before. When on an uncomfortable journey like this, you will meet such a lot of people that 'would so wish to go with you;' but when the time comes, they prefer to warm their toes by the fireside; though in Bangkok it must be confessed they require but little of this latter luxury. Hence the energetic vagrant sees, and very frequently *knows*, more about the countries that he visits than fifty mere lazy gaberlunzies, who live years in the same regions without any higher aim than the gathering of almighty dollars—when they can get them! I am aware that this is preaching heresy against the opinions of some old fossils, but it is a fact all the same.

'Gie's Peebles for pleesure,' said the patriotic old Scot, after he had been a week in Paradise. Well, whatever Peebles may be like, it must be confessed that nobody, except, perhaps, a very devout Buddhist, will ever visit

Mount Phrabāt a second time for the mere 'pleesure' of doing so; a remark, however, equally true of many other places equally interesting and equally uncomfortable. My Chinese interpreter and myself were thus tramping barefooted in front of the buffaloes, when Chang, as I called him, drew my attention to a peculiar din in the distance far away. It sounded at first like the confused buzzing of insects, such as one hears often enough in Eastern lands at certain times of the year. But soon came the sound of the clashing of cymbals and the beating of tom-toms, mingled with the distant murmur of voices, that made it plain enough that it was insects of the human species that accounted for it all. It was near midnight at the time, and this at last was the holy Mount Phrabāt, at which neither Chang nor I had ever been before, or will likely ever be again.

By the way, Chang, my Chinese interpreter, did not like to be called by that name, as he was rather a stickler on the importance of proper names; but, as I could never keep his real name in my memory for two minutes, I had to adopt this course of a nickname. He was a tall, strapping fellow, with a very pronounced hare-lip; and as very tall people are notorious for their vanity (especially when with a hare-lip), Chang, as became such a personage, resented the liberty I was taking with his name. But when I humbly told him that I could not keep his real name on my tongue, that he was very strong and tall, and that there was a countryman of his, a Chinese giant, called Chang—in short, when I told him that it was on account of his big size that I called him Chang, I hit the nail of vanity straight into his temples, and he succumbed forthwith. So easy, indeed, it is to conquer the world—if we only knew how!

But though it was Chang's ears (for he had rather large and flabby ones) that first caught the noise, it was I, unfortunately, that first picked out the evil odour, which became very unpleasant as we walked further into it. This was, however, in the day's work; for I did not visit Phrabāt with the expectation of sleeping on downy beds sprinkled with rose water, but prepared to take matters as I found them, and with the best grace I could muster. We took the carts well into the outskirts of the seething throng, and then Chang and I went to see what was to be seen. Chang was not a bad interpreter, but he had the fault of being too good a linguist, and therefore fonder of showing off his own attainments than of interpreting my simple questions. Chang, in fact, was too good at both Siamese and English, and, like other good people of his kind, he was not averse to showing off his own goodness in this respect; for interpreters, after all, are only mortals, in spite of all the profound learning that their heads contain.

There was a tremendous crowd, walking promiscuously to and fro along the narrow paths and passages of this unique locality; and for almost all of them the naked earth formed their sleeping couch and the heavens their canopy. But I am sorry to say that they did not at all seem to be thinking of religion. True enough that in one place we discovered a yellow-robed *phra*, or priest, with shaven head, and holding forth to the people in peculiarly modulated tones, something like the bleating of a lamb. He was not preaching in the manner we call preaching, or giving his own opinions on religious concerns; but was rather reciting (like the parson who steals his sermons) and rehearsing portions of the ancient Pali scripture, which all the priests and most of the laity get up by heart; for it must be remembered that the whole male population here must to a certain extent be priests some time or other. This *phra* had a goodly congregation listening to him, but nothing very extraordinary. On moving at random further round some corner, we came across a much bigger and more fervent crowd—for they were listening to a play! thus reminding one of the old saying, that where God builds a church, the Devil builds a chapel, and that, also, the latter has generally the larger congregation.

Chang said that the play was very dirty, and it *must* have been dirty for Chang to say so; for a play is generally very gross before an Asiatic thinks it either lewd or immodest. And so I had the good fortune this time of seeing the gestures and grimaces without understanding their import. Though this pilgrimage is undertaken as a homage to Buddha, it must not therefore be supposed that it must necessarily mean a humble spirit and a contrite heart. Yet the subdued lights of the countless tapers burning in the open moonlight, the babel of voices, and the eternal din of musical instruments, had a very pleasing, if not edifying, effect on a stranger visiting Phrabāt for the first and only time. For this was the night and this was the hour at Phrabāt, the holiest place of the Buddhist religion, which numbers more worshippers than any other religion in the world. We were not able to find out that night where the famous real footprint of the Buddha was; nor did we know that we should be permitted to see it, even if we did know where it was. It would probably have been more interesting to have seen it that night, as it was the climax of the ceremony, but we were of course groping in the dark and feeling our way. And so Chang and myself, after various aimless wanderings, had to return at last to the carts again.

I felt the stench at first very acutely, and made Chang and the drivers remove the carts further away, as I thought that this would lessen the evil, but it rather increased it. However, after the buffaloes were taken out, I laid down in one of the carts and soon went fast asleep. Some time later Chang, the evil genius, woke me up, and said that he was told it would be safer for me to take the carts inside than leave them in this comparatively lonely spot, where they could more easily and more secretly be attacked. There could be no reasonable objection to a proposal like this, and so after telling Chang to take the carts wherever he liked, I laid down and tried to sleep again. He brought the carts, and me in one of them, to near the middle of the great gathering, where a number of other carts were also congregated. To my surprise at first, I found that the stench here was less offensive than at the outskirts, but the reason was not far to seek, on reflecting on the mode of conservancy at this holy place. No wonder that the holy city of Mecca has been proved to become a dangerous focus of cholera during the pilgrim season; and Phrabāt is another Mecca, though resorted to by Buddhist instead of Mohammedan worshippers.

There was another potent reason why I did not feel the stench so much, and that was because I was getting used to it, as eels are to be flayed. This accommodating power of the nose is a wonderfully wise provision, for without it life, under certain conditions, would become intolerable. The nose in this respect may be aptly compared to the conscience, for though both the conscience and the nose give timely warning, yet if their admonitions are disregarded, they cease to warn, or do so with a feebler voice. And so they accommodate themselves to the necessities of the situation, as their purport in the main is not to make the present life either miserable or unhappy. In this respect we can personify the nose and the conscience, and fancy them respectively upbraiding reason after the following fashion :—

> I've warned you once, I've warned you twice,
>   But you so heedless grew,
> That when in vain I warned you thrice,
>   Then I got heedless too.

CHAPTER VIII

> They bowed and vowed,
> And vowed and bowed,
> That rude-looking rustic, and pagan crowd;
> And racked their bones,
> With sighs and groans,
> Before their grim idols of stocks and stones.
> The Idolater.

Toilet *al fresco*—Chang with the Hare-lip—His Vanity—An Unsuspected Stranger—Comparisons of Languages—Buddhism a Religion of toleration—Visit to the Real Phrabāt or Sacred Footprint—Watching the Worshippers—History of Phrabāt—First discovered by a king—Defects of the Footprint—'A Blind Man's Blot'—Description of the Buddha—Judging his size by Inductive Philosophy.

THOUGH late (or rather early) of retiring, we were not late in getting up in the morning. The natives felt curious as they watched me making my simple morning toilet, and eating my equally simple and frugal breakfast. But what fetched them most was when I began to shave. Indo-Chinese of the male sex, and of all sorts and conditions, are so generally deficient in the way of beards, that they sometimes cherish a hair or two growing out of the top of a wart, as if they were of real personal attraction. No wonder then that they were amused to see me shaving, with all the facial contortions essential to the proper performance of that most poetic operation. But though they laughed and giggled away, they appeared to be very good-humoured, and why should they not laugh as much as they pleased?

After these functions were over, I wanted to take a photo of Chang with my kodak, but felt awkward in asking him, as I was afraid of hurting his feelings. Not that there was any fear of Chang objecting to his shadow being taken, for such reasons as already noted in a previous chapter, for he was one of the ever-increasing army of Orientals, that are too civilised and too 'like master,' to have any compunctions on that score. But I was afraid that he might object on the score of his hare-lip. I had therefore to resort to stratagem, which, as it turned out, was not at all necessary. The four Siamese boatmen had been left behind with the steam launch at Tarua, but there were two Chinamen with me at Phrabāt, namely, a Chinese cook that I had taken all the way from Bangkok, who scarcely spoke a word of even 'pigeon' English, and Chang, who spoke English remarkably well, in spite of his natural difficulty of pronouncing the labials to perfection.

To avoid Chang taking any possible offence, I proposed to take the photo of the two of them together, though I really only wanted Chang's alone. After setting them together in this way, I asked them to separate a bit, so as to get the cook tacitly out of the field of view. But no delicacy of this kind was at all necessary, as Chang, with a lordly wave of his hand, spurned away his brother pigtail, with the remark that he would like a photograph all to himself, without the encumbrance of his less remarkable countryman. He then put on his very best smile, curled his upper lip, or rather what remained of it, and I took his photograph. I am sorry it turned out such a failure, like almost all the photographs I took with that stupid kodak. Chang, to tell the truth, was more than usually vain, I think, of his personal appearance, and except the pronounced blemish alluded to, he was really a fine, active, and intelligent fellow. But I felt rather sorry for him when the moment of disillusionment came, for he was all the time labouring under the impression that I was able to hand over to him the image of his handsome person at once, which of course I was not able to do. And what havoc he played with the hearts of the simple Siamese maidens on that pilgrimage! for he appeared quite a gay Lothario among them all.

Here I was, all by myself, at this religious excitement, among those swarming heathens, without a single European within a long distance off, although there is no excitement or hatred so strong as the fanaticism produced by religious impressions. But a surprise awaited me in the early morning. After taking Chang's photograph, he and I were wending our way among the carts, when I caught a glimpse of a wonderful *solah-topi*, or sun-hat. The natives of the East are fond enough of heavy, unwieldy turbans and puggarees to cover their heads with, but that *solah-topi* never graced the attic regions of a mere native. That was certain beyond dispute. The particular *solah-topi* mentioned is never seen in India, and seldom or never west of the Malayan Peninsula. It is so very big, especially at the back, that it requires a very big man to set it off to advantage; and as it is so seldom seen elsewhere, it may be considered a speciality of Bangkok and surrounding country. Its proportions are out of all reckoning, and the largest and roundest moon-face looks under it like a mouse peeping out of a haystack.

But when I did get a glimpse of the underlying features, they were white and pale enough in every respect. The stranger's cart had just arrived, so that I was alone during the night right enough; but yet his presence surprised me. Shuffling my way through the carts in this person's direction, 'What in the world are *you* doing here?' I exclaimed, as if I had suddenly come across an old companion on the top of Mount Everest. 'Well,' he replied, 'I guess I am trying to spread the gospel among the heathen.' Yes, the inevitable missionary again! And as he satisfied all curiosity as to his purpose, there remained none as to his nationality, for that saucy phrase of 'I guess' settled that once and for all, and pointed him out as a freeborn American. He had been slowly travelling during the night so as to be at Phrabāt in time to distribute among the natives the gospels in their native tongue. Each of the gospels could be had separately, and I noticed that he charged a small sum for each of the copies, with some certain exceptions. The amount was such a mere trifle, about a halfpenny or less, that I wondered why it was worth his while to charge for the copies at all, when he charged so absolutely little for them. His reply was satisfactory enough, namely, that the natives would value the book more, and would feel more inclined to read them when they realised that they paid for them, that they cost them something, and that they were now their own undisputed property. How human this feeling! And I fancy it is not at all confined to natives of the East.

Rev. Mr. C—— said that some of these gospels had been translated (for the first time, I think) by himself, and that he found the translating business rather difficult, as the Siamese language, he said, though apparently primitive, is really a figurative one; so that literal translations of some passages became meaningless or uncertain. This can easily be understood. For there is no valid reason why a primitive language should not be a highly figurative one. Hebrew is a primitive language, yet what language can be more figurative? Indeed, many learned people maintain that poetry, the particular province of figurative language, is rather marred than otherwise by the modern encroachments of science and art, with the exact and too rigid vocabulary to which they give rise. The great Creation around us, the heavens and the earth, the land and the sea, and the joys and sorrows of the human heart, have always been with us, and have always been, and always will be, by far the truest sources of figurative inspiration.

As Siam itself is suggestive of a transition country between Burmah and China, so do the Siamese alphabetical characters appear to be a sort of a transition stage between the simple and beautiful round character of the Burmese and the irregular, pictorial character of the Celestial Empire.

I noticed at Phrabāt that the priests, of whom there were crowds, had no more objection than the mere laity to possess themselves of these gospel pamphlets, for the Buddhist religion in this respect differs wonderfully from the Mohammedan one, which is the most militant religion extant. The only marked exception to this rule, as regards Buddhism, exists in the case of Thibet, where the Buddhists are very reserved and seclusive, partly on religious grounds, and partly, probably, for political reasons. Besides, Thibet is the region where the Mahatmas prevail, with Koot-Hoomi at their head, and, perhaps, Madame Blavatsky at their tail, and they no doubt influence the people of Thibet in their hostile attitude to strangers, who would fain venture to peep below the hood of their holy lamas. But in all the rest of the Buddhist world toleration is very common throughout.

In Burmah, indeed, and I think in Siam, everybody at some period or other of his youth becomes a priest, from the king downwards, and he can cease to be a priest whenever he chooses. But when a priest, he has to wear the characteristic and sacred yellow robe, be known as a *phoongyee* in Burmah and *phra* in Siam, and he must beg his food and live in a monastery known as *Kiung* and *Wát* in these countries respectively. In this way, these monasteries are not for religious instruction only, but are also the recognised seminaries for secular education. And so well do they carry out the latter portion of the programme that, as regards Burmah at any rate, elementary education is more generally disseminated there than in almost any other country in the world.

After accompanying Mr. C—— for some time while he was distributing his tracts Chang and I began to prowl about on our own responsibility. And at last we fell in with the very temple where the famous footprint of the Buddha was placed. It is only a comparatively small temple, called the *Medop*, whatever that means, rather handsomely built on the spur of a hill, and with doors inlaid with mother of pearl and other gems of various figures and designs. This is the place, then, where Buddha placed his footstep, during a hasty visit to earth some centuries ago. The doors were shut when we arrived, and surrounded by a crowd, as one sees round the doors of a theatre during the first night of a promising play, or round a bank door on the morning of its going to fail! Chang and I mingled freely with this crowd, scarcely imagining that they should allow my unhallowed footsteps to enter the sacred temple itself. But I would try. Shortly afterwards the door opposite which I was standing was opened, and I was carried inside with the crush, whether I would or not. Here, then, at last, before my very eyes, was the very holy footprint of Phrabāt that I had come so far to seek.

It appeared that Gotauma Buddha paid a visit in the flesh to Siam some centuries ago, and in proof of his presence he left the print of one of his holy feet here, deeply imbedded in the solid rock. The place that he chose for this great manifestation was the northern, or north-western spur of a short isolated range of hills, that extend in this region in a general direction of north-west and south-east. It was no less a personage than the king of Siam himself who first discovered the sacred footprint. Though he was a usurper, and had murdered the previous king, yet the great favour shown him by this revelation was enough to cover a multitude of sins. Neither is it revealed how king Phra-chow-song-tam proved that the footprint really belonged to Buddha, or whether the king saw Buddha himself as well as the footprint. This is rather a pity, as we have no authentic account as to what sort of physical semblance Buddha bore at that time. But people must not too narrowly question the truthfulness of kings, and as king Phra-chow-song-tam (I love to dwell upon the pretty name) did not condescend to do so, I shall humbly endeavour to enlighten the reader as to what sort of fleshy form Buddha bore during his transient visit to this highly favoured country. But that's in the sweet by-and-by.

At any rate they built a temple in that very spot, and called it Phrabāt, which being interpreted from Siamese means simply a footprint, or *the* footprint, that is to say, the holy footprint ; while they called the temple they built themselves by the name of Medop, for reasons which I dinna ken. Scattered here and there, in the neighbourhood of this Medop, are various other 'works of merit,' as they call them, and pagodas of the usual kind, so dear to the heart of the Buddhist co-religionists. It was after climbing one of these pagodas to get a good 'level' photographic view of the Medop itself, that the natives at one time gathered round, expecting that I should fall when coming down. And though I did not fall, yet it was a pity that the photograph turned out such an utter failure after the trouble I had taken to get it. This, then, is the sacred place of annual pilgrimage, not only for the Siamese themselves, but for all the surrounding tribes who hold by the tenets of Buddhism ; and the pilgrimage always comes off at this time of the year, and culminates with the full moon, which on this occasion had happened the night before.

And so, after the place was filled, every one approached and made obeisance at the sacred footprint, whenever he or she was able to come near enough to the edge of it. I quietly got near it myself at last, squatted down in a very devout way, with my right elbow resting on the raised rim of it, and watched the people as they came and went. The hollow representing Buddha's footprint here is almost exactly five feet long, while it is eighteen inches broad at the toes, and fifteen towards the heel. And I should say that the impression is fully two and a half, or even three feet deep. The devotees approach this impression devoutly, each provided with a piece of gold leaf carefully folded over in grosser material, while sometimes the worshippers have small sticks decorated with miniature flags, on which rude figures are drawn of serpents, crocodiles, dragons, and so forth. Each worshipper as he approaches the edge of the Phrabāt, or Footprint, goes down on his knees, and places his hands palm to palm with the thumbs pointing upward, something as a swimmer does before diving. He then repeatedly raises his hands in this position to his forehead, and mutters some kinds of runes appropriate to the occasion.

This custom of Buddhists of placing their hands in this position is so common among them, even as a form of salutation to their fellow mortals, that it is strange that no verb has ever been invented in English adequately to express it. It is not clapping of hands, for that involves noise and repeated action, nor is it folding of hands, for that involves the idea of grasping. For want of a better word, then, I shall use the word '*palming*' to express this attitude, and to '*palm*' the hands will be understood in this book to mean the placing of hands together, palm to palm, in the position just described. For instance, when a Burmese or Siamese servant is speaking with deference to some lordly superior, he does not respectfully stand up in the presence of the great one. He does the very opposite. He flops down on his knees, with his body bent forward, and '*palms*' his hands in profound humility and attention, in front of his forehead.

As I watched these simple people muttering their mystic runes, and casting their little offerings of gold leaf into the footprint receptacle, I could scarcely refrain from asking myself, 'What is religion?' Opinions differ so much about it, though it is the profoundest and most important of all themes, and on which hang by far the most vital of all issues—the final destiny of man. Not that the Buddhist ideas of the final destiny of man are very much like ours, but that is a deep and wide subject that cannot be touched here. As already remarked, the edge of the footprint is a little raised above the level of the ground around it, as the Buddha's foot probably made a splash, and so raised the margin of the solid rock ; and resting my elbow on this edge, I could have remained sitting there as long as I liked, so far as any interference on the part of the worshippers was concerned. For nobody seemed to take any heed, though they watched me with not a little curiosity when I was outside. And so when each did his share, as he thought, of this divine worship, he retired to the open air again. And I followed in due course.

Fixed on the inner wall of the Medop, there is a plate model of the footprint, covered all over with the inevitable gold leaf. And the best description of this plate would be to suppose it to form the sole of the boot that Buddha wore on the occasion. It is about a couple of inches thick, and of the superficial area already recorded. The under surface of the plate, or that which would be next the ground, is divided into a number of separate areas, impressed with various symbols possessing different virtues. Besides this plate, preserved in the holy shrine itself, there are a few consecrated casts of it in other places in Siam, and considered so holy that, though they are not altogether esteemed as sacred as the real article, yet several smaller pilgrimages are made to them by people who have not so many sins to cleanse, or who cannot or will not otherwise afford to undertake the greater pilgrimage to Phrabāt itself. One of the very holiest of these casts is to be found in a temple at Paknām, where my Dutch 'casual' and myself tapped the German birthday feast on a previous occasion.

From an artistic point of view there are several defects in the Buddha's footprint, as represented in this cast, and which I hope all pious Buddhists will pardon me for pointing out. In the first instance, it is so large and shapeless as to belong to the class of feet facetiously known as 'flippers,' for nobody admires large flat feet even on women. Again, all the toes are exactly the same length. Wherever you wander through the Buddhist world, you will always find the images of Buddha with not only the toes but also the fingers all of the same length. Tapering fingers, falsely supposed to represent sense and culture, are entirely absent from the images of Buddha, and yet

Buddha was a great æsthete. But putting aside the toes and fingers, what really offends the dilettante observer is the entire absence of an instep exhibited by this sacred footprint, for the cast that represents it is as flat as the flippers of a seal. People do not sufficiently consider the vast importance of the instep in the human economy. Buddha, in fact, would not have passed for a common recruit in a marching regiment, his feet being so flat, and so destitute of instep. The importance of the instep is one of these coming events that has not yet been fully recognised; but that is because the world is still in its infancy. We have been advancing a bit lately though. Palmistry, of course, is already an old and most reliable science; and recently the tips of the fingers, and more especially the thumbs, are marked out as unfailing indications of identity and character. Why the thumb more than the other fingers? Surely the index finger, from its very name, ought to be the better indicator of the two, and if it isn't, the thumb should be called the index finger, and the index finger should be called the thumb.

Not long before leaving India on this journey, I was much afflicted with a new craze, and though it was far from my own seeking, I wish good luck to it. This was nothing short of taking the finger impressions in Indian ink of every recruit passed into the army, in order to facilitate the recognition and recovery of deserters. The majority of these impressions that came under my observation looked to me uncommonly like one of Mr. Gladstone's blind man's blots. Why, I could not distinguish a man from a woman by them!

Scientists, again, seldom think of the instep, yet this much neglected feature is one of the most important, and its time is coming like Christmas. For it is the instep that more particularly imparts these numberless peculiarities of grace and carriage, that comprise a great part of true physiognomy. Observe that man with the brisk step and energetic spirit. Turn him up, and you will be sure to find a high instep. And that fellow with the slow steps and flabby features. Well, you needn't turn *him* up, poor beggar, for he has flat flippers. You may depend upon that without requiring to adopt the process of turtle-turning at all. It is not the flat feet that reflect the flabby face, but the flabby face that reflects the flippers. Why are the fair sex, especially the French, so fond of high-heeled boots? Just to give them an extra swagger by an artificial instep. They never think that this is the case, but it is. The time will come when people will be valued by their instep, and yet Buddha, according to this plate, has no instep at all. It must not be forgotten, however, that the nose has quite lately got into great prominence (as it should) in matters anthropological, judging from last year's annual gathering of the British Association, and that the 'nasal index,' as they call it, is fast becoming the index of many other qualities besides. This nasal index has sprung from India, too, the original starting-point of many other myths. But it is strange that it never struck the lecturer, that a sharp nose is not always a sign of intelligence, as it has from time immemorial been associated with approaching dissolution, and the babble of green fields. However, I shall stick to my last—or rather to my instep—as by far the more important factor of the two, but I must leave it for the present to the calm contemplation of the thoughtful reader, without going into any further details.

Now let us begin to dissect the Buddha, or rather to construct him from the means at our disposal. His footprint, I say, was five feet long, eighteen inches broad at the toes, and fifteen at the heel. And what do we gather from this? Wait and see. By the power of natural induction inherent in the human mind, man is capable of arriving at certain conclusions, based upon certain definite premises.

It was by this divine faculty that our old friend Robinson Crusoe concluded, and concluded rightly, that some people landed on his lonely island, from the discovery of human footprints on the sandy shore. It was from this faculty that the famous naturalist, the late Professor Owen, concluded the previous existence of a gigantic bird (the *Dinornis*) from simply getting hold of a single shoulder blade or so. And not long thereafter, several skeletons of this kind of bird, which he had described unseen, turned out of their cold, cold grave, just to please him, and to please me too, when I saw one or two of them in New Zealand on a later occasion, looking like the skeletons of great big camels. It was thus that James

Watt conceived the brilliant idea of the steam-engine by witnessing a storm in a tea-kettle, and that the mighty intellect of Sir Isaac Newton grasped the profound law of universal gravitation by watching an apple fall from a tree. Assuredly there is nothing great on earth but man, and nothing great in man but mind.

Finally, it was in this way that the ancients calculated the size of the mythological hero, Hercules, though I do not quite know how fine and large they made him. And hence arose the figurative classical expression of '*Ex pede Herculem*,' which may be briefly stated as the method by which to judge of unknown quantities by quantities which are already known. It is thus that I have calculated the size of Buddha at the time he visited Phrabāt, and here he is.

Speaking in general terms, a masher six feet high should have a foot ten inches long. It should really be a little more, but let that pass, as the figure ten is a convenient one, and I must have due regard to the feelings of my imaginary dandy. His shoulders should be one foot ten inches broad, or a little more. Now, if a ten-inch foot gives one foot ten inches for breadth of shoulders, what breadth of shoulders should a flipper five feet long give? It is a question of simple proportion, and the breadth of shoulders should be exactly eleven feet. By the same method of calculation, the height of the Buddha should be thirty-six feet! Think of it. It is not so easy to calculate the cubic bulk or displacement of Buddha, as he might have had a wasp-waist or a pot-belly, which would make all the difference. He died, however, it is said, after he was eighty years old, and by surfeiting himself too heartily with pig's pork, of all other foods for a slender waist! Taking, then, one consideration with another, I have calculated that the cubic bulk of Buddha, when he visited Phrabāt, must have been about the same as a dozen or fifteen large white elephants. No wonder that he made a deep impression on the solid rock. Such be thy God, O Sir Edwin Arnold!

While I cannot help smiling at the sylphlike proportions of Buddha at this time, I must not forget to mention that his footprint is not the only one of note in the legendary lore of the world. There is said to be a footprint of Adam on Adam's Peak in Ceylon, which he left there as he stepped from that (supposed) Garden of Eden over to India across Adam's Bridge. The Hindoos, however, maintain that it is not the footprint of Adam but of Brahma; and I am sure I cannot make up my mind as to which of the two legends is the correct one.

While lately rambling on the Appian Way outside Rome, I came to a small church where they showed me a piece of marble on which were imprinted, according to the faithful, the impression of both feet of our Saviour side by side. The impressions are somewhat larger than natural size, and beautifully impressed on the solid marble. This took place when Christ, after the Resurrection, met St. Peter escaping from Rome for fear of his life. St. Peter said to him, '*Domine, quo vadis?*' (Lord, where are you going?) Christ replied, '*Venio iterum crucifigi*' (I come to be crucified again). Thereupon St. Peter returned to Rome for whatever fate might be awaiting him there. It was on this marble that our Saviour was standing at the time. Such is the tale; but the Bible, I think, says nothing of St. Peter having ever visited Rome.

CHAPTER IX

> This man would guide you; would he?
> I cannot see how could he,
> But yet beware that should he,
>   The day you'll ever rue;
> For by the great Apollo,
> The victim's blood will follow,
> And scream from hill and hollow
>   With shrieks of horror due.
>
> *The Guilt of Blood.*

Return from the Shrine—'My Father was an Englishman'—Lost sight of the Missionary—The Menam a Misnomer—The ex-tutor of the Crown Prince—Captain Bertuzzi Imprisoned—West and Välloo—Search for Passports—The Royal Palace—The Emerald Buddha—Prince Damrong—White Elephants—Trial of Phra Yott—Short Cut to the Millennium.

AND then we returned from the fair. The whole of this month is counted for righteousness by the Siamese in the way of pilgrimage to Phrabāt, but the day of the full moon, and that preceding and following it, are esteemed the three principal days. As this was now the day after the full moon, there were vast crowds that evening on the road from Phrabāt back to Tarua again; and it was there that I had left the steam launch 'Guinèvre' and her crew. I knew that some of the rickety country carts were not unlikely to break down on the journey, and that a block and obstruction might be the natural consequence. I was therefore anxious to leave as soon as we could, and, if possible, to keep in front of the other carts. But the drivers could not be prevailed upon to start before the cool of the evening, for fear of injuring their precious buffaloes by the heat. However, when the multitude of carts did manage to start at last, ours was among the first half a dozen to do so. The missionary and his cart were coming along with me a portion of the way, but somehow or other

I lost sight of him later on. We stopped three or four times at small villages, to rest the lazy buffaloes; and as it was very droughty weather, Mr. C—— and myself, with more zeal than discretion, indulged in eating raw cucumbers, when we could find them, so as to keep us as cool as cucumbers are supposed to keep people.

In one or two of these places we noticed what we thought was a young Siamese girl, hovering round us with more than usual curiosity. Observing this, we at last made signs to her to come and sit down beside us on the verandah. But she turned up her nose indignantly at this proposal. The missionary then spoke to her in Siamese, when she again turned up her nose and replied in a pet, 'My father was an Englishman.' We then discovered that the father of this girl was really an American, a fellow-countryman, therefore, of my present 'casual' companion, and that this girl could speak more or less English, though in manner and dress she looked just like a Siamese girl of the period, performing the sacred duty of a pilgrimage to the Buddha's holy footprint.

Then the moonlight night came on, but yet our progress was unpleasantly slow. We reached Tarua back again some time after midnight. I had by this time lost sight of both the missionary and of 'My father was an Englishman.' His cart was quite near mine for a long while, but whether it eventually broke down and fell to the rear, I was not able to make out. Where he was going to I did not exactly know, but I wanted to say good-bye to him, or, if he was going down the river anywhere, I would have given him a passage on the 'Guinèvre' towards his destination. So Chang and myself waited on the bank of the river at Tarua for fully an hour, but I never saw the missionary again. And to this day I do not know what has become of him, whether his cart really broke down, whether he was spirited away by the Siamese, or whether he himself spirited away 'My father was an Englishman.' The reader must not think that I am making this remark seriously, as I have always had a great opinion of the courage and self-sacrifice of missionaries, though others, I know, consider missionaries and mischief-makers as equivalent terms. I only make the statement for a laugh, which, indeed, often does good to one's soul. At any rate, I would willingly myself have run away across the country to the China Sea, with my two Chinese servants, but, alas! they would not run away with me.

It was then I realised the great topographical advantage that Phrabāt possessed over Bangkok, as a starting-point from which to cross the wild interior of Siam. But I was helpless, for I had only taken supplies for this journey alone. Besides which, I had no servants, for the two Chinese who came with me to Phrabāt had only intended to come with me for this trip alone, and were by no means prepared to face the more interior wilds of the country. At this time of the year the stream at Tarua is only a small tributary that falls into the Menam lower down, and was quite shallow. So we ran the 'Guinèvre' on a sand-bank once or twice, but managed to get her off again without any damage, and reached the ancient capital of Ayouthia in due course; and here my friend Chang returned once again to his ordinary course of life, instead of breaking the hearts of the simple Siamese maidens up the way of Mount Phrabāt.

I stayed for a little while at Ayouthia to see some of its ruins, and climbed to the top of some tall old building to have a look round the country. The city was abandoned in 1767, and is now almost entirely in ruins. It is virtually situated on an island, with the network of the river surrounding it on all sides. This portion of the country is in fact a mere mesh-work of land and water. Though the real meaning of the word Menam is *Mother of Waters* (*Ma*, Siamese for *Mother*, and *nam*, for *water*), yet the Menam is by no means a large river. The Red Indian word Mississippi has, I think, something of the same meaning, and apparently with much greater right, as it is the longest river in the world, and rivals the Amazon itself in the amount of water it brings to the ever-craving sea. Indeed, the Menam only deserves the name of river after the confluence of these many streams below Ayouthia; and as such, it is not more than one hundred and fifty miles long, if even so much; while the other Mother of Waters, the Mississippi, has got the magnificent length of 4,350 miles!

The real great river in these regions is the Mekong, of

which the British public have heard so much of late, and of which they are not unlikely to hear still more in the near future, in connection with the Franco-Siamese question. But I shall not say anything more about it here, till I reach there myself on this rambling journey. Having done with Ayouthia, then, we kept on to Bangkok, where the 'Guinèvre' safely arrived without any further misadventure.

When I reached Bangkok I found that the arrangements with the Crown Prince's tutor had fallen through, as he had become too anxious to get home as soon as he could, and could not therefore join in such a wild-goose chase as mine apparently was. I was sorry for this in a way, because he spoke Siamese fluently, and by going together we should be much more comfortable in many ways. Besides, I had for some time back relied on his coming, and did not, therefore, exert myself in procuring an interpreter, so much as I should otherwise have done. But when looking on the business from another point of view, I was not sorry at all. For a person may be a good tutor, but yet a poor traveller, and I should be sorry to be hampered by anyone who might not be prepared for any hardship or emergency that might occur on the journey.

I also found on my return to Bangkok that my late would-be companion, Captain L. Bertuzzi, had just been clapped in prison pending trial for the fearful crime of murder. Somebody else, however, came to the rescue. The same gentleman who had previously warned me against Bertuzzi now stepped in again, and said that he would try and get an interpreter who would be prepared to accompany me, and this he did the very next day.

The following morning there appeared on the scene a small Eurasian, who looked quite a boy, but who was really much older and wiser than he looked. He wore one of those huge hats, to which I have already alluded, and he looked so very small under it, that he reminded me of the puny little heir and the great steel helmet in the *Castle of Otranto*. But it might turn up rather handy, as on the journey he might be able to use it for a bed at night, and for a sunshade during the day. However, I was not in a position to pick and choose, but to take the goods the gods provided, and take my chance as to how they would turn out. Besides, it is a difficult task to judge at first sight of what stuff a man may be made of. The name of my proposed interpreter was West, and his mother was a Siamese lady, while his father was an American, exactly the same as 'My father was an Englishman' (already alluded to in this chapter). Indeed, I think that West's father was one of the pilots that originally started the business with Pilot Jackson, already more than once honourably mentioned in these pages.

West now in his turn procured through one of his friends the services of a Madrassee cook, named Vălloo, who will probably make the reader smile before the end of the story; and I was now as happy as the proverbial king. I had at last obtained all I wanted in that line, and my only fear was that they would desert me before starting; and so I was naturally anxious to start at once.

I had now to procure passports to permit me to proceed through the interior of the country. Some said that a Siamese passport was not worth the paper on which it was written when I did reach the wild interior, but I subsequently found that this was a mistake, and that my passport was of great use to me. Moreover, if anything really did happen, I was anxious to have the passport in my possession, to prove that I was practically authorised to enter the interior. The difficulty, however, at this time was to get a passport, and not as to whether it would be of any value when I got it.

I duly applied to the British Consul, who appeared lackadaisical enough about it, while I was now getting fidgety to start without delay. I also wished to have an opportunity of visiting the King's Palace before I left, but, though I wrote to the consul on this subject, I was not able to do so.

I intended to start on a certain day if I could at all manage it, but there was no sight of the passport, though I had applied for it four or five days before. The morning, therefore, before my proposed start, I went to the British consulate to inquire, but there was no word about my passport. One of the assistant consuls met me in an outer room, and told me that the Siamese private secretary to the Minister of the Interior was then with the consul on some business in an inner room, and so I waited till he came out. He spoke English well, and, as he was just then returning to the Palace, he faithfully promised to speak personally to the Minister of the Interior about my passport, and that it would be forwarded without delay.

I was now starting without being able to visit the Palace after all. That same day, however, some friend came to know of this, and said that he would see what could be done that evening. (He was an English official in the Siamese Government service.) In the evening the two of us drove up to the Palace accordingly, and I was able to see whatever any visitors are allowed to see within the Palace precincts; for the very interior, where the King lives with his fair ones, is never of course seen by any traveller, nor by anybody else save the inmates thereof. The Palace was very interesting, and well worth a visit. I once saw the Golden Palace of Mandalay, after being just vacated by King Theebaw, the last King of Burmah; and I also at another time made one or two assaults on the Imperial Palace of Pekin, to see what the Celestial Emperor was like, but I am sorry to say that I was ignominiously repulsed on each occasion. I am not able, therefore, to speak with confidence of the Imperial Palace of Pekin; but I am able to say with certainty that the royal Palace at Bangkok is vastly superior to what the Golden Palace at Mandalay was at its best.

To a European who has never been in the so-called 'gorgeous East,' and whose eyes are more accustomed to solidity than to glitter and glare, it is not easy to describe the Palace at Bangkok. There are, of course, the inevitable pagodas covered over with gold leaf, as becomes the royal residence of a Buddhist country; and one entire pagoda is said to be covered in with gold sheet, and not with the tissue gold leaf only. But I have my doubts about this, though it was impossible to say from a mere cursory inspection of it like mine. The finest structure of all is the pagoda containing what is known as the Emerald Buddha. Except for the purpose of airing the interior, or for the admission of a very occasional stranger, the doors and windows of this pagoda are never open, for fear of tarnishing the decorations. This was also said to be the audience hall of the king on very important occasions. As we happened to visit this pagoda as the sun was just mellowing the evening sky, the effects on the interior were very pleasing.

The walls and roof are covered over with frescoes of various designs, representing historical and allegorical scenes connected with Siam, and the import of which is to a great extent lost on a mere European. The doors and windows are also massive, and beautifully inlaid with mother-of-pearl and more or less precious stones. But the distinguishing feature, in particular, is the Emerald Buddha, which is placed on a gorgeous structure some fifteen or twenty feet above the ground, and is said to contain a valuable emerald in its forehead. But the Buddha, which is a small one, is placed so high above the spectator that he scarcely gets a good view of even the Buddha itself, let alone the emerald.

And so we two prowled about, along with another official we picked up at the Palace itself. Later on, the three of us went into a club within the Palace enclosure. This was a club to which all servants of the Siamese Government of a certain standing were eligible, whether Siamese or Europeans; and Mr. C——, who brought me there, belonged to it himself. When standing in the billiard-room of this club, who came into it but the man of all others that I wished to see, and this was His Royal Highness Prince Damrong, a name, by the way, of somewhat equivocal signification, if it were an English one. He was brother to the King of Siam, and was also Minister of the Interior of that remote kingdom, so that it was he who granted or refused passports to travel through the wilds of the country. He remembered about my passport at once, about which his private secretary had told him, and said that it would reach me in the course of the same evening. He asked me a few questions about my prospective travels through the country, and I congratulated him on his fluent English; and so the Prince betook himself to billiards, while the three of us duly took our departure.

It was after this that we went to see the White Elephants, which are considered so sacred in Buddhist countries. There are said to be fifteen or twenty white elephants within the precincts of the royal palace of Bangkok, but we only saw five, as we considered the careful inspection of five sacred white elephants quite enough at one time. When we went into the *keddah*, or stables, where they were kept, we found that each had a separate stall for himself, entirely shut off from the stalls of his fellows, so as to prevent them tickling one another with their tusks, which are rather dangerous weapons to scratch with. These five elephants were considered the choice of the lot, and were arranged on one side of the *keddah*, while the others were arranged round the corner; and as we had seen enough, and it was growing late, we did not go to see the others at all. Moreover, one elephant is so much like another, even when they are sacred white elephants, that you don't know where the difference comes in.

When we entered the first stable, the mahout in charge of the sacred animal shouted the words *chouk, chouk*, to his elephant, when that intelligent creature solemnly raised his trunk in front of his nose, and saluted us with great precision. The salutation of this sacred white elephant is the one depicted on the cover of this volume. Perhaps I should not say that the elephant raised his trunk in front of his nose, because an elephant's trunk *is* his nose, and a variety of other things besides. All the elephants we visited saluted in the same way in obedience to these mysterious words of *chouk, chouk*. Beauty is not the special point in favour of elephants, as they are altogether too unwieldy to be things of mere beauty only. The massive head, the large, ragged, and jagged ears, the coarse, pachydermatous hide, and the small, oblique, piercing eyes cannot by any manner of means be called beautiful. Yet they are wise and shrewd, as well as strong; and they are often very gentle and affectionate in their disposition. And I may state that it was from these very same stables that the docile and famous white elephant, 'Jumbo,' originally came, as a present from the King of Siam to Her Majesty the Queen

It was for a long time thought that elephants would not breed in captivity. But they do occasionally. They take a long time to grow, twenty or twenty-five years, and the few of them brought up in this way become extremely tame. I once saw a young one, two or three years old, that used to abandon his mother, to partake of the hospitality of Indian servants in the way of plantains, potatoes, and such-like delicacies. His mother was one among others that used to pass daily along a certain road in Mandalay, on some work or other; and hence the many temptations to her precious little baby, that used to follow her in her daily pursuits. But when she would miss him and call for him, or when he himself would think he was playing the truant too long, off he would immediately start with a peculiar trot and whimper of his own.

Well, if beauty is not the distinguishing quality of elephants in general, it is certainly not the strong point of sacred white elephants in particular. In the first place, they are not even white, for they are much nearer being black than being white anyway. The five that we saw possessed a colour that is seldom admired by any one, and that is a colour generally known as mouse-colour. In some places the hide exhibited more or less pronounced patches of a pinkish hue, which is highly valued among elephants, but of which I saw but little on this occasion, though I have often seen the pinkishness alluded to among water-buffaloes in various parts.

Indeed, these sacred white elephants looked to me very much like other elephants, only more so. I have heard it said that there is some peculiarity about their huge flat feet (without an instep), and that there are some other minor distinctions. But even then it is hard to account for the devotion paid to them. We do not admire people who have six toes or the colour of a mouse. Yes, but these people, you know, are not sacred white elephants. Intelligent Siamese Buddhists deny that the Siamese go the length of worshipping white elephants. But there is no doubt they look upon them with great awe and veneration. Indeed, I have read in a book (and it, therefore, must be true, though I scarcely believe it) that the principal white elephant in Siam ranks very high in the order of precedence in that kingdom, which is as follows:—King, first queen, chief white elephant, crown prince, &c.!

We were just leaving the Palace as the sun was setting. As we were passing out, a band of Siamese minstrels were playing the Siamese national anthem, and the great royal ensign was being hauled down on the flagstaff; and in this fashion we quitted the Palace precincts, well pleased with our random visit there.

During my short stay at Bangkok this time a legal trial was taking place, of which the reader has probably already heard. This was the trial for his life of a Siamese official named Phra Yott, and I was able to attend the court during his first days of trial. A brief notice of the case may therefore not be out of place here, as the cause that led to it was the occasion of much internal disturbance in Siam itself at this very time. It was also the ostensible reason why the French men-o'-war silenced the Ocean-butterfly Fort, and forced the Menam up to Bangkok, and why French troops occupied the island of Koh-si-chang, and still occupy Chantaboon. While yet most important of all to us, it may be counted as remotely the cause that is said to have brought Great Britain and France on the verge of war not long ago, and may do so again in the near future, for unfortunately this last 'cloud in the East' has not yet altogether vanished away.

So the trial of Phra Yott was admittedly a very important one; and so far as the casual observer could see, the case may be briefly summarised as follows:—The French recently occupied a district of north-east Siam named Kamoun, and of which the above Phra Yott was the civil commissioner. This region is in the vicinity of the Upper Mekong river, and is said to form a portion of the larger province of 'Luang Prabang, of which more will probably be heard during the settlement of the Buffer State between the eastern territories of Great Britain and France. The French seem to have occupied this district of Kamoun without any bloodshed, and so Phra Yott's occupation, like Othello's, was gone. Later on Phra Yott was sent by the French out of the portion of the country which he previously governed, accompanied by his assistant, Luang Annarak, and some forty or fifty followers, all unarmed. The exodus was escorted by a French inspector of police, named Grosgurin, in command of some twenty Annamese soldiers serving under the French Government.

All went well for the first four or five marches, till the parties reached the village of Kieng Chek, where they stayed two or three days on account of the illness of the French petty officer in charge. At this place, however, Phra Yott met some Siamese troops, who were on their way up to reinforce him, and with orders to him to resist the demands of the French in Kamoun. The party of Phra Yott and of Grosgurin, both at Kieng Chek and on the previous march, appear to have occupied different camping-grounds, though near one another.

Phra Yott maintained that he had not submitted to the

French occupation of his country, that he became the creature of circumstances for the time being, and that he was deported from Kamoun against his will by the French authorities. He could offer no resistance when the Siamese party remained unarmed. But having now received his reinforcements, and his orders to resist the French, he accordingly refused Inspector Grosgurin to command him any further.

It seems that it was Phra Yott's assistant, the said Luang Annarak, that first gave out this decision, whereupon Grosgurin, who was at the time ill with fever, sent for Luang Annarak, and promptly placed him under arrest, perhaps as a hostage for the future behaviour of Phra Yott's party. At any rate Phra Yott, now with his armed men, went over to Grosgurin and demanded the release of Luang Annarak, which was refused. It was then that the firing on both sides began, and evidence varied as to which party fired the first shot, but the firing eventually resulted in the death of fifteen or sixteen of the French native party, as well as of poor Grosgurin, who was the only European among them. The loss on the Siamese side was less, but I forget it. This was the whole business that eventually led to such complications.

The ordinary observer, unacquainted with the quips and cranks of mother Themis, will naturally conclude that much of the guilt of Phra Yott depended on the circumstances under which he acted. If he was simply taken by the French, as he said, deposed from his authority, and ousted out of his country, he was compelled to submit for the time being, for the simple reason that he could not help it. When assistance arrived, however, with orders to resist, if he should be accounted guilty because he did resist, then many a fine and brave patriot has in past ages deserved to be hanged. Nay more, Phra Yott denied that he had even given the order to fire at all, and that the *melée* began without any instructions from him whatever.

The French, on the other hand, maintained that Phra Yott was a bit of a tyrant, who oppressed the natives over whom he ruled, and who were therefore very glad to get rid of him. This may or may not be true, but it is one of those vague kinds of complaints that anybody can make against anybody else with whom he is not on amicable terms.

II

Besides, the accusation had no bearing on the case whatever, as it was not pleaded that he was oppressing any people over whom the French had any jurisdiction in any way. Granted that he was an oppressor, and there is no evidence that he was, is it likely that the French deported him out of his own special country on this account? They wanted his district—and that was all. And so the fate of Phra Yott will be told in a future chapter, as it does not conveniently come in within the compass of this one.

This hypocrisy on the part of governments would be very amusing were it not so cruel, and is too prevalent among ourselves to blind the eyes of anyone who is not born blind, or does not care to see. It has led to the death of poor Lobengula, the African chief, although as a ransom for his poor life he gave 1,000*l.* (perhaps all he had) to a couple of cruel hounds clothed in white English skins; and every lover of justice must regret these outbursts of false-righteous indignation on the part of governments, when they have some poor beetle to crush, in the way of untutored races. There is a good deal of the cowardly bully about governments, as about individuals. They pounce upon the weak, while they shrink from the strong.

And, moreover, goodness and badness are only comparative. If every state that governs its people better than its neighbour were therefore and on that account entitled to annex the same, the said neighbour's territories, we should soon be on the straight way to the Millennium, provided of course that the other states would not object. The logical conclusion of such a state of affairs would naturally be that the bad states would be annexed by the good ones, the good ones by the better ones, and the better ones by the one only best of all. This is a consummation devoutly to be wished, but will it ever happen? I am afraid we shall have to look for the Millennium in some other direction.

CHAPTER X

> They heaped upon his hapless head
> All sorts of crimes, and sternly said
>   'Twas he who stirred the strife;
> While he declared that all the while
> His conduct was devoid of guile.
> Though now, alas! in durance vile
>   He pines away for life.
>   *The Ill-fated Patriot.*

Phra Yott continued—The charges against him—Their punishments—Siamese judges—Prince Bitchit—Phlegmacy of Asiatics—Its moral effects—Chewing the cud—Moors and Arabs in Europe—The smoking lady.

PHRA YOTT was arraigned before a criminal court, composed of six Siamese judges and presided over by H.R.H. Prince Bitchit; and the charges laid down against him were categorically as follows :—

(1) Wilful and premeditated murder, committed by himself or by his orders on a French officer, called M. Grosgurin.

(2) Wilful and premeditated murder, committed by himself or by his orders, on an unknown number, supposed to be between sixteen and twenty-four Annamite soldiers, being a part of the detachment commanded by the said Grosgurin.

(3) Severe wounds or bodily harm, wilfully inflicted by himself or by his orders, on Bhoon Chan, Cambodian interpreter, and on Nguyen Van Khan, Annamite soldier.

(4) Robbery, committed by himself or by his orders, of arms and ammunition, and also of the personal effects of M. Grosgurin and of the Cambodian interpreter, Bhoon Chan, and of eighty-two piastres which were in the latter's trunk.

(5) Arson, committed by wilfully setting fire or ordering to set fire to the houses where M. Grosgurin and his soldiers were quartered.

All the aforesaid crimes being aggravated by the circumstances that the nature and gravity of these crimes were such as to create a cause of war between Siam and France.

And as I am on the categorical tramp, I may mention

the punishments by which his crimes were punishable by Siamese law, and which were duly laid down in connection with the case; and these were in their order:—

(1) Death.
(2) Mutilation.
(3) Scourging with fifty strokes.
(4) Imprisonment, and at the expiration of the term of condemnation to cut grass for the elephants.
(5) Quadruple fine.
(6) Triple fine.
(7) Double fine.
(8) Simple fine.

And from these eight different sorts of punishments, the one to be selected which is in proportion to the case.

Such, in plain English, was the formidable array of crimes and punishments which poor Phra Yott had to contend against on this important occasion.

The court-room, where the case was tried, was in one of the large public buildings within the enclosure of the walled city; and it was only a comparatively small room, though honoured with so great a trial. On the elevated daïs sat the six Siamese judges, in the centre of whom sat and presided H.R.H. Prince Bitchit. To the right hand of the court and below the daïs sat the French advocate, the French consul, and a French legal expert, who had come all the way from Saigon to watch the case. To the left of the court and facing the French party sat the defending pleaders, consisting of an English and a Cingalese lawyer, while the Crown Prince's ex-tutor acted the part of interpreter, in preference to coming with me through the wilds of Siam. Immediately in front and behind the judges was the Recorder's table, with three or four people sitting at it; and this party seemed to me to act the part of a 'buffer state' between the other two parties, and thus prevented a fresh collision on the floor of the court house.

Last, but not least, there sat in front of the Recorder's table no less a personage than Phra Yott himself, who was being tried for his life for all these crimes mentioned above, and who was the immediate cause of all this hullaballoo, the echoes of which have not yet quite died away. It is needless to say that he was the observed of all observers. He was dressed in a blue coat and waistcoat, and a skirt that bore some distant resemblance to a kilt, but folded up behind in Siamese fashion, while on his feet he wore the daintiest little pair of pumps, and the long white stockings, reaching above the knee, which are so very much affected at the present time by the real Pink-'uns of Siam.

There's Phra Yott for you, and make the best of him. He sat only a few yards in front of me, and was as cool as the proverbial cucumber, chewing his betel all the while with appreciative gusto. He did not appear bloodthirsty or ferocious in any way, and had nothing in his appearance to distinguish him either as a felon or a hero. After the usual preliminaries had been gone through, and after Phra Yott had pleaded 'Not guilty' to the series of charges laid against him, he left the Recorder's table, and went to sit beside his counsel to the left of the court, and still under the guard of a Siamese soldier, who always stood behind him.

By this time he had got tired of chewing his betel-nut, and so he calmly took out of his pocket a great big cheroot, and commenced to smoke it there and then ! The scene would strike any European with surprise, if unacquainted with the ways and manners of Eastern nations—to see the prisoner, tried for his life, and yet pulling away at his cheroot in the open court, as if the results of the trial were a matter of mere indifference to him. Most Europeans would have their throats a little too dry for smoking under the circumstances, and I should have liked very much to have possessed the brush of a ready artist, to depict the scene which I am now trying to describe with the more humble material of a scribbling pen. I hadn't even my kodak with me, and to have a 'snap-shot' at a court of justice with a kodak would be outrageous indeed.

It is difficult to know whether to praise or to blame the marked coolness of Asiatics in situations like this one. Whether they think it is fate, which they cannot avert, and to which they must therefore meekly bow down ; or whether it is mere physical insensibility, the results are equally notable. Their indifference probably arises from a combination of these causes. For the Asiatic is certainly more of a fatalist than a European is, and he is also less highly developed in his nervous organisation, being more of the salamander sort of disposition, so to speak. These qualities prove of great value in sickness to him at times, while at other times they are his very bane without an antidote.

By this means the Asiatic, like the Salamander, recovers wonderfully from wounds and surgical operations, which would kill Europeans on account of their more sanguine disposition, and more inflammatory blood, not to mention the baneful effect of alcoholic stimulants, which the Asiatic in his primitive state seldom or never touches. But on the other hand he yields sooner to exhaustive diseases, says it's his *kismet* (fate), and makes it so. Why, then, can't Asiatics as a rule face Europeans on the battle-field? for certainly they love life and fear death less than their pale-faced fellow creatures. Just in part because they are fatalists, and want therefore the mental and physical courage that defies both fate and man as long as it is possible to do so.

Nor must we ever lose sight of that indefinable something known as 'moral influence,' for no people are ever cocksure of victory from well-known antagonists; and the moral influence in such a case is tremendous, as it tends to make the strong stronger and the weak weaker. Why, it is this idea of moral influence that prompts John Chinaman to fire crackers to frighten away the devils, that prompts the soldier intentionally to shout when charging an enemy, and that prompts a dog to bark when gathering the sheep! Yet we must all bow down to fate some day or another, because we cannot get out of it. And while talking in this high falutin style, we must not forget that Europe was at different times nearly overrun by the Moors of Africa and Arabs of Asia; and that the flower of Europe, the Crusaders, fell for several generations in their vain efforts to wrench the Holy Sepulchre out of the hands of mere infidel Saracens.

But the smoking portion of Phra Yott's drama brings to my memory another smoking reminiscence, illustrative of the difference between Asiatic and Europeans in matters of modesty and taste, as well as in matters of more serious import. In 1887 the Queen's Jubilee was celebrated in Mandalay, then newly annexed, and people from far and near gathered round to see it. In the building where the proclamation was to be celebrated, there was a temporary structure erected to serve the place of a daïs or platform. And on this raised platform was Sir Charles Bernard, the then Chief Commissioner of Burmah, along with those whose rank or vanity led them, so to speak, to seek the top story. Conspicuous in the front row on the said platform might be seen a Shan *sawbwa* or chief, with two of his wives, one on each side of him. European petticoats had scarcely yet invaded these remote territories, and all the European officials were dressed in uniform, or in the absence of uniform, were wearing the best dress they could muster, while Sir Charles himself was decorated in all his bravery of gold lace. He rose to make a well ordered and apparently well studied address. He spoke slowly, and appeared a little nervous on the occasion, for he was not only proclaiming the Jubilee of the Queen, but also the permanent annexation of Upper Burmah to the British dominions.

Suddenly when he was in the middle of his speech, I observed the elder of the two Shan ladies clapping her hands two or three times, as is the fashion with the great people of the East, when calling their servants. She was promptly attended by a young boy (or was it a girl?), who made his way across the lower floor, immediately in front of the platform, till he reached opposite his mistress. She wanted something which he fetched and gave her, and soon after, my beauty was smoking and fuming away in great style, with a big cheroot in her mouth.

The sight of the Chief Commissioner arrayed in all his glory, delivering his important address, and this lady of the land smoking and puffing away within a few seats of his right elbow, looked highly ludicrous, and brought many a titter of applause from those of the audience capable of appreciating the incongruity of the situation.

CHAPTER XI

Before you start on your campaign
  Look well unto your larder;
For armies on their bellies[1] fight,
  And aye will fight the harder,
When they have quite enough and more
Of rations of all sorts in store.
The Soldier's Complaint.

My passports at last—Departure from Bangkok—Supplies left behind—Landing at Paknām—Uncomfortable cabin—Disturbing influences—A welcome message—Reach Pechim—Corporal of the Guard—Chowmuang of Pechim—Twenty sons and thirty daughters—Prolific royalties—The strolling players—Siamese superstitions.

But what has become of my passport all this time? Well, the passport promised by Prince Damrong did not arrive that night after all; but, sure enough, it did early the next morning, and I was very glad to get it. Besides this Siamese passport I also procured another one from M. le Myre de Vilers, the French minister at Bangkok, in case I should travel through the French territory of Cambodia. This same M. de Vilers is the French minister that, at the time of my writing, is making such a noise in Madagascar, and is evidently an ardent promoter of the extension of the French Colonial Empire.

I could now see my way gradually getting clearer. I had advanced to West and Välloo a portion of their prospective pay, in a guardless impulse of sudden generosity, as I felt so pleased to get them engaged at last. Second thoughts afterwards suggested to me that I had probably made a mistake, and that this very engagement 'bounty' of mine might not unlikely ruin the very purpose for

---

[1] This has now become a physical as well as physiological fact; at any rate as regards the Thin Red Line.

which it was intended. Both of them had now the
'bounty' in their pockets, and if they wished to abscond,
how should I be able to get a hold of them in such a city
of klongs and canals as the city of Bangkok? I was not
so much afraid about West as I was about Välloo. The
day I engaged him, I told him to remain about the hotel,
in case he might be wanted at any time. He faithfully
reported himself the same evening, but he was not very
steady on his pins, as he had gone to the bazaar, and had
there been in company with Sir Simon Shumshoo, the John
Barleycorn of eastern nationalities, and had there
apparently spent his advance freely.

I seriously warned him, and he promised, of course.
But I had got suspicious, and I now began to think what
I ought to have thought about before. Before engagement he had shown me a certain number of characters
from people he had previously served, and if I had kept
these, or could now get a hold of them, I would feel more
confident that Välloo would come up to the scratch when
the moment of starting came round. I could not get a
sight of him for the whole of next day, as I suppose he
was suffering from a headache; but West, who found out
where he lived, was able to wriggle the characters out of
him, and then I felt more at ease about Välloo.

The paddy-boat tug, with which I intended to sail,
was starting at noon of the day on which I got my Siamese
passport, and I was anxious not to miss her, as I was now
losing time by any further delay. This kept me busy all that
morning in making whatever arrangements were necessary.
West and Välloo presented themselves faithful to their
promise. I had previously drawn out with the hotel
manager a list of what I would require, and subsequently
got the luggage, and, as I thought, the supplies, on the
landing place, ready to be shipped into the small launch
that was to carry us to the larger tug, for the latter had
promised to whistle for me when she approached the hotel
landing, in dropping down the river.

Under these happy prospects I was having my last
luncheon in the hotel, and the hour was high noon; when
I suddenly heard the warning whistle, and went hurriedly
on board. We were off at last then, with West and
Välloo as gay as crickets. I thought nothing of my

supplies, for who ever thinks of ham and eggs when sailing out of harbour on a voyage of discovery? But West did think about the creature comforts, and asked me about them. I gave him the paper list on which they were recorded, and he went to take an inventory. He came back to say that no supplies had come on board at all with the exception of a few tins of preserved soup!

My joy was immediately changed into mourning; for what on earth could be done? We had been steaming down the river for a couple of hours by this time, and were approaching the little village of Paknām already mentioned. To ask the tug to return to Bangkok was out of the question, for she was a regular trader, duly advertised in the papers, and cram-full of Chinese and other passengers, besides what little cargo she could carry. It was a very bad beginning to a journey of this kind, and augured but ill success to us. Indeed, the country was so disturbed at the time of starting from Bangkok, that there were not wanting evil prophets there, who predicted the direst results to our little unprotected expedition, and were ready to lay down their bottom dollar that we should never reach the China Sea, but would have either to turn back, or perhaps get killed on the journey. These evil prophets, however, were happily and I hope pleasantly disappointed, as the mere existence of this volume is enough in itself to confirm and testify.

We were then very awkwardly situated, however, and did not know what on earth to do. To proceed without any provisions at all would be courting almost certain failure, and it would never do to return back again. We could have landed at Paknām and again returned to Bangkok by the steam tram car, but I could not endure the idea. For once West and Vālloo had returned to Bangkok again, who knew but that they might give me the slip altogether? And though I certainly intended to use them as Izaak Walton was wont to use his frogs, namely, as if I loved them, yet now that I had them in my clutches, I should feel very sorry to lose sight of them again on any pretext whatever.

I induced the skipper of the tug to put in to Paknām all the same; and West and myself went on shore to forage for food. All we could get of any service to us consisted of a few crabs and water-melons, the former of which were very good. It was getting very late in the evening, and the skipper of the tug was getting very urgent to start. We had scarcely left the river's bank when a steamer of the Scottish Oriental Line, called the 'Devawongse,' hove in sight on her way to Hong Kong. It was only a few hours ago that I had said good-bye to the captain of her, as I was starting from the hotel. I knew the ship would anchor for the night off Mosquitto Point just opposite, as all out-going ships do. So we hailed the 'Devawongse,' and went on board of her as soon as she came to anchor. But the captain unfortunately had little of what would be of any use to me on such a journey. There was therefore nothing to do but go on and trust in Providence, for I had detained the little tug far too long already.

Night fell apace. The tug 'Hong Kong' would be some twenty or thirty tons, or perhaps even more, as it is difficult to judge of the size of ships by the naked eye only. Her cramped deck was literally strewn with passengers and passengers' luggage, and she was by no means a first-class clipper wherewith to travel. There was a sort of sheltering hood in the middle of her, and on each side of the ship, beneath this hood, there were two narrow bunks for her crew, and for any benighted passenger, willing to pay extra for the privilege of stowing himself away in one of them. The only seat, or rather bench, in the ship was the lid of the water-tank, placed immediately to the right of the man at the wheel, while on the other side of the steersman was a broken chair without any back to it.

Such was the craft in which I proceeded from Bangkok to Pechim. Perplexed as I was about my provisions, I forced my narrow cork mattress into one of these bunks, and then squeezed myself inside after it. It was an unpleasant place to sleep in, for it was intolerably hot and stuffy, and still worse, it was so full of fleas that I was soon driven out of it again. I then turned somebody out of the broken chair, and took my place beside the man at the wheel, who was steering his tug from the front of the hood, and within a few feet of the bows of the little vessel. Between him and the said bows were some half a dozen Chinese passengers, lying quietly on the deck, and all of them apparently fast asleep. There was a slight choppy sea on, nothing to speak about, but enough to make the little craft toss more or less in the trough of the sea, and to make the sea spray occasionally splash over her low bulwarks. I was feeling a wee bit squeamish at this time, with the tumbling of the tug, when she took a sudden lurch, and shipped a sea that soon dispersed the sleepers, and rather cured me of the nausea, by watching the heathen Chinese scootling about in the water.

Later on the same night we made the entrance to the Bang-pak-kong river, up which we proceeded, and the banks of which were for some considerable distance in quite a twinkle-twinkle of fireflies, so common in swampy low ground like that along which we were now sailing. This river, we found, assumed different names according to the portion of the country through which it passed, and higher up still, the Bang-pak-kong is known as Pechim-Menam or Pechim river. Though the word 'Menam,' therefore, literally means the 'Mother of Waters' in Siamese, it is evidently used as a kind of general term for any main stream whatever. And as people's ideas of a main stream must differ immensely according to their range of knowledge, even so must differ the general meaning of the word Menam; for the Menam itself, that waters Bangkok, and which according to Siamese notions is above all others the 'Mother of Waters,' would scarcely form a first-class tributary to some of the very largest rivers in the world, and is not nearly so large as the Mekong on the east side of Siam, which has the much less pretentious meaning of 'Boundary Water,' and of which more anon.

I felt drowsy at last, and, stretching myself on the lid of the water-tank, I soon forgot fireflies and fleas, as well as my provisions and heathen companions, and fell soundly asleep. The next day we called at a place called Patrieu, where I made a cursory inspection of a large rice-mill belonging to the owner of the 'Hong Kong' tug. There was said to be a solitary European at this place. We did not happen to see him during our short stay, but we afterwards saw in the papers that he was murdered a short time after our visit. Indeed, crime was said to be rather rife in Siam at this particular period, though the reports thereof were probably much exaggerated.

Later on the same day, the tug took in tow several of

those unwieldy paddy-boats, which did not tend to accelerate the very modest speed with which we started. Yet, in spite of the rice-boats, I spent the greater portion of that day in the capacity of the man at the wheel, to while away the time; and I can now almost claim a pilot's certificate on the Menam, the Bang-pak-kong, and a portion of the Mekong, as the reader will see when we get there.

During the following night we arrived at Pechim, with no less than five rice-boats still hanging to our stern. It was at Pechim that I was going to land for my cross-country journey, and this was the ultimate limit of the voyage of the 'Hong Kong.' It was too late to go on shore that night, never knowing where to go. But on waking up in the morning from my water tank, like a hot-weather walrus, I was pleased and surprised to find a Siamese messenger waiting for me. This was a servant from the acting Governor of Pechim, who had received orders from Prince Damrong, Minister of the Interior, with instructions to make every necessary arrangement for my overland journey.

This was a very pleasant surprise, because at the time of leaving Bangkok, I did not know there was any telegraph communication between Bangkok and Pechim at all. Nor did West know, no, nor even the learned Vālloo. But it was true, all the same. I went with the interpreter to see the Governor shortly afterwards, and he came with us to show the rest-house where we were going to put up during our stay at Pechim. These rest-houses—some of them, of course, more primitive than others—are to be met with in various places over the whole of Siam, and are known in the language of the country under the name of *sala*; and the *sala* at Pechim is about the best of them all.

Shortly after reaching this *sala* I received another equally welcome message from the manager of the hotel at Bangkok, regretting the mistake about my provisions, and offering to send them in another tug that was sailing in a day or two, if I would wait at Pechim to receive them.

I need scarcely say that I was very glad to receive the last-mentioned message, as it relieved my mind considerably; and though the mistake at Bangkok kept us at Pechim for four whole days, it was the only reasonable thing that we could do under the circumstances. And for the intending traveller the moral of this unhappy tale is, that when bound on a random journey like this, he ought to look at everything for *himself* ; as, after all, it is he who really suffers if anything goes seriously wrong, For though the mistake on this occasion occurred probably through the negligence of the hotel servants, yet I had to blame myself in not checking the articles before starting, or even asking West to do so. But this is the twice-told tale of being very, very wise after the event, and I shall therefore say no more about it.

So there we stuck at Pechim for four whole days, feeling the time very long, and wishing very much to be jogging on our way. The *sala* at which we put up was as comfortable as could be expected, and is probably one of the best throughout the country. There was a bedstead in it, of elaborate construction, and so large as to contain a couple of giants at least, with a few of their wives and concubines.

On the evening of our first day at Pechim, a small group of Siamese youths came up to the *sala*, and began squatting themselves down about the verandah. On inquiring who they were, we were told that they were our guard during our stay at Pechim. They consisted of eight unarmed Siamese soldiers and two ordinary king's messengers. To confess the truth, they were more or less of white elephants to me, and I should much have preferred to have been quietly left alone, or with two or three at the most. After it got dark, as there were so many of them about the open verandah, I told West to give them a gentle hint that a couple of them would be quite sufficient to watch during the night, and that the rest of them might go home. But the corporal of the guard said that they could not go home without the necessary orders from their own proper authorities. As this was a praiseworthy trait of discipline I said no more on the subject, as any further suggestion upon my part might possibly be misunderstood, and I was anxious to avoid any misunderstanding of any kind whatever.

On waking the next morning at early dawn I went out on the verandah, and there were my innocent young guards all fast asleep. They were, in fact, mostly raw recruits, who had lately come into Pechim from the outer-lying villages to learn the goose-step for the first time. And from what I could learn from West's interpretation, there was a kind of conscription going on then, and for the first

CORPORALS OF THE GUARD.

To face page 110.

time in the history of the kingdom of Siam. This was probably on account of the hostilities that were then pending between this country and France.

As we had nothing to do at Pechim, we sometimes wandered about the straggling town on the bank of the river. Pechim appeared an old place, and to have been at one time more prosperous and larger than it is at present. It had been walled in and more or less fortified at some previous period, and there was still remaining a kind of walled citadel, where the 'chowmuang' of the place lived almost alone.

He is not far from the madding crowd, however, as the citadel, such as it is, is quite beside the bazaar on the right bank of the river, called here by the name of Pechim-menam. It was this 'chowmuang' that was to provide transport for us, and his particular office I found difficult to understand. My interpreter tried to make out that 'chowmuang' meant a 'little king,' as he used to say; or, say, a feudal lord or country laird.

He was not the governor of Pechim, for that functionary had just gone down to Bangkok with the Governor of the province of Battambong, probably to consult on political matters at this grave crisis with the French; as Battambong was one of the rich provinces of eastern Siam over which France was then casting amorous eyes. Neither was he the second governor, for *he* was there as large as life, living on the opposite side of the river. I say 'as large as life' advisedly, as he was much the largest Siamese I have ever seen; and his name was Phra Pitsac, while the chowmuang's name was Phya Yo-athai. Phya is a higher personal rank than Phra in Siam, while there is no hereditary rank at all in the country except those of the king and princes. This second governor was nearly six feet high, and, as he was also big made and fairly fat, he would probably weigh fifteen or sixteen stone—quite a phenomenal height and weight for the Siamese, who, though often well knit together, are generally short, and seldom run to excessive corpulence.

But the chowmuang, who was an old man, probably over seventy years of age, appeared superior to either of the two governors, whatever his real office was. He might be the feudal lord of the soil, but not necessarily, as I afterwards came across chowmuangs in small villages, who could not possibly be feudal lords, and in fact my inquiries about the business were rather a failure, as I did not like to carry them to the verge of curiosity.

I knew that something of the same kind of system prevailed in Dutch Java, where everything is done through the *Woodanas*, or native chiefs, but really originating with the Dutch so-called Residents in their districts, who literally recommend, but practically command, whatever instructions have to be carried out. The same sort of system also prevails to a certain extent throughout British India. But these cannot properly be compared with the system obtaining in Siam, as both India and Java are conquered countries, ruled over by alien authority, whereas Siam is an independent country (and I hope it will remain so) with a homogeneous people, without any racial differences between the rulers and the ruled.

At any rate, the old chowmuang of Pechim came one morning to see us at the *sala*, and next evening I returned his visit inside his citadel, accompanied by West, as I always was, for purposes of interpreting. He appeared quite a genial old greybeard, and very willing to do all he could to make us comfortable.

Throughout that journey how often and often have I repeated the very same questions and received the very same replies? West did not understand this at first, and, like Chang at Phrabāt, instead of interpreting my questions and *vice versâ*, he would answer them himself without any further reference. But when I explained to him once or twice that these questions were frequently put for the mere sake of *talkee-talkee*, or having something to say, he seemed to see through the business better, and improved in this respect as we went along.

I forget now how it was that, among other topics, we at last fell into the topic of wives and children. This would be a forbidden subject of conversation in India, both among Mohammedans and Hindoos alike, as they are very reticent about these matters. Not so, however, with the frank and free Buddhists, among whom the fair sex enjoy all the freedom prevalent among Western races, with neither harem nor *purdah* to confine them, and without let or hindrance to their conduct in general affairs. This freedom of the women is indeed a marked and pleasant feature in the social life of both Burmah and Siam.

I understood from the chowmuang that there was no law forbidding a Siamese from having quite a number of wives, but that most people were content with one only, except of course the king, who was rich, and could have as many as he liked. When I told him that no one in my country was allowed to have more than one wife, not even the king himself, he was rather amused ; and his merriment was still further increased when I told him that quite a considerable portion had never a wife at all, and included myself among the category.

I casually remarked that with so many wives the king of Siam must have a lot of children, when he replied that he did not think he had so very many, only about twenty sons and thirty daughters ! I do not know, indeed, how many children the king of Siam has got, nor do I suppose that the chowmuang knew either. But the present king's father had eighty-four children, which should surely secure his posterity unless massacres should be resorted to to a very enormous extent. While visiting the King's Palace a few days previously, I saw five young yellow boys walking along, and each with a servant behind him. My companion recognised them, and I asked him who they were. They were five sons of the present King Paramindar Maha Chulalongkorn. They were all about six or seven years of age, and must have been born within two or three years of one another, so that they must almost all have had different mothers.

But prolific in this way as are the kings of Siam, they are beaten hollow by the late Moung Lohn, King of Burmah, and father of Theebaw, the last king of that country, who required to be deposed a few years ago, and who now lives a harmless enough life in India, without any further opportunity of cutting off the heads of his cousins and his aunts. King Theebaw himself, when we annexed the country, had only five children in five years of married life, and three of these had already died. But the pious monarch of immortal memory, King Moung Lohn, had 110 children, namely, forty-eight sons and sixty two daughters, from fifty-three recognised wives, besides his offspring from odds and ends of concubines !

I

No wonder that such kings are liable to become silly yet Solomon, who must have been a most henpecked monarch, was also the wisest. Under such a condition of affairs farewell to domestic affection, and a long farewell to domestic happiness and peace. A person must possess a vast amount of the milk of human kindness, who can afford to distribute it in such endless ramifications. For no man, though even a king, can love so many wives and children ; nor can so many wives and children love one man, though even an emperor !

The chowmuang was very intelligent, and had a map of Siam hanging on the wall of the verandah ; and he had a very fair idea of the bearings of places depicted thereon. We were examining my proposed route to the ancient ruins of Angkor Wát ; and as he traced it out with his forefinger on the map, there could be no possible doubt about his rank, as one could easily see by the length and transparency of his finger nails.

It was getting late in the evening before we left the chowmuang, and West and myself turned back again through the long straggling street of the main bazaar. The Siamese, like the Burmese, are extremely fond of the drama, and especially of plays of a comic or burlesque character. They generally act in the open air, or nearly in the open air, and their stage decorations are of the simplest and most primitive kind. On our way back we met a company of these actors, powdered and painted in great style, and preparing for a play that evening at the corner of a street. There were lots of masks and false faces, with other paraphernalia of the stage. I tried on some of these masks, but none of them were big enough. Some of them were intended to come down over the head, and at last I got one big enough to slip over mine. It was obviously intended for a stage monarch, as it was very gaudy, and surmounted by a miniature pagoda. The eye-sockets, however, did not hit off my eyes, and I could scarcely see at all when having it on. But pretending to be a terrible bogey, and playing Blind Man's Buff with the actors, I am sure we gave as much pleasure to the spectators as if it were a real play.

They are also great believers in superstition and demonology in the town of Pechim, and we saw some houses in the outskirts with buttressed cactuses in front of their doors, to guard them against evil spirits. It is a strange belief among many uncivilised people, that evil spirits can only go in a straight line, the same as is said to be the case with mad dogs.

One would think that evil spirits, being so canny, would be particularly handy in dodging round the corners. Yet this is not the case ; for they don't seem to be dodgy in that way at all, but go as it were straight in a bee line, till they reach their victim, or squash themselves like jelly fish against the first opposing obstacle in the way. So practical a form does this belief take that, among the Shan and Kuchin mountaineers, the bamboo-lined passages leading up to their dwellings are made winding and crooked on purpose, so that the evil spirits or *Nats* will not be able to find their way when wishing to do them any harm. But primitive man seldom attributes any great degree of 'cuteness to the evil spirits that haunt him, and in the stage of Fetishism, the worshipper sometimes whips his fetish to bring him better luck next time.

CHAPTER XII

> Onwards on, there's no returning,
>   Till the goal is reached afar;
> Though thy lips be parched and burning,
>   Think no more of fair Braemar.
>   *The Highland Recruit.*

'March, march, Ettrick and Teviotdale'—Bivouac in Open Fields—The Láös Mountains—A Melting Atmosphere—Village of Chandakān—Initiating Priests—Straggling Bullocks—Country Waggons and Country Tracts—The Forbidding Mudfish—Tactics of Tactoo — Its Geographical Distribution — A new-born Baby—Vicarious Lying-in—A Dying Sufferer—The Evils of Quackery.

THE expected tug arrived from Bangkok at last, and we were so anxious to make a start that we actually left Pechim at four o'clock in the evening, the acting governor coming down to see that the transport was all right. I had pitched my tent once or twice near the *sala*, to show my new servants how to pitch it again when required, and was rather surprised when the governor said he had never seen a tent pitched before. This tent I afterwards abandoned, as I found it too cumbersome and unsuitable for the journey.

There was no elephant transport, which is quite a common means of conveyance in Siam, for the governor of Battambong, as well as the head governor of Pechim itself, had quite recently gone to Bangkok, and they had taken all the elephants with them. As the ground was flat with pathways for wheeled carriage, we contented ourselves with three carts, which were afterwards found to be insufficient, and were increased to five. The carts were different from those we had at Mount Phrabāt, and not nearly so good; but they were the best we could find, and we could not therefore justly complain. They were skeleton carts, with their sides composed of upright bamboo bars, and gradually widening above; so the floors of them were much narrower than their tops, and they were also very long in proportion to their breadth. They were, in short, the usual carts common in this portion of the country for carrying rice, which of course is the staple produce of Siam ; and they are generally loaded with this rice after their ends and sides are protected with matting, so as to prevent the rice from escaping through the openings between the bars.

We were so late of starting that we could only cover six miles before nightfall, and had to bivouac in the open fields. But we *had* made a start, and that was everything. The night was warm enough, to be sure, so that we were in no great danger of catching our death from cold, though we were liable enough to catch the malarial fever which is rather common in this as in all other tropical swampy countries. In fact we travelled through the country at about the hottest time of the year in Siam, where April is the hottest month, whereas June is the hottest month of the year throughout the greater portion of Hindustan.

But at this particular time I considered myself seasoned, like the conspirator Catiline, who was said to be equally patient of both heat and cold. For I had been less than six months in Europe during the previous eighteen years. And of the rest I had passed some three years in Aden, that delightful spot which is said to be separated from the unmentionable place by only a thin sheet of brown paper, and I had even passed a portion of the merry month of June on one occasion, along with only one other European, in a grass hut in a cholera camp on the outskirts of Jacobabad, which at that particular season of the year is the real place with the thin paper partition, and not Aden, the evil of whose climate has been very much exaggerated. Nay, more, I had been during that time in Canada too, when the thermometer was going down 55°–60° Fahr. below freezing-point. So that I had therefore endured the two extremes, as it were, of heat and cold, without feeling very much the worse of either the one or the other.

The whole journey in this respect offered a remarkable contrast to the one I had been previously meditating— namely, the lofty Pamirs, with their towering mountains and eternal snow. However, I subsequently came to prefer this one for the sake of its greater novelty, if for nothing else, as there had been plenty pioneers among the Pamirs of late.

We bivouacked in the neighbourhood of a small village called Wat-Kitétt, where some of the inhabitants came out to see us, and some half a dozen of them brought their sleeping mats out with them, and stayed with us during the whole of that night, lying down peacefully on their mats within a hundred yards of where I was trying to sleep in the open on my cork mattress. We started at daybreak the next morning, and, after fording a tributary of the Pechim river, we duly arrived at the village of Chandakān. These two marches were comparatively short ones, and were by far the shortest we had on the whole journey, for it would have been a mistake to try long marches on the first few days out.

During our second day's march we came in sight of some of the Lāös mountains, to the north and to our left-hand side. They looked between 2,000 feet and 3,000 feet high from the route we were taking, with a regular even summit, stretching for miles and miles away, like the top of an elevated plateau, but I could fancy they were not quite so smooth as they looked to us in the distance.

The weather was very warm, and, after lying down on the bamboo floor of the *sala*, I found myself getting uncommonly hot, and gradually bursting into a profuse perspiration. Perspiration is supposed by some people to be an indication of health and physical vigour. Nothing could be further from the truth; for, except in the case of very fat people, anything over ordinary perspiration is an indication of weakness, and not of strength. But I had not grown so suddenly more than usually weak, nor more than usually fat, and I could not account for this uncomfortable perspiration that I found creeping over me, as I felt like fat Will Waddle when he got his bedroom over the baker's oven. The cause was similar too, for, on getting up and looking around to account for the roasting, I found Vālloo cooking my dinner immediately below the place on which I was lying down.

The village of Chandakān is a straggling and large one, with houses along each bank of the tributary which we had just forded, but with most of them at a distance of a mile or more from the east bank of the stream. Our next march was a very long one, as we covered twenty miles or even more. The bullocks also proved recalcitrant on this journey, so that we were very late in arriving at our destination. Invariably getting up at the very dawn, we generally managed to start at or before sunrise, and on the next morning at ten o'clock we found ourselves at a village called Bang-yan, and there we stayed to have our simple breakfast and let the animals have a rest.

We stopped longer than we expected, for at this village we witnessed the ceremony of preparing young aspirants for the Siamese priesthood. There were five candidates, four of whom would be under twenty years of age, while the fifth would be considerably over fifty. We mentioned before that a good pious Buddhist may become a priest or cease to be a priest at pleasure. But a candidate must go through those ceremonies all the same, and as long as he remains a priest must conform of course to the rules of the order, of which celibacy is one, and living on alms is another. Three older 'phras,' or priests, were putting the neophytes through their facings, which consisted of much muttering and posturing of various kinds. The word 'phra,' by the way, though generally used for a priest in Siam, is by no means confined to that order, but is also a title of rank among the laity, as in the case of Phra Yott, for example, who was not a priest but a civil official. Indeed, the king himself is a phra, and his full title is Phra Bat Somdetch Phra Paramindr Maha CHULALONGKORN Chula Chom-Klao Chow Yuhua, which I hope the reader will be able to remember better than the writer. But, in case he cannot, he will naturally be pleased to find out that His Majesty the King of Siam is generally known under the name of CHULALONGKORN only.

The elder priests were kneeling, and, when questioning the candidates, screened themselves by a large fan which they placed between them. Part of the trial consisted of vows and responses from the candidates, and partly in repeating long rigmaroles of something, which were probably passages from the ancient Pali writings. Then the company, led by the priests and neophytes, marched in procession three times round the small temple, but yet the ceremony was not over. I tried to take a snap shot at this procession with my camera, but it was not successful. And I wanted badly to take the photo of one of the neophytes, who looked rather picturesque with his shaven head and new canonicals, but the ceremony took too long, and we had to go away before it was all over.

We had opened the bullocks from the carts, as we generally did during our midday rest, but every one seemed so intent on this ceremony, that the bullocks were allowed to go astray, and we took some little time to find them again. We managed to start at last, leaving the priest-making ceremony still going on, and arrived on the banks of a stream within a couple of miles of the village of Papróng, where we put up for the succeeding night. Shortly after leaving this shelter, we had to ford the stream three or four hundred yards higher up, and as the banks were very steep, it was with some difficulty that we were able to get the carts across it.

About half-way on the march to Sakhéo we crossed another ravine that gave us some trouble, and the carts at last began to break down. Next day we arrived at Wattaná, after a very tiresome journey, as the carts were continually breaking down, till at last one of them got completely disabled by one of the wheels coming off, so that its contents had to be carried in on the shoulders of the drivers. Yet the Siamese get on with these rickety carts well enough, for though they are always breaking down, the drivers are always ready with their choppers to set them up again, out of the forest that almost invariably surrounds them.

We were now approaching a portion of the country supposed to be destitute of water at this time of the year, as we were travelling through it at the very end of the prolonged dry season, when all the water was supposed to be lapped up by the sun. We therefore cut down several joints of the largest bamboos we could find in the forest, so as to fill them with water in case of emergency. Indeed, these hollow bamboos are the usual means of carrying water in this country when going on a long journey. And when cutting them down, one could not help observing how very suitable they were for the purpose. They are so light and so easily cut and trimmed, while a couple of joints of the very largest of them, after boring a hole through the soft partition between them, can readily contain a considerable quantity of water. The interior surface of these hollow bamboos is also so beautifully clean, and of such a rich cream colour, that when you put water into them, they almost invite you to drink without your being particularly thirsty, provided of course that the water itself is good, which is not always the case. I need not mention the numberless purposes to which the universal bamboo is put by the children of the tropical forest, for they are very various, and have already been described by travellers over and over again.

At Wattaná we got some fresh fish which was very repulsive to behold, but very excellent all the same. Valloo at first hesitated to cook it for me. The fish, I think, is not uncommon in Siam and elsewhere, and I bespeak it to the wearie wanderer when *it* is very fresh and *he* is very hungry. I forget the name of it, but am sure I have often seen it in bazaars both before and after this time. It lives by burrowing into the mud at the bottom of lakes and tanks, hence its very muddy appearance; and it is frequently caught by stamping with the naked feet, and in this way feeling for the fish embedded in the mud.

I afterwards on this same trip came across the very same fish, at the house of a planter, with whom I put up for a few days, near the old town of Malacca, on the Malayan Peninsula. He showed me where he used to keep this fish in a large cistern partially filled with mud and water; and he declared that when let loose on the ground, they would find their way to the nearest mud pond, with the homing instinct of a carrier pigeon. I even think he told me that he saw an example of it himself, but I cannot trust my memory, and it may sound to the reader as dangerously bordering on a traveller's tale. Be this as it may, the fish is certainly very tenacious of life on dry land, and is no doubt very shrewd in finding out his way.

This was Saturday evening, and we rested the next day at Wattaná, putting up in a small shelter with *attap* or dwarf-palm roofing, which in fact is the usual mode of roofing in this country. After nightfall I heard the shrill cry of a tactoo within a few feet of where I was lying down. It was there sure enough in the roof beside me, but I could not see it in any way, as these peculiar lizards are invariably shy of revealing themselves in public. As the shelter altogether was but a small tiny shanty, I thought I should be able to get hold of this tactoo, to know what manner of beast he was, as I had never been able to see a tactoo properly, though I had often enough heard one. But though I offered a reward for any one who would catch it for me, nobody would try to catch the beast, as they said it would bite them. I have only seen a tactoo once, and not very well then; but people who have properly observed it say that it is beautifully marked, with green bars across the back, and to be altogether a pretty lizard of about a foot long with a broad flat head.

I mention the tactoo on purpose: (1) because it is like the heathen Chinee—so peculiar, and (2) because of the wrong idea prevailing about its limited geographical distribution. This lizard is to be found in no portion of India, and Englishmen first came across it when we first occupied a portion of Lower Burmah, after the first Burmese war, and before we were at all acquainted with Siam. It was so peculiar and characteristic, that it was immediately supposed to belong to Burmah, and to Burmah alone.

As a matter of fact, however, the animal has got a fairly wide distribution, for I have myself heard if not seen it in Upper and Lower Burmah, in Siam, Laös, Cambodia, and, if I mistake not, on the southern coast of the island of Java. Tjillitjap (pronounced 'Chillichap'), the remote corner on the south of Java, in which I think I once heard the tactoo, and on the climate of which I commented at the time, has since been abandoned by the Dutch garrison there as uninhabitable, thus verifying what I thought of it when passing through the place as a mere stranger, some years ago, and without knowing anything at all then about its vital statistics (*vide* 'Toil and Travel,' p. 139).

So much then for the tactoo's supposed confined localisation. Its cry is so peculiar that when once heard it can seldom be forgotten. The animal is very fond of concealing itself among the roofs and rafters of dwellings, as well as among the branches and foliage of trees. And wherever it is, it is sure to make itself heard, though very shy of showing its colours.

The noise it makes begins with three or four sharp strokes with its tail on whatever object to which it may be sticking at the time; then there is a short pause, to be followed several times by the peculiar, almost articulate cry, from which it generally receives its name in the different countries which it inhabits. Though it is known to us as *tactoo*, on account of its cry, it is known in Siam as *Tokáy* for the selfsame reason, while in other places it is known as *tau-tau*. I had frequent chances of hearing this lizard on this journey, and listened carefully to hear what it did say; and there is no doubt that what it tries to say resembles the word 'tokáy' more than any other. But perhaps it changes its language with the country, like the people themselves, and that it says 'tactoo' in Burmah and 'tokáy' in Siam. Meanwhile the particular tokáy, then under discussion, hearing his fate plotted in this open manner, soon gave us the slip, and we neither heard nor saw him any more.

As we halted at Wattaná for a whole day, we prowled about the village to while away the time. We at last came across a small grass hut, and found there a mother and a newly-born baby. The child had been born the night before, and when we crept inside, and squatted down on the grass floor, we found the mother as glib and talkative as possible. She was already sitting up on her humble litter, and did not seem at all much the worse of her late adventure. Immediately beside the shakedown was a brisk fire (hot though the weather was), and on the top of this fire was a great pot, from which the patient was constantly helping herself with some infusion or other. The litter was so near the fire that the poor woman perspired freely, which her frequent potations from the pot rather increased than otherwise.

She drank such quantities of this fluid that we naturally inquired the reason why, and then found out that all women in this interesting condition drank freely of this liquid, for the purpose of what I cannot explain here in the unconventional language in which it was translated to me. I therefore had a sip of it myself, to see what it was like, and found it but slightly coloured and of a distinctly astringent taste. They had several chips of wood in the pot, from which they prepared the infusion, while a stock of the same material was lying near the bed for replenishing purposes. And so we took a few of the smaller chips with us, and also the next day made the guide show us in the forest the kind of tree from which these chips were prepared.

None of the men in the village ever put in an appearance to molest us in any way. But the women-folk are said to be brimful of curiosity, and accordingly one of them peeped in to have a look at us, with a child about six months old in her arms. Both the women kept up a running conversation with the interpreter, with a cordiality that I envied, for I was entirely out of it, except the few remarks that West would explain now and then. We found that this roasting of the mother, and her frequent potations, were the custom among women in this condition, and that it had to be endured for several days to promote rapid recovery! This particular one was to be kept separate like this for a fortnight, after which she was to return to her usual mode of living again. Both the newly-born infant, and the other one in arms, were girls, and as I was going away, I placed a silver *tical* in the tiny little palm of each of them, and expressed, through the interpreter, a hope that the young daughters would live long and marry fine husbands, an expression of sentiment that appeared to gratify both the parents.

These terrible ordeals must tell heavily against poor women on these important occasions, for many of them are not only senseless but absolutely dangerous; and at the best appear very ludicrous to people with their eyes a little more wideawake. Among some of the Dyaks of Borneo, which I had so lately visited, as well as among various other tribes, still more curious customs prevail about childbirth and children, such as the custom that when an infant is born, it is the father and not the mother that lies up and begins to complain; for almost immediately after, the mother goes about her business, while the father gets (?) very ill, and betakes himself to his sleeping mat, there to be the object of sympathy and congratulation. It is a merciful providence with such simple races, that childbed among them is a matter of far less serious concern than among races more advanced in civilisation. In this respect, at least, the specific curse of Mother Eve seems to have fallen much more lightly on them, poor bodies! This particular process of what may aptly be called *Vicarious Lying-in* is very wide-spread over the world, and perhaps prevailed at one time in France, as it is scientifically known in Europe under the French name of *La Couvade.*

But it is as natural to die as to be born; for when we visited some other dwelling there was quite a different tale to tell. On ascending the few steps that led to the bamboo floor of this house, we noticed a boy of nine or ten years of age lying on a mat, and quite senseless. Very little observation was required to see that he was suffering from *hydrocephalus,* or water on the brain, and that he was in all probability dying. It looked so helpless and pitiable a sight, that I felt very sorry I could do nothing to relieve his distress, and could not help reflecting on the universality of that dread tyrant Death, for we meet him wheresoever we go.

> Thou art where billows foam,
>   Where music melts upon the air;
> Thou art around us in our peaceful home,
>   And the world calls us forth—and thou art there!

So sang the gifted Mrs. Hemans, and there are but few of us who have not felt his bitter stings.

I had a small case of medicines with me to guard against contingencies, and the villagers would sometimes come to know this, and that I was a Medicine-man; and it was natural that they should ask for medicines from the strange physician, whether there was anything wrong with them or not. But I put a stop to this practice at an early stage, for the very good reason that I detest quackery, and could not reconcile myself to be giving quinine tablets for a pain in the stomach, perhaps, or paregoric elixir for a stitch in the liver. France in this respect is far ahead of us, as she discountenances all quack doctors and patent drugs. Medicine, no doubt, is a convenient profession to travel with through wild regions, as it tends to conciliate the natives, and there is also the delightful advantage, that before your prescription has time to do much good or harm, you are possibly jogging along on your journey, with the pleasant prospect of never seeing your patient again. However, all the medicines on earth could not save this poor boy, and on inquiring about him before starting next morning, I was not surprised to hear that he had died during the night.

CHAPTER XIII

> A merry crew they were indeed,
>   Who never would to aught give heed,
>   And always seemed so gay;
>   You'd think, to look upon the crew,
>   They never had a thing to do,
>   Except to laugh and play.
>
> *The Weavers' Wives.*

West and his ghost stories—Warlocks of Wattaná—Their *Aqua fontana*—Siamese shanties—Dropsy and its diagnosis—Love-making philtres—The prowling Pontianas—'Gog-og-oo!'—Pontianas pursuing West—Arrival at Arrānh—Origin of 'Farrang' —Crossing the watershed—A gay villager—A modern distillery—The web and the weaver—A bantering wife—The Lady of Láös.

It was during this halt at Wattaná that West, the interpreter, suddenly burst upon me as a teller of ghost stories, in which he faithfully believed. I'm a bit superstitious myself, and it was then that I discovered that West was a great believer in witches, warlocks, and all sorts of hobgoblins.

During the course of that last trying day's march, I must have spoken roughly to one of the drivers, as the transport had been giving us such a lot of trouble. I forget what I said exactly, but it broke no bones, and must have been very harmless to the driver, as it must have been spoken in English. West warned me, however, and said that the people about here were known to be very revengeful, and that though they would not kill us on the spot, perhaps, they would do so afterwards, as they were very skilful in witchcraft.

One particular method which, he said, they had of killing people, was by poisoning the drinking water of the wells in such a way that the person who drank of it did not die then, but at whatever time the poisoners liked, so as to take away suspicion from the criminals. Though I could believe they could poison the water, even without witchcraft, I could scarcely believe they could regulate the fatal event, even with witchcraft. It would be too much like the clockwork of an infernal machine, with which the sorcerers of Siam have not yet become acquainted. Of that I was certain, but I should like to hear what West thought about it. I was lying as usual on the cork mattress, on the bamboo floor, with a hurricane lamp beside the pillow, while West was leaning against one of the large posts that passed through the floor, and on to the roof of the shanty.

But to avoid repetition, perhaps it is as well to give a brief description of these dwellings, premising that the same description is equally true of Siam, Borneo, Burmah, Malay Peninsula, and various other equatorial places that I need not mention. These climates being generally moist and swampy, the ground is often soaked or even flooded with water. And so the houses are constructed on piles firmly driven into the ground. And the number of these will of course vary according to the size of the building and the pleasure of the builder.

In the great majority of cases, the floor on which the family live is raised five or six or more feet above the general level of the ground. This floor at times consists of planks of wood, but much more frequently of split bamboos placed side by side, and levelled out by pressure. There is seldom or never two storeys to a house in the country districts, but the floor is often divided into compartments, separated from one another by matting partitions, or by split bars of the ever-useful bamboo. But though the houses consist of only one storey, yet one portion of the floor may be fixed to the supporting posts on a slightly higher or lower level than another portion. There is scarcely ever any furniture, and as there are no seats, nor stools, nor chairs, the people, except when they are working outside, pass their days and nights squatting down on mats or on bare bamboo floors, or sitting on a more raised portion of the floor with their feet dangling to a lower level one.

Mats, skins, water-pitchers of dammered bamboo lacework, comprise most of the furniture in any of the houses, while the roof and walls invariably consist of grass or of *attap* made of palm leaves, and stretching between the rafters, as well as between the upright poles already mentioned. Sometimes there is no fireplace on the raised floor, and sometimes there is. When there is, it is only for cooking purposes, and never with the idea of keeping one warm; for that, indeed, would be superfluous in most of these climates. The hearth, when there is one, consists of baked clay in the middle of the floor, and surrounded by fenders of any wood that comes handy. Leading up to this inhabited floor, there will be a primitive ladder of a certain number of rungs tied on by thongs of bark, or perhaps there will only be a piece of timber with notches here and there, for the naked feet of the people to get hold of.

Such is the typical dwelling in any of the countries noted, and in many others besides. Except in the large towns, the houses are seldom arranged in any regular order, and it is therefore often very difficult for the stranger to get any satisfactory idea of the size of a village, as the houses are built anyway throughout the forest, so that when you are visiting one house, you may not be able to see any of the others. Needless to say that these combustible houses frequently get on fire, but they are so easily rebuilt from the forest, that there is seldom much wailing about their loss. It was West's ghost stories that led me into this digression.

Well, there was West, leaning against one of those supporting poles, with the lurid lamp-light shining in his face, and quite convinced that the poisoners of Wattaná could give any of us their *aqua fontana*, and arrange that we should just die on the precise day on which their worships would please. I felt sceptical at first if West was in earnest; but he was, as could easily be seen by his serious face. I therefore asked him to sit down and tell me what other strange things they did in these queer countries.

It was Saturday night, and we were resting on the morrow after a hard week's work, so that a ghost story would be very refreshing. The light, being behind my pillow, left my face in shade, and fell with a dim religious tinge on the interpreter's serious countenance. This was lucky, as I must have frequently appeared very grave when I did not at all feel so.

One of the most successful methods of poisoning adopted

by these warlocks consisted of fids of flesh taken out of the rump of a live elephant. Neither mutton nor beef is of any good for this purpose. These fids of elephants' flesh are beaten with a stick, while repeating sundry incantations over them, till they get reduced to the size of small balls, when they acquire the curious property of flying about anywhere at the operator's will. They are, however, generally harmless, except under certain conditions; and they generally go to work by making noises about the house of the victim, after the usual method of a good old 'Brownie' of more northern countries. Then, some time or other, the victim asks unguardedly, 'Who is doing that noise?' or some words of that sort, when one or more of the attenuated fragments immediately jumps down his throat without further ceremony. It is then that the trouble commences, for the balls gradually swell to their former size, and as they are quite indigestible, after all the curses heaped upon them, no wonder that the patient soon dies in great agony by a general swelling, which is always mistaken for dropsy by the doctors—but isn't.

Among the most interesting remedies possessed by the witches of this country was an aromatic oil procured from a dead person who 'died in confine,' as the interpreter always put it. By rubbing this oil over the eyebrows a person can see through anything, even through a stone wall. It is a good thing that the preparation of this oil is such a secret among the witches, as it sometimes might reveal far too much to people. And then there was of course the philtre or love-potion, which by rubbing over a coin before giving it to the only girl that ever you loved, she immediately abandons all and follows her lover. My informant did not know whether this philtre had any effect on the sterner sex, as he was not so interested on that side of the question. He also gave me a portion of the recipe for this valuable preparation; but as I doubt if it is complete, and as it might play havoc with the hearts of some readers, I naturally hesitate to write it down here. Most of the ingredients, moreover, would be quite inadmissible in plain English print, though I could get over this difficulty by resorting to Latin for the occasion. On the whole, however, I think it is better that the prescription should perish in its own stew!

But of all others the *Pontiana* was my informant's pet aversion for a ne'er-do-weel sort of warlock, for he had had personal experience of this malignant kind of spirit himself. '"Pontiana"?' I said; 'that's almost like *Pontianak*, the name of the big town in Dutch Borneo.' 'Yes,' he replied; 'and that's because there are so many Pontianas about it.' 'And pray go on,' continued I, 'and tell us all about the Pontiana.' The Pontiana, then, according to the story, is essentially a woman who 'died in confine,' as West used to put it, and a most malignant creature she is. But to prevent her evil pranks from having full play, a pin is always driven through the sole of each foot before burning or burial. This precaution prevents the Pontiana from resting comfortably on the ground, although it does not prevent her from roosting among the branches of forest trees.

Though born in Bangkok, West had travelled a bit, and had accumulated a certain amount of information of sorts, especially of the diablerie kind. He was at one time living at Singapore, for instance. On one unfortunate occasion, when living in that city, he and a friend of his, on a bright moonlight night, went out into the outskirts of the town to shoot flying-foxes, a variety of the very largest kind of bats prevalent in parts of the East. They suddenly heard the shrill voice of the Pontiana shrieking, 'Gog-og-oo!' Courageous though they were, they immediately took to their heels, for who could listen unmoved to the fearful voice of the Pontiana? They were, however, promptly pursued by the 'Gog-og-oo!' of the fiend, till they reached the inhabited suburbs.

His friend had unfortunately got the start of him in their sudden stampede, and, what is more, he kept it; so that the Pontiana, with her 'Gog-og-oo!' kept fluttering about his ears in the most maddening way, although he could see nothing. At last, in his despair, he remembered that evil spirits were dreadfully afraid of gunpowder, and so he let off his musket, which was on full-cock at the time; and no sooner did he do so than the Pontiana vanished at once. Yet, though he and his friend had thus narrowly escaped the clutches of the Pontiana, they had not escaped the attention of the police, for a few of them, having heard the report of the gun among them, promptly arrested both himself and his friend in the very midst of their frantic excitement.

However, after telling the native police that they had just been pursued by a Pontiana, and that the gun had gone off by accident, they were allowed to proceed on their journey without further molestation, secretly vowing, no doubt, that they would never again go out to shoot flying-foxes, let the moon shine never so brightly. Such were some of the stories to which I listened that Saturday night, and which vividly brought home to me the simple-minded kind of caravan with which it was my lot to be travelling through this remote country.

On Monday evening we arrived at Arrānh. Throughout the last few days' journey we occasionally got glimpses of the Láös mountains to the north, but the forest on our way was generally so thick that we could not see any great distance on either side of us; but on the last journey we appeared to be leaving the mountains behind us altogether. We were very well received by the chowmuang of Arrānh, and I told West to ask him if he had ever seen a 'Farrang' or European before. He had seen one Farrang in his life, he said, and that was five or six years ago when a Farrang came to the village, and that he did not know whence he came or whither he was going. His servant who was sitting on his marrow-bones behind him confirmed his master's statement, and said that he had seen the same Farrang, but none of the others present had ever seen a European before.

It is strange that the word 'Farrang,' almost universally applied to Europeans in the East, really means a Frenchman, which sounds rather odd, as far more English-speaking people than French travel through remote Eastern regions. Yet such is the case; and even in India, so long in our own possession, the word generally used is Ferringhi, which is only a corruption of the word Farrang. This village of Arrānh was the largest since we left Pechim, and contained perhaps thirty or forty houses in all, situated on both sides of a river with high precipitous banks.

We were now in an interesting locality, for we had just crossed over the watershed that separates the streams that finally fall into the Gulf of Siam from those falling into the Mekong river, and finally into the China Sea. For the river, near the source of which Arrānh is situated, goes to the great lake Tele-Sap, of which more anon, and from which proceeds the river that finally falls into the Mekong at Penhom-penh, the capital town of Cambodia.

We, that is the interpreter West and myself, invariably prowled about the villages in the cool of the evenings, whenever there happened to be a village to prowl about; and so we did about Arrānh. We put up on the north or left bank of the river, but later on crossed over to the other side, to have a look at the place, being guided about by an old villager who seemed to be the boss of the village, next to the chowmuang himself, and who appeared a little 'elevated' at the time of our visit.

The people throughout our journey hitherto appeared very sober and steady, and if I offered anything to an occasional chowmuang, he would only taste it, and pass it on to some one else. Arrānh, however, appeared more or less an exception to this rule. When prowling about the houses on the other side of the river, what did we come across but a woman preparing the native liquor known generally as Shumshoo, but known under the name of Larong in this region.

We wanted to see how the thing was done, by lifting off one large iron pot that seemed placed over the mouth of another one. But the old woman would not let us do so, saying that it would spoil her brew; so we did not insist, as I was always anxious to avoid giving any cause of offence to the natives in any way. While straggling still further on, and still guided by the old villager, we came across another woman, just preparing for the same business, and in the act of placing the apparatus in position. This simple form of still may exist or have existed in our own country. But as I never saw it before, I may briefly describe how the thing is done in this remote corner.

There is first a trench dug in the ground, a few feet long, and gradually deepening at one end. In this deeper end is placed a wooden fire, and over it is placed the apparatus. This last consisted of two large pots, each capable of holding a few gallons of water. One of the two pots is filled with rice in process of fermentation, mixed with a considerable quantity of water, in which the rice has probably been soaking for some days previously. This pot is placed immediately over the fire, and over the mouth of it is placed the upper pot of about the same size, and with three or four holes in the bottom of it. The rim of the lower pot, along which the upper pot touches it, is hermetically sealed by means of wet cloth placed between. There is thus an open communication between the two pots by means of the holes in the bottom of the upper one.

The upper pot is quite empty, with neither water nor rice ; but through the side of it, about the middle, there is a small round hole. Through this hole, from the inside, is placed a narrow tube, ending outside in a small spout, and on the inside enlarged into a round slightly hollowed disc, placed flatly in the pot, and the edges of which nearly touch the sides of the pot roundabout. The mouth of this upper pot is closed hermetically with a hollow metallic lid, in which cold water is placed on the outside, and easily replenished whenever it gets warm, so that it answers the purpose of a condenser.

This constitutes the whole apparatus which, when I saw it working, seemed equally simple and efficacious. And this is the way the thing is done : the fire is lit and heats the lower pot, and the steam containing the delicious larong passes through the holes into the upper pot, thence rises to meet the cold under surface of the lid, and immediately condenses and falls in drops on the flat disc mentioned. From this the gathering fluid passes through the tube piercing the middle of the upper pot, and from the spout at the end of it the larong drips, drips, in precious little dew-drops, into whatever vessel is placed to receive it. There is your shumshoo or larong for you, ready for action, and you may take it or may leave it, just as you please. I tasted a little of it on this occasion, and did not think it particularly palatable.

We then returned to our own side of the river, over a rickety and creaky wooden bridge, that was fully twenty-five or thirty feet above the bed of the river, which was then dry, or only with dirty-looking yellow stagnant pools of water. But the height of this bridge indicated plainly enough how this river rises in the rains, till it eventually overfloods the country. When we returned to the northern side, I tried my hand at weaving. I have already described how the houses are raised on posts, and that the inhabited floor is generally several feet above the ground. The space beneath that floor is open all through, except the supporting poles, and contains all sorts of questionable articles, such as the sucking-pigs and squealing grunters mentioned when treating of the Dyaks of Borneo. On this journey we sometimes met with primitive handlooms in these open spaces, and more than once I tried my 'prentice hand at weaving; and so I did on this occasion.

The loom was very small and the web very narrow. My legs were not particularly nimble in working the foot-strings, and my hands too were coarse and clumsy in passing the shuttle to and fro, while the thread was so fine and easily broken, that I repeatedly broke it without feeling that I did so. This state of affairs did not at all seem to please a middle-aged woman to whom the web belonged. She was a little shy at first, but afterwards came up in a bantering way, and catching hold of me by the shoulders, tried to take me away from the web, which I was evidently spoiling. I returned the compliment by catching her in turn, and trying to seat her beside me on the plank, so as to teach me how to weave properly, much to the amusement of the people who were looking on.

This woman had never seen a European in her life before, and I only mention the incident as an indication of the genial disposition of this simple race; for it looked more like an old-world lover's quarrel than a squabble with a purpose. By this time, too, I was indeed becoming quite proficient in the language, and was specially fluent and free with such phrases as *Kopjai* (thank you), *Lakōn* (good-bye), *Sŭbbhai* (how are you?) and *Soe ügain* (you're very pretty!).

Further on our way we met two girls, ten or twelve years old, and one of them stopped to speak to our merry old guide. She was his daughter, he said, but that he had a bigger and a prettier one than that. We soon reached his house, and there on the verandah was the buxom girl of which he spoke, without being at all overburdened with overflowing drapery. The interpreter talked to her for a little while, and from the hearty way she laughed I concluded that the conversation amused her not a little. Thereafter the rhyming Jingo seized me, and thus I jingled to the Lady of Laös :—

The Lady of Láös.

'You wear but little garments on,
　　My pretty heathen maid,
You wear but little garments on,
　　Your bloom to hide and shade;
Your legs and arms are far too bare
　　For pretty maids like you,
And oh, your breasts, though fresh and fair,
　　Are far too plain in view.

'You know that beauty is enhanced
　　By being but half revealed,
While man is oftentimes entranced
　　By graces half concealed;
For Cupid is a skittish child,
　　That hates the shining glare,
And scorns the commonplace and mild.
　　For what is wild and rare.

'Go, then, my pretty, pretty maid,
　　To clothe your naked charms,
And cover with some sort of shade
　　Your breasts, your legs, your arms;
And I shall love you ever more,
　　With all my soul and might,
And roam with you on sea and shore,
　　Your own true lord and knight.'

But quoth the maid: 'I cannot be
　　Except what nature meant,
A plain and simple maiden free
　　Of powder and of paint;
For since I lack the subtle art
　　Of counterfeit and sham,
Perhaps 'tis better for my part,
　　To be but what I am.

'Besides, a little bird, you know,
　　Once whispered in my ear,
That British beauties often show
　　Their bosoms quite as clear;
Then take this little hint from me,
　　However far you roam,
That precept should, like charity,
　　Be practised first at home!'

CHAPTER XIV

*Oh! sad was my heart when my wife ran away,
But soon it was equally blithesome and gay,
When once I discovered that now I was free,
Without such a slovenly slattern as she.*
                              The Grass Widow.

The parasitic parricide—Its mode of germination—Two-tree Tank—Abandoned village—Foul-drinking water - Dissensions in the camp—'Amn't I a man, too?'—A bump on the rump—Vālloo, the dark delinquent—Forest camp-fire—Vālloo vanishes—The Tragedy of an Omelette—Vālloo recovered—Helplessness of native coolies.

THE next inhabited village was nearly forty miles away from us, but we hoped to cover the distance in two marches, in spite of impediments. So we made a start in the very early morning, as we invariably did, with the regularity of clock-work ; for we turned in early, and the labourer's sleep is both sweet and refreshing. Not very long after leaving Arrānh we got into more open country, compared with the forest that had almost continually surrounded us for several days past, and we could just see the last of the Lăŏs mountains receding in the distance far away behind us.

Before noon we made our usual halt near a small, muddy tank, which would probably be considerably larger during the rainy season, but was at this time of year nearly dried up. While Vālloo was cooking I lay on my back under the shade of a large forest tree, and gazed dreamily towards the sky. I observed that the tree bore two kinds of leaves, and that there were actually two kinds of trees with only one stem. It was, in short, a particularly good example of those parasite trees that one occasionally meets with in the Malayan Archipelago and elsewhere, though I don't remember its name, if ever I did know. I called West over to point it to him as a curiosity. But West, casting his eye

PARASITIC PARRICIDES.

To face page 136.

in the near distance, said that there was another of the same kind over yonder. It could not be, I thought, as the tree in the distance displayed only one kind of foliage. Yet the interpreter was right, as we discovered on going over to it. For there were two of those peculiar trees within one or two hundred yards of one another, and conspicuous to the traveller, as there were no other forest trees about the tank at all.

The main difference between these two trees among themselves consisted of the fact that the parasite on the tree under which we were lying was in its infancy, while the parasite 'over yonder' had already crushed its foster parent and was growing in its place. This variety of parasite resembles the Rata of New Zealand in being a parasitic parricide, or killing the foster parent that rears it; but whether their mode of germination and other characteristics are the same I am unable to say. This, at any rate, is a remarkable tree in its mode of growth, which, in these two instances, could be judged with some accuracy, as the two trees were in two distinct stages.

The seeds of this kind of tree are carried into the forks of the branches of other forest trees, the usual mode of transport being probably by birds. Here decayed vegetable mould gathers round the individual seed, and it takes root firmly, stretching most of its string-like filaments towards the ground, along the bark and stem of the poor deluded foster parent. From the same seed branches also spread outwards and upwards, so that the tree actually consists of roots and branches, without any stem in the proper sense of the term, though the roots eventually join in such a way as to put on the appearance of a single solid stem. For the long, slender filaments of roots eventually reach the ground here and there along the stem of the victim. There on the ground these roots fix themselves firmly, and grow so thick individually round the parent stem that they eventually appear to coalesce, and hold the foster stem enclosed, as it were, in a cylinder, the hollow of which grows less and less, till the foster stem is at first crushed, and finally decays and disappears altogether.

This is an interesting and remarkable fact in the vegetable kingdom, and which shows that the struggle for existence goes on in the vegetable as well as in the animal world.

The parasite at last entirely replaces the original foster tree, and spreads its branches far and wide, while the united roots put on the appearance of a single, solid, though not very smooth stem. It finally looks like a large forest tree, something in general appearance like a mango, with outspreading heavy branches, but never a very tall stem. In another village (Kallán) I believe we saw one or two specimens of this treacherous tree after the last remains of the original tree had completely disappeared.

But the special thing of interest in the two trees now under observation was, that the one we noticed first was a very young parasite, and that only a few of its cord-like roots had as yet reached the ground, while several other filaments were making their way in that direction all round the foster parent's stem. On the other hand, the roots of the other tree had long ago reached the ground, had grown so thick round the parent stem that they had partially coalesced, and in the fatal cylinder thus surrounded the stem of the poor victim was already quite dead. And so were the branches, for they grew neither buds nor leaves any more, while both they and the stem were alike gradually fading out of existence.

It must, however, take many, many years from the first lodgment of the parasite seed till the final disappearance of the unfortunate foster parent. If anyone, then, happens to travel in the direction of 'Two-tree Tank,' as we called it, any time during the next twenty years, he will certainly be able to see for himself both these parasites, with one if not the two foster parents still clutched in their faithless arms. The strange trees cannot possibly be missed, as they are the only trees on the pathway between Arränh and Sisophon, and only some nine or ten miles from the former place.

We had already begun to feel the want of potable water, for the water both here and at Arränh was thick and undrinkable. We had with us a large and simple filter, that could contain a couple of bottles of water. But the thick fluid here filtered through it so slowly, that it was almost useless to us. That same night we reached about half-way between Arränh and Sisophon, near the site of an old village that had been abandoned some years ago; and it may be remarked that deserted villages in these countries disappear rapidly, on account of the perishable and movable nature of the bamboo material of which they are mostly composed. The only vestige of the previous village now visible was a water pond, that was gradually filling in with mud and *débris*, and was filthy beyond measure.

Camping out for the night at the same place we met a small party of natives with some water-buffaloes, which had been let loose, and on going over to look at the condition of the pond, we found it was only twenty or thirty yards across, and that it was mostly covered with the vegetable fungus that sometimes grows on the surface of dirty water in these low latitudes. Wading in this vegetable fungus were the water-buffaloes of the natives, with only their noses above the water, and blowing and puffing away, as is their usual custom when they can wallow in muddy water, which they love so much. The water looked so foul and repulsive, that Vālloo had to cook the humble *chowpatties*, or wheaten bannocks, with a bottle of soda-water, a little of which we had with us in case of emergency.

Vālloo asked in the evening what he was to cook for dinner, and seeing that he had fresh eggs in a basket, he was advised to make an omelette among the other delicacies of the sumptuous banquet. Though we were not at all scarce of provisions yet, we were naturally anxious to make use of whatever eatables we came across on the journey, as we could not possibly know when some serious difficulty might come across our way. When the banquet came up at last there was no omelette, and Vālloo said that the *sab* (meaning West) would not allow him to cook it. I thought this strange, but did not care to say anything about it, except telling Vālloo that in future when I told him to do anything, he was to do it, whatever the *sab* said, or at any rate to tell me about it at the time.

Thereupon Vālloo went away, and I thought no more about the business. A little while later, however, West, who was lying down in the dark in one of the carts, came out and asked if Vālloo had been using his name during the conversation. I prevaricated a little, and said that Vālloo had not made use of his name, which was literally true. But he remarked that he thought Vālloo meant him when he used the word *sab*. I then told him what Vālloo had said, as he was speaking in Hindustani, which West did not understand.

I was very desirous of keeping West and Vālloo on good terms with one another, as they were my only companions. But dissension appeared in the camp at a very early stage. In our marches the sun was very trying during the day, and, as the carts had hoods and were not full, I left one of them nearly empty for West and Vālloo to occupy during the most oppressive portion of each day's journey. It was for this purpose, and to keep them light, that I had increased the number of the so-called carts from three to five. But these two servants did not pull on well when thus jumbled together in one cart, and West evidently did not like poor Vālloo to be packed with him, so 'huppish,' indeed, is human nature in all its grades and conditions.

On recognising this feeling, I got the waggons so arranged that each of them could go into separate ones, when oppressed by the heat. This difference, however, led to an ill feeling, which I was sorry to observe. Vālloo being the weaker vessel, I felt a little inclined towards him, especially that he was more alone, as he did not know the language of this country. I was myself then the only companion that he had; for, though his mother tongue was Tamil, he could speak Hindustani to me after a fashion, for I have never been particularly proficient in that language myself. This proffered kindness to Vālloo, however, failed in its purpose, like the good intentions of many other people: for Vālloo unfortunately took advantage of it.

A few days previously he came up to me with a complaint against the interpreter, and concluded his speech with the very quaint Hindustani expression of *Ham nae admi hai bhi?*' (Amn't I a man, too?) Though I should be sorry to deny the poor beggar the proud prerogative of being a man, yet the expression surprised me, as I had never heard it from a native before. It was evident enough, I thought, that Vālloo was getting cocky. Moreover, I plainly saw that Vālloo on this occasion was not telling me the truth, and I told him so with such good effect that he went away penitent enough, and with the usual entreaty of *Māf karo, sāb* (Forgive me, sir), that so frequently ends these interviews. Well, I forgave him on the spot, and told him not to be making a fool of himself, or that worse might happen.

When West, then, on this occasion said that Vālloo was not telling the truth, I called Vālloo back again, and then again became convinced that he was misleading me a second time. Suddenly remembering the *Māf kāro, sāb*, of a few days before, and the way I had freely forgiven him, I regret that I got very much annoyed, and, rising from the matting on which I was lying down, I inflicted on Vālloo a smart harmless kick on the rump with my bare toes, that had neither shoe nor stocking on at the time, and again forcibly enjoined upon him not to be telling me lies.

Vālloo yelled and vanished, still rubbing the offended member, and I lay down and thought no more about the matter. Before putting out the light I had an occasion to call for Vālloo; but Vālloo was not to be found, and no amount of calling could bring him back again. At first I thought that Vālloo might have sulked for a moment, but when he did not turn up, I got somewhat anxious about him. Though never in the habit of being unkind to natives, yet who knew what had become of Vālloo?

Vālloo was a Madrassee, and the natives of India, in their otherwise normal health, are in the habit of carrying with them enormous spleens that are extremely brittle—an affection, strange to say, very rare among Europeans in this peculiar land of contrarieties. People are particularly prone to suffer from slight injuries when affected with this kind of spleen, which bursts on the slightest provocation, landing the aggressor into all sorts of pains and penalties. I, of course, knew of this weakness, and, on the principle of 'Live and let live,' I had seldom or never touched a native. Yet who knew but that this might be a very serious exception, which might undo all previous leniency? for natives are said to die for spite sometimes, so as to let in their unkind masters under the section of the criminal code that is headed 'Murder and Homicide.'

The camp-fire of the travelling natives already mentioned was burning brightly four or five hundred yards away from us, and perhaps Vālloo in his sulks had gone over there to soothe down his wrath. And so we sent messengers over once or twice, but neither the messengers nor the strangers could see anything of Vālloo. Our resting-place here was nearly clear of forest, for almost the first time, and with only a few bushes between us and the camp-fire of the strangers. Over we all went at last—drivers, interpreter, guide, and all; and we diligently searched the bushes, and cried for Vālloo long and loud. But—

> Though 'Vālloo, Vālloo,' oft we cried,
> Yet Vālloo never once replied.

At last I grew quite uneasy about my dark delinquent, and could scarcely sleep a wink through the whole night. The reader, reading this simple narrative in a cosy nook, may laugh over this business, and I cannot now help smiling over it myself. But it was at the time far from a laughing business in those lonely wilds. Vālloo, I feared, was foolish enough to do anything silly, and if he had really run away I felt certain that he would never reach back alive. For he could not speak the language of these Laös tribes, and he was also considerably taller, thinner, and darker than the natives of this country, who feel not a little contempt for the natives of India.

He was, therefore, I thought, probably fleeing from a condition of comparative safety to almost certain death. For as long as he remained with the caravan he would probably be safe enough, as the natives were not likely to attack us, and, if they did, poor Vālloo would not be the principal object of their fury; whereas, being now a solitary wanderer, a deserter from his master, and unable to talk the lingo, his life would not be worth a couple of days' purchase among them. This naturally made me anxious about him. I would be in duty bound to report his loss whenever I reached the outskirts of civilisation again, and I could picture myself arraigned at a court of justice—as well I might be—for the untimely loss of this fair and promising fellow citizen. And, oh, that bump on the rump, how I regretted it!

I felt so anxious about him that I was up some time before daybreak, to see if he had returned to camp. But though the morning returned, returned no Vālloo. We always had native guides from place to place, and our present guide had come with us from Arrānh, which we had now left nearly twenty miles behind. One of the drivers said that he knew the way to Sisophon, and so we sent the guide back to Arrānh with all the speed he could manage, with instructions to the chowmuang to do all he could to catch the dark delinquent, and send him back safely to me, for which he, the chowmuang, would have his reward.

So the guide started back again, and we prepared to resume our journey, as the only thing to do under the circumstances. But the guide had not gone back more than half a mile, when our attention was drawn to something in the distance. Who was this but Vālloo, who had been lying down during the night in the long grass half a mile or more away from us; and there was the guide along with him. For he had caught Vālloo, who was then in full retreat, with a bundle of some rubbish slung across his shoulder, and with a bottle of water like Hagar when she fled into the wilderness from the presence of Sarah. I went out to meet him, to make sure with my naked eyes that it was really Vālloo, and nobody else that I was seeing. On meeting me he was evidently afraid of getting a drubbing, which he richly deserved; but I was so thankful to get him again, that I felt more inclined to kiss his swarthy features than to punish him in any way. I encouragingly clapped him on the shoulder, and told him not to be afraid; whereupon the valiant Vālloo suddenly burst into a flood of tears. This episode I have taken the liberty of calling *The Tragedy of an Omelette*, which, though amusing enough to write about, was far from amusing to me at the time.

West and Vālloo got on better, I think, after this unpleasant occurrence, and I was very pleased to see it, as their petty little bickerings sometimes annoyed me; for West was a little too peevish to Vālloo, while Vālloo on his side was a 'wee bit daft,' as they say in France. I do not know to this day how he managed originally to reach Bangkok from India, but he was by no means an ideal rover. It is said, with some appearance of truth, that the greater bulk of coolies that emigrate from India's coral strand have no idea whatever where they are going to; and though I did not think of asking him, I am certain that Vālloo, though a Madrassee, had not the faintest notion in the world as to whether Madras was north, east, south, or west of the country through which he was now travelling.

There is good reason to suppose, says the *Saturday Evening Journal*, that an emigrant often has no idea where he is going, but the Government does its best to protect him. The recruiter tells a man that he will take him to an exceptionally sacred shrine of Juggernath, and gives him an advance of money. When the coolie agent asks the coolie in clear terms if he wants to go to Jamaica, the recruiter whispers, 'Say yes; the sahibs speak of Jamaica when they mean Juggernath.'

And as for poor Vālloo, he probably thought that, in order to travel across a strange country, he had only to close his eyes and see rainbows in his retinas; but he found it quite a different task in reality. So much then about Vālloo for the time being, for he will crop up again by-and-by.

CHAPTER XV

Wearie wanderer, faint not yet,
　Though the fates look dark and drear;
Think not yet thy star has set,
　Though it shines not bright and clear;
Trust in the arms that are mighty to save
From depths of the sea and the gloom of the grave.
　　　　　　　　　The Wearie Wanderer.

Arrival at Sisophon—The ancient Kingdom of Kumēr—Sisophon a frontier garrison town—Scarcity of water—Where now the Pitcher-plants of Borneo?—Cocoanut milk as a substitute for water—Village of Penhom-Sok—Going astray—The young Chow-muang—China a paradox—Ceremony of Kohn-chúk—Monster bird with four legs—A Chinaman and his wives—Milk at a discount—Reach Siäm-Réäp.

WE arrived at Sisophon late that evening on account of our awkward delay in the morning. We were now in a different country altogether, though still within the jurisdiction of Siam. For we had left Siam behind us some days before, and our journeys of late were through the country occupied by the Läos tribes, who mostly occupy the mountains to which I have several times alluded, while some of them have descended to the lowland plains to the south; and it was among these latter that we had been wandering of late. Our last night's halting-place was in fact the boundary spot between the Läos tribes and the ancient Kingdom of Cambodia or *Kumēr*, as the natives themselves call it, and this was the reason why that village had been deserted, as the people on either side of the boundary would not let the people on the other side of it live in peace in this intermediate spot. And so both Sisophon and Arränh are nearly twenty miles away from this boundary line, the latter in Läos and the former in Kumēr or ancient Cambodia; or rather, I should say, to

L

speak by the card, that the present Cambodia once belonged to the ancient Kingdom of Kumēr.

The very name even of the ancient Kingdom of Kumēr is scarcely know to Europeans; and the history of it is much wrapt in the mists of tradition and fable. Story says that it was once the most powerful country in the Far East, not even excepting China, and it is in Kumēr that there still exist by far the most remarkable ruins in further Asia, to which I shall refer more in detail by-and-by. This ancient kingdom is said to have once extended, not only over the portion of the country now described as Kumēr or Cambodia, but also over Tonquin, Annam, Cochin-China, and Siam, even including the Malayan Peninsula. But its glory has departed long ago, like that of many another ancient country.

The same river on which Arrānh is situated passes also through Sisophon, and is there known as the Sisophon-menam, which proves clearly, as mentioned before, that the word 'Menam,' though literally meaning the 'Mother of Waters,' is conventionally used for any main stream whatsoever. This same river flows on to the great lake Telé-Sáp, and on a tributary of it to the south-east is situated the town of Battambong, the largest town in this portion of Siam. Sisophon itself, though not so large as Battambong, is larger than any of the villages through which we had passed on our way through the Laös country, and is a frontier military station. Here lives, when he's at home, the Governor of the province of Battambong (or Prattamong, as the natives pronounce it); but he was at this time at Bangkok on some business or other.

Sisophon is the furthest town east, in this latitude, that is held by a Siamese garrison, as by a recent convention (1893) between France and Siam, the provinces of Battambong and Angkor are to be considered neutral territory, not to be occupied by troops of either nation, though it is not denied that the provinces and their revenues essentially belong to Siam. Sisophon was decidedly more picturesque than the villages through which we had lately been passing, as there were several small hills and hummocks in its vicinity, though none of them of any great consequence.

Next day we left Sisophon, and after the usual midday halt, arrived the same evening at Prah-nit-prah, where we came across some fruit-trees, including pomegranates and the well-known cocoanut trees, the former being still unripe, while the latter were in full fruit. This made us more or less independent of the foul water which was our portion for some time back. Where were then the Travellers' Palms of Borneo, and the Pitcher Plants thereof? They were nowhere to be found, for they only grow where there is no need of them, and where it drips, drips, drips every day without ceasing. After Prah-nit-prah, we were always coming across odds and ends of cocoanuts about the villages, and we used to take numbers of them with us in the carts, in order to slake our thirst by the way, as the weather was uncommonly hot at the time.

We must have drank the milk of scores and scores of them during the next few days, and I gradually got so familiar with them that I could easily distinguish between a good and a bad one, a young one and an old one. We opened them with a chopper, and I noticed that the thick outer covering of the young ones is much softer and more homogeneous, cutting up like hard cheese; while that of the older ones was much tougher and more fibrous. The young ones were also heavier, and more valuable to us, as they contained more milk; whereas the older ones contained less milk, but more meat inside. For when the nut gets old, the outer covering grows harder and more ropy, while the milk inside is gradually deposited to increase the white substance or meat portion, which gets thicker and thicker at the expense of the milk, till there is comparatively little of the latter remaining. But we did not require the meat, and a little of it goes a long way, as it is particularly filling at the price.

The bad quality of the water depended, of course, on the unfavourable season of the year we were passing through, when the water was nearly dried up everywhere in these regions. For at other times and seasons there would be no lack of water, as a considerable portion of the country is actually deluged during the rainy season, and for some time thereafter. However, as we could not change the seasons of the year, we had to adapt ourselves to matters as we found them.

Our next night's halt was at Penhom-sók, a village to which we went by mistake, through some blunder or other.

The portion of Kumēr through which we were now passing was much more open and cultivated than our route through Laös; for though we frequently passed clumps and patches of trees, there was not that same interminable forest as we had lately come across. The country also appeared more inhabited, as shown by tracks and pathways branching here and there to different villages, whereas among the Laös tribes there was scarcely ever a branching path to either side, which went far to prove how sparsely inhabited that portion of the country must necessarily be.

The chowmuang of Penhom-sók came to see us shortly after our arrival, and was a young man of not more than twenty-five or thirty years, whereas most of the other chowmuangs were old, or at least middle-aged men. It was after reaching Penhom-sók that we found we had gone astray, and that we should not have gone there at all. We had no map, and perhaps the young chowmuang was not very familiar with maps, if we had them; but he was quite able to point out on the floor the relative positions of Sisophon, Penhom-sók, and Kallán, and to prove that, in order to get to the last-named village, we had now to travel over two sides of a triangle instead of one, which, he said, was not at all necessary. He was quite correct in his explanation, and as he traced out the route with his beautifully long clear nails, anybody could see that he was a person of importance.

This young chowmuang was much more familiar than most of the others we had come across, and observing Vālloo, that prince of *chefs*, in possession of such quantities of enamelled plates, cups, and saucers, he thought he might get some of them. But we could not give him any then, though he was told he would be welcome to the whole lot when the journey was at an end. These simple people are by no means bashful in asking things, but remarkably frank and open on such occasions. However, there is one blessing in the fact that they are seldom hurt by refusal. This same habit, I am told, is very common among the Dyaks of Borneo; but with those who know them best, they possess the reputation of being extremely honest; and that though they would not hesitate in asking for a thing, they don't mind being refused, and that they never dream of stealing anything, however much they may like it. This is a great blessing. I went to Borneo for the purpose of seeing some of the most depraved savages, but I returned with a different opinion, in spite of their childish passion for head-hunting, and a few other harmless recreations which we need not talk about.

As this random narrative proceeds, it will be seen, much to my regret, that all people are not so honest as the Dyaks of Borneo, or the simple-minded people of the kingdom of Kumēr.

After lying down that night (for we generally did so early) we were disturbed by the beating of *tom-toms* and the music of minstrels. We dressed again and went to see what it was all about, when we found that none of the stars had fallen, but that the young son of one of the principal villagers was in preparation to undergo the solemn process of *Kohn-chūk* on the morrow. Generally speaking, there is no caste in any of the Buddhist countries, thus offering a great contrast to the Hinduism of Hindustan; and though various grades of rank are bestowed on individuals, there is no hereditary rank whatever outside the king's family. There is a remarkable exception to this in China, where people are often ennobled after they are dead, an amusing example of which took place in the case of Sir Robert Hart not long ago, when not only himself but his dead father and grandfather were ennobled by the young Emperor, and I hope that the grandson, if not the grandfather, will duly appreciate the honour.

Yet, in spite of this funny paradox on the part of China, which is more than usually paradoxical in most things, the previous statement holds generally true, till Japan some twenty years ago began to adopt Western methods, including pot-hats and breeches. Japan, however, much as it is deservedly admired by Sir Edwin Arnold and others, can scarcely be called a typical Buddhist country, because, though Buddhism is more prevalent than any other religion, yet it is not even the State religion, but *Shintoism*, a kind of religion that is not easy to define, and to which the Emperor of Japan himself belongs. Perhaps this may partly account for the greater homogeneousness of these races; but be the cause what it may, there is no doubt that the Burmese and Siamese are among the most genial of races that one can meet anywhere.

Well, then, it was a young son of one of the village magnates that was to undergo this ceremony. These youths have got their heads shaved while they are young boys, up to twelve or thirteen years, except a small tuft on the top of the forehead, like the tuft on the scalp of the Red Indians. About the age above stated, this tuft is removed with due religious (?) ceremonies; and then the hair is allowed to grow all round, and the boy becomes a man, for these sons of the tropics ripen early in life. It is cynically said among us that the tailor makes the man; but in these places it is evident that it is the barber that does so. I am glad that it is the Siamese and such like harmless boys who have got this tuft on the top of their heads, for if it were British ones, it would be sad to think how often it would lead to their heads being kept 'in Chancery' while striving with other boys equally pugnacious.

To cut off these tufts, or *Kohn-chuks* as they are called, at the holy Mount Phrabāt is a very sacred business, and I saw several of them when up there; but it is not always easy to perform the sacred office at that holy place, as it is a far cry indeed from Penhom-sók to Mount Phrabāt and *vice versâ*. Though the real ceremony was coming off the next morning, we stayed a little while with the merrymakers, with their music of *khongs, tapòns, ranàts, basilis* and *tom-toms*, the mere mention of which is sure to enliven and enlighten the reader, and which really discoursed a weird and wild kind of music, which was far from being unpleasant to listen to.

Next morning, just as we were starting, we heard a blunderbuss go off, which was the announcement that the ceremony had just been performed. These ceremonies must be common enough among the Siamese, though I never saw it among the Burmese, their next-door neighbours and co-religionists. It is prevalent, however, among all the Cambodians as well as the Siamese; and when visiting the Palace at Bangkok, I was pointed out the preparations for this same ceremony on one of King Chulalongkorn's sons, while on one of the two occasions I afterwards visited the King of Cambodia's palace at Penhom-pénh, this same ceremony was actually taking place on one of King Noròdom's sons. So that the ceremony of *Kohn-chuk* must be of very frequent occurrence with these extremely prolific royalties.

Shortly after leaving Penhom-sók that morning, we opened on an extensive plain, interspersed, as far as the eye could reach, with enormous ant-hills, some of them three or four feet high, and looking in the distance like miniature troops in loose skirmishing order, or like the 'standing-stones' of Druidical associations. And this leads me to a story, brief if not pithy. Once upon a time we were dwelling in tents among hills in the far north, and surrounded by hostile tribes. A little while before they had cut up a small outpost some five miles away from headquarters, by coming down from their mountains suddenly in the middle of the night, and as suddenly disappearing there again. But at the time referred to, the troops were going out the next morning in that same direction, for the purpose of firing at improvised dummies, which had been previously erected here and there by parties told off for the purpose. That night, when enjoying a quiet smoke after dinner, outside the mess tent, a warning suddenly came in that the tribes were upon us. Immediately some troops were on the move to meet the enemy. But behold, it was only their own innocent dummies that they were going to fight with, and which were coming down upon us in this loose skirmishing order. I forget now who brought in the first news, but the false alarm at any rate turned out a ridiculous fiasco.

There were thousands on thousands of these large ant-hills, extending for over twenty or twenty-five miles ; and so, as the particular locality of Penhom-sók had seldom or never been visited by Europeans, I took the liberty of calling the locality by the name of 'White Ant Plains'; and there must be such countless millions of ants in this vicinity as to render a great part of the ground quite unfit for cultivation.

That night we reached Kallán after crossing two streams, the banks of which were so steep that one of the drivers got injured when crossing over one of them. Kallán itself is situated on the further east of these streams, mostly on the left bank ; and the river, so far as we could learn, was the one we had previously come across both at Arrành and at Sisophon.

This being another Saturday night, with nothing to do on the morrow, the interpreter whiled away the time by a fresh instalment of ghost stories ; but as we have so many other things to speak about, the reader will have to content himself with the instalment already given.

The *sala* where we put up at Kallán was not far from the chowmuang's house, and in the evening, before it got dark, and before sitting down to the ghost stories, I wandered about the village alone to see what it was like, as the interpreter had gone away somewhere to forage for provisions. When thus prowling near the chowmuang's house and not knowing it was his, I saw a very funny little bird, quite callow, with scarcely any feathers. But what was most surprising about him was the very strange possession of not less than four legs. A bird with four legs I had never seen before, and so I tried to catch this curiosity. The people round about, seeing me trying to catch the bird, came and helped me, and we did at last manage to catch him. West turned up soon after, and the chowmuang said that the bird had been received two or three days previously from another village, as a present to his young son of four or five years old. The bird itself could only be a week or two old at the most, and might turn out anything, though I had a shrewd suspicion that he belonged to the common or garden barndoor fowl.

But whatever species he belonged to, common or uncommon, what was certainly not very common about him was the possession of four legs, two of which, however, were useless, though nearly as large as the normal ones, and projecting behind in a very curious and awkward way, as the supernumerary claws were always catching in something or another. The bird being such a curiosity, the chowmuang was willing enough to part with it, as he probably thought it might bring evil fortune over the whole household. And so, after giving a small present to the young son in exchange, we got one of the chowmuang's servants to make a cage, and I brought 'Jimmy' (as I called him) with me, with the intention of giving him as a present to some zoological garden or other ; but I had to part with him in Singapore, as will be noticed in due course.

Here, almost for the first time since we left Pechim, we came across Chinese ; for though the prolific Johnnie almost overruns the more valuable parts of Siam, as the rabbits do in Australia, yet he is not fond of travelling on his own account for the mere fun of doing so, and one would therefore scarcely expect him in such unprofitable regions as those we had lately been traversing. A certain one of these Chinese seemed a person of consequence in Kallán, and kept a shop, to which we paid a visit and were rewarded for our courtesy by a present of fresh eggs, which Vālloo duly converted into an omelette, as on another memorable occasion.

It seemed, therefore, that the inland Siamese, Láös tribes as well as the Kumerēse or Cambodians, were familiar with the domestic fowl, a familiarity which will not surprise anyone to hear. But what will probably surprise many people to hear is the fact that these very same people never make any use of milk in any shape or form whatever. They did not breed sheep or goats, so far as we could see, and the jungly nature of the country would probably preclude the breeding of sheep, at any rate. But they breed plenty of cattle—for the sake of the bullocks only; and, as a matter of fact, cattle, next to rice, form, perhaps, the greatest export from Siam, from which scores and scores of them are shipped at Bangkok every week in the year.

Milk being the natural food of man in his early infancy, and the first for which he has any natural liking, it seems strange to us that any people could exist, familiar with domestic cattle, sheep, or goats, and still remain ignorant of milk and its useful ingredients of butter and cheese. Yet this is the fact, not only here but throughout the greater portion of Eastern Asia.

The Chinaman referred to had a Kumēr wife at Kallán, from whom he had five children; and I am not quite sure but he had two Kumēr wives. At any rate, he frankly, almost proudly, told us that he had a Chinese wife and one child 'o'er the border' there, in his own Celestial Empire, where he had left wife and child while pursuing Dame Fortune in the kingdom of Kumēr. Among his other accomplishments, the interpreter spoke Chinese apparently as well as Siamese itself, and he asked the Chinaman if his Chinese wife, with the dainty little feet, would not be jealous of the Kumēr one, and *vice versâ*, when the Chinaman dismissed the idea with a lordly wave of his hand. He occasionally visited the Chinese wife, he said, and there was no jealousy whatever between his wives—oh dear no; which goes far to show that women in the East are not built on the same model as their Western sisters. But the statement may be taken for what it is worth, being made by an interested party and a Chinaman to boot, for women are women all over the world, however much they mask their nature by custom and stifle their feelings by the grim law of necessity.

Siäm-Réäp was our next intended destination, and was said to be nearly forty miles away; and so we started from Kallán early on Monday morning, hoping to reach Siäm-Réäp some time on Tuesday evening, which we did, after staying a night on the way. The track was very soft and sandy on this journey, for though the White Ant Plains extended even beyond Kallán, we afterwards traversed a portion of the country sometimes flooded during the rains by the great lake Telé-Sáp, of which we shall speak shortly, for we are now approaching quite near it.

Siäm-Réäp was perhaps the largest place on our journey. It is impossible, however, to give a fair idea of the population of these places, where no census is ever taken; and the population of Indian villages warns one of how futile the attempt might be, as they generally contain at least three or four times the number of people that the ordinary observer would put down to them. Not, however, that there is any great comparison between the teeming honeycomb villages of India and this very sparsely inhabited country. Further, to show how difficult it is to judge of population when there is no proper census taken, it is only necessary to mention that Whitaker's Almanack for 1894-5 gives the population of Siam at four millions, while the 'Bangkok Directory' for the same year gives it as nine millions, and adds that 'the actual population in all probability far exceeds that number.' Whitaker's Almanack is probably under the mark, but it is really impossible to say.[1]

Like Pechim, Siäm-Réäp contains a fort, with its wall

---

[1] While passing these pages through the press, I again consult Whitaker's new Almanack for 1896, just out, where it says that the population of Siam is 'variously estimated at 7½ to 88 millions'!—thus supporting the opinion previously expressed in the text, and also proving how uncertain the statistics of this country are.

evidently built of vitrified bricks, looking like pumice-stone, and in a very good state of preservation. This town of Siäm-Réäp is supposed to be very ancient; but with the exception of the wonderful ruins in its vicinity, and which we are just approaching, and perhaps the fort, there is but little to distinguish it at the present period from any other equally large town throughout the rest of Siam. The morning after we arrived here we had a host of visitors, curious to see the strange 'Farrang,' and more curious still to see the strange bird with the four legs, the sight of which amused them considerably.

CHAPTER XVI

> The day grew dark and darker still,
> And nature seemed to droop and die
> When all at once was heard the shrill,
> Wild shrieks that rose and rent the sky;
> And then the pagans 'gan to prance,
> Like maniacs in a mystic dance,
> And blood like water freely flowed
> To quench the thirst of that grim god.
>
> *The Fatal Eclipse.*

Ancient ruins of Angkor-Wát—March thereto—Don Quixote and Sancho Panza—A plague of Mosquitoes—The Moon being eaten by Rahú—Description of Rahú by Father Sangermano—His great size—Not big enough to swallow the Moon—A partial Eclipse—Invisible at Greenwich—Angkor-Wát relegated to Owls and Bats—Though I ate the Lotus I did not forget my Country!

WE were now within six or seven miles of the curious but comparatively unknown ruins of Angkor-Wát, by far the most inaccessible and most interesting ruins of Further Asia. The few English people who have ever heard of them are under the impression that they are situated in Modern Cambodia; but they are really placed in the ancient kingdom of Kumēr, or Ancient Cambodia, the history of which is so much wrapt in obscurity, and are some forty or fifty miles north of the northern boundary of the modern country.

We had scarcely ever met a pony during the whole of our journey across the country, for the children of the forest have but little use for this kind of animal. Nor would they have been of much service to us even if we had them, as, contrary to the general prevailing opinion, they are generally such mere cats that there would be no pleasure in riding them; while our marches were otherwise so slow and tedious that, as we had generally to keep within touch of the baggage, riding on such animals would be even more tedious than walking itself. But one of the officials at Siäm-Réäp lent us a couple of ponies, and on them Sancho Panza the interpreter and myself proceeded to the ruins in due course. Here, indeed, a pony was of some real use, as the pathway was so soft and sandy as to make walking as tiresome as walking along a sandy sea-shore.

We sent out the baggage during the day, but as the march was only a short one, we did not start ourselves till the afternoon, and we reached the ruins at early twilight. There, on one of the eastern gates of it, on the second landing, I watched the full-orbed moon slowly and solemnly rising out of the far-away flat forest, to the still farther east of the ancient shrine. It was an impressive sight enough for the solitary stranger visiting these strange out-of-the-way ruins, but a still stranger spectacle was to follow that same evening. We put up in one of the usual wattle *salas* near the ruins, and on ground that looked very swampy and feverish. It was frequently remarked on the journey how little we had suffered from mosquitoes. But here was a very marked exception, for the mosquitoes were swarming and buzzing round us in crowds; and there is nothing better calculated to disturb one's equanimity than the incessant buzzing of mosquitoes.

True enough that when the blood gets thin by prolonged residence in tropical climates, the bites of the mosquitoes do not raise those angry lumps that they do when the blood is sanguine and pure. But still, people continue to look on them as old enemies, whose biting and buzzing they cannot easily endure, however long they remain in malarious countries. After dinner, then, we began to make ready our mosquito curtains. But when we opened mine, behold it was full of holes, however they happened to come there. It is much better to have no mosquito curtains at all than to have one with holes in it; for the mosquitoes are wonderfully clever in getting in through these holes, but not at all so expert in getting out of them again, even if they tried to do so, which they seldom do.

We extemporised supports for these curtains, of a primitive kind, so as to hang over the mattress which was lying on the bamboo floor, and were trying to patch up the holes with some fine twine that we had, West pinching the holes between his fingers and thumb, while I tied the knots around them. Though the ruins themselves have been abandoned times out of mind for religious purposes, yet a large number of Buddhist priests live near the ruins, and inside the wide moat that surrounds them all.

After dinner, then, when engaged in this useful but prosaic process of knot-tying, we suddenly heard tremendous shouting and *tom-tomming* a little distance away. We went out in a hurry to see what the uproar was about, and found a group of natives, with their *tom-toms* and other instruments, actually baying at the moon, which was going through the interesting ceremonial of an eclipse !

Most of the people of the country through which we had travelled spoke more or less Siamese, though their own tongue might be that of Läös or Cambodia, as the case might be. At least, those who came in contact with us spoke enough of it to supply our daily requirements. But the priests here spoke no Siamese whatever, but only the language of their own country. We had provided, however, for this contingency by procuring at Siäm-Réäp the services of a Kumēr guide and interpreter, who could speak Siamese to the interpreter already along with us ; so that conversation now became considerably mixed before it reached my ears in the English tongue.

We asked them what they were making such a fearful noise for, when they pointed to the moon, which we had not noticed before, and said that a black man called Rahú was eating it up, and that they were making this deafening din to frighten him away. Strange that all races think black men worse than white ones, even when they are not white themselves ; and we ourselves paint the Devil black, though some people say that he is not so black as he is painted. So strong is the idea of colour among some of the simpler races who believe in a future life, that they pin their faith on becoming white men in their next stage of existence, if they behave themselves properly in this one.

But when the natives on this occasion mentioned the name of the black man Rahú, a faint glimmer came into my memory that I had read or heard of Rahú before, and after returning where I am now writing I was still further enlightened on this profound subject. It happened in this way. Several years ago, when in Upper Burmah, I came across a curious old book translated from the written manuscripts of an Italian priest called Sangermano, who served as a missionary in Burmah about a hundred years ago, and long before we had any footing in the country at all.

The other day I was casually looking over this book a second time when I suddenly came across my friend Rahú, and noticed that I had previously noted on the margin of the book the worthy father's description of him, and this is what I had read and marginally noted some nine long years before :—

> We must now speak of the eclipses of the sun and moon, of the phases of the latter, and the causes that produce them. It has been mentioned above that the Burmese, besides the seven principal planets, admit of an eighth called Rahú, which is opaque and dark, and for that reason invisible to us. The size of the monster is 4,800 *juzena*. Its body measures 600 *juzena*, its breast 12 *juzena*, its head 900 *juzena*, its forehead and mouth 300 *juzena*. The size of the feet and hands is 200 *juzena*, and that of the fingers 50 *juzena*. When this monstrous planet is instigated by envy towards the sun and moon, probably on account of their clearness and splendour, he descends into their respective paths, and, opening his horrible mouth, devours them. Should he, however, retain them for any length of time his head would burst, as both the sun and moon irresistibly tend to prosecute their course; he is therefore obliged, after a short time, to vomit them up. Sometimes he places them under his chin, at others he licks them with his tongue, and sometimes covers them with his hand; and thus are explained the total and partial eclipse of the sun and moon, together with their immersion and emersion. Every three years Rahú goes to meet the sun, and every six months the moon.

To enlighten the reader still further, more particularly as to the size of Rahú, it may be mentioned that a Burmese *juzena* is about eight miles long, so that he can calculate the size of Rahú in plain English for himself. And it need only be said here that he is far and away a bigger bug than Buddha, even according to the *ex pede* measurements given in a previous chapter. But fine and large as Rahú is, yet, if his measurements be carried out rigorously in English miles, it will be found that he is not nearly big enough to swallow either the sun or the moon.

It will also be observed from the above that the superstition about the black man Rahú is common among the inhabitants from Burmah to distant Kumēr, and even further, for it is prevalent among some tribes in India, from which the name Rahú probably started at first, and means the 'gobbler' or 'seizer.' Indeed India seems to have been the cradle of a great many myths and mysteries. The occurrence of this eclipse was on March 21st. It was again almost exactly full moon, for we had just taken four weeks and a day to cover the distance from Mount Phrabāt to this remote portion of Indo-China. We watched the eclipse for a long time with not a little interest, while the natives were trying to frighten Rahú away, which, by the way, they did at last, and no doubt thought themselves wonderful magicians at the end of it all.

It was a partial eclipse, thanks to the native *tom-tomming*, for we watched it till we were quite sure it was on the wane again. But we were probably asleep before it entirely cleared away, as the whole business must have occupied several hours altogether. I wondered at the time whether the eclipse would be down in almanacks or not, and whether it would be visible at Greenwich; but judging from the great difference in longitude, I concluded that it could not possibly be seen in the British Isles, as it would be broad daylight in that favoured country during the whole time that the eclipse would be seen.

Roughly speaking Angkor-Wát is about 105° east of Greenwich, and is therefore almost exactly seven hours anterior to it in point of time. The middle of the eclipse was between nine and ten o'clock at night, which would correspond to two or three o'clock in the day in the British Islands, and therefore the eclipse could not possibly be visible there as it would be broad daylight. Since returning from the journey I have looked in an almanack for this purpose, and find that the event is noted right enough, but, as I suspected, put down as invisible at Greenwich. It was really an impressive sight to watch this unexpected eclipse at this out-of-the-way and unfrequented old ruin, with the atmosphere as still as death, and without speck or cloud throughout the whole vault of Heaven. And so I marked down the event as a somewhat interesting red-letter day in the course of my life.

We spent the best part of three days wandering about these wonderful ruins, but were driven off at last by the mosquitoes, such are the fuzzy-wuzzy little things that are capable of marring our contemplation of the old and romantic.

The ruins of Angkor-Wát are sometimes known under the name of Nakkon-Wát, the latter being the more common name in Siam, while the former is the name used in Kumēr itself, as Angkor is the name of the province where the ruins are, and the word *wát* means a temple, or, rather, a monastery, like the Burmese word *kiung*. It takes some time to make one's self fairly acquainted with this extensive and complicated structure, and I despair of imparting to the reader a fair conception of what it is like, as it bears no resemblance to any other kind of building with which he is likely to be familiar.

We were up very early the next morning, wandering about the place, but instead of meeting *phras*, or priests, sitting on their knees, palming their hands and muttering some nonsense in true orthodox style, we, alas! found sweepers gathering in baskets the bats' guano that had fallen during the previous day and night. How, indeed, had the mighty fallen! And to what base uses can the most sacred objects be put at last, like Cæsar filling a bung-hole, or the sacred Angkor-Wát being made the solitary habitation of owls and bats! Alas, alas, the mutability of all things under the sun!

The building must have originally been built for a monastery, though nobody in the country itself knows anything about the business, except in the way of tradition and fable; and as it is now entirely deserted, and seldom or never visited by the natives themselves, it is no wonder that these creatures make it their home and habitation, where the bats may sometimes be seen suspended from the roofs of the corridors, to which they impart a very foul and unflavoury smell. Though to describe a great ruin like this is a very difficult task, yet I annex a ground plan of the place for the reader's edification.

The ruins are placed on what is practically an island, three or four miles round about, and surrounded on all sides by a small river, or, to speak more correctly, with a wide artificial moat communicating with the small river Khontai-Khom, on which the town of Siäm-Reäp is situated, six or seven miles further down towards the south. Across the said wide moat, on the west side, is a large, wide and stone-built causeway that completely divides the moat at that place, without any passage for the water, unless it flows over it, as it probably does at certain seasons of the year. This is the only way of entrance on foot to the sacred island, which is elsewhere all surrounded by the moat already mentioned, and which looked very beautiful at the time of our visit, as in some places it was literally covered with the handsome oriental variety of water-lily known as the 'lotus,' and which was then in full and varied blossom.

This magnificent lily abounds in various parts of the East, and varies considerably in colour, from a dark pinkish hue to nearly pure white. It is above all others the sacred flower of eastern lands, in whose worth and praises so many fables have been told and songs have been sung; and it is certainly a very pretty sight to see a whole field of them floating gracefully on the surface of the water. I was aware of the ancient lotus-eaters, who forgot their country by eating of this seductive lily; but as we don't eat lilies, I did not hitherto know what part of it they ate, and treated the whole story as a mere fable. But here I discovered, for the first time, that the lotus really grows a kind of more or less succulent fruit of a peculiar conical shape, and which was freely eaten in this country. And so I, too, ate one of them, and with much fear and trembling, lest I also should forget my country. But why, man, bless your soul, I was more homesick after eating it than I was before!

CHAPTER XVII

> Is this the sacred shrine
> Of days of old langsyne,
> Where priests and vestal maids were wont to bend the knee?
> Alas! how ruined now,
> With ne'er a knee to bow,
> But left to bats and moles, and lone as lone could be.
> *The Ruined Abbey.*

Description of Angkor-Wát Ruins—Its Ancient Grandeur—Its Bas-reliefs—An old-world Tug-of-war—An undeciphered Tablet—*Bomb-bomb*—Scattered Sculptures—Angkor-Thóm—Rozinante comes down—Angkor-Wát Built by Angels—Compared with Borobodo in Java—Borobodo a Buddhist Shrine—Overlapping of Symbolic Sculptures—The same of Religious Forms—The Theory of Evolution and of Devolution—The Cannibal who first ate an Oyster—First View of Telé-Sáp—The 'Roderick Dhu' and the 'Lady of the Lake.'

AROUND the ruin, and some three or four hundred yards away from it, there is a wall twelve or fifteen feet high, and in an excellent state of preservation. It is impossible to follow this wall all throughout, on account of the dense jungle growing about it here and there. But I followed the outside of it as well as I could from the south-west corner to the south gate, and counted 753 steps, representing half the length of the wall in a west-east direction. Making due allowance for the more or less tortuous way that I was compelled to take, this rough measurement would make the wall in this direction something like three-quarters of a mile long. Our Kumĕr guide said that the walls, as well as the buildings, were square, with equal length of sides; but whether he was right or wrong about the walls, which we were not able to measure thoroughly, we found that he was quite wrong about the buildings themselves, for I measured them afterwards, and found that, with the exception of the central platform, they were really oblong in figure, with the longer sides directed east and west, and the shorter ones north and south, as may be seen from a glance at the accompanying ground plan.

Inside the park-like wall is another wall, only a few feet high; and inside this again, only a short distance

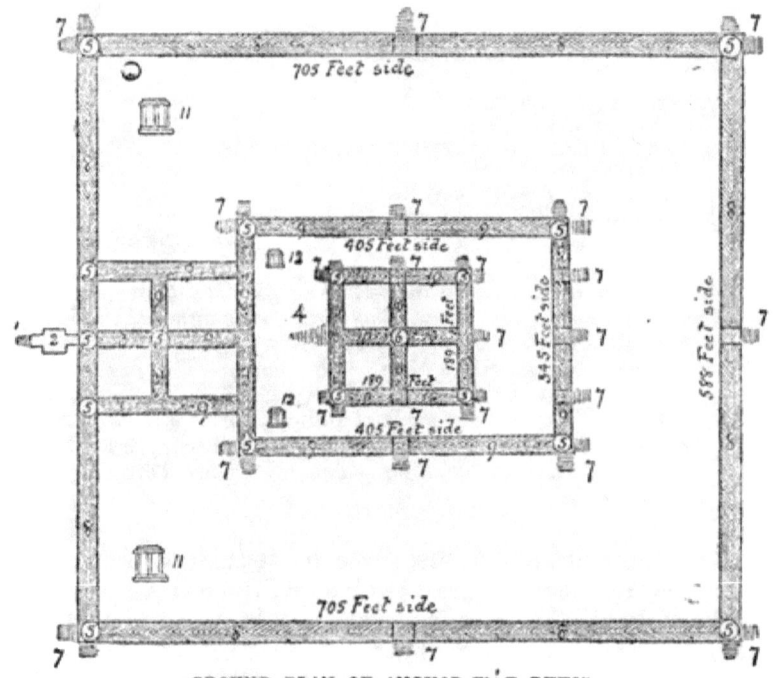

GROUND PLAN OF ANGKOR-WÂT RUINS.
From a Sketch by the Author.

(1) Ordinary causeway, leading across moat into the Ruins. (2) Elevated main entrance. (3) Roofed stone staircase, leading from first to second platform. (4) Stone staircase, but not roofed, from second to third platform. (5) Towers at corners, &c., of the various platforms. (6) Great central tower, being the highest point of the Ruin. (7) Stone stairs leading from corners, &c., of platforms, there being two at each corner. (8) Roofed outer corridor, the outer wall, as it were, consisting of a double series of pillars, and on the inner wall, facing outwards, are placed the beautiful bas-reliefs, nearly half a mile in extent. (9) Roofed corridors of second platform. (10) Roofed corridors of third or central platform, which is quite square. (11) Temples in the outer court. (12) Temples in the inner court.

from it, is the magnificent ruin itself. I happened to have a measuring tape with me, twelve yards long, but by attaching a piece of twine to it we were enabled to get a length of twenty-seven yards. With this combination we measured the building as shown in the figure, and the measurements may be relied on as correct enough for all practical purposes.

By looking at this figure the spectator will see that though the outer contour of the building is oblong, and also the second platform, yet the central or third platform is a complete square, some sixty-three yards wide on each of its four sides.

Neither of the outer two walls alluded to as separate from the building is represented in the figure at all, nor, of course, is the surrounding moat—only the ruin itself, then, and nothing more. The building is so complicated and extensive in its structure that it would be difficult to describe it, even by pens more familiar than mine with the ins and outs of architecture. The outer walls of the building, represented in the diagram by double lines (8), are on a raised platform ten or twelve feet from the general level of the ground ; and from the middle of the west wall (to the reader's left), the causeway (1) leads to the raised main entrance (2) of the structure. The spaces between these two lines (8) represent the roof of the corridors, supported on the outer side by a double row of columns (represented in the figure by the outer line), and on the inner side by a substantial wall (represented in the diagram by the inner line), on which the extensive bas-reliefs are to be seen.

These bas-reliefs are raised three or four feet above the ground, and are about four or four and a half feet wide. Speaking roughly, they look to the naked eye about half as wide again as the frieze of the Greek Parthenon, to be seen in the Elgin Rooms of the British Museum. The sculptures are somewhat less 'relieved' from the general surface than the bas-reliefs just mentioned, but they are apparently quite as finely chiselled and in a much better state of preservation.

It was on this inner wall that the measurements of 705 feet by 588 feet were taken, extending from the outer doorpost on the one side of the building to that on the opposite side.

Bas-reliefs abound on the walls almost everywhere throughout the ruin ; but it is on the outside of this inner wall of the corridor that they are particularly abundant and extensive. Taking the sum of the four sides, there is nearly half a mile of almost continual sculpture on these four walls alone ; and representing various scenes, most of which are of a warlike character, while one side in particular is occupied by what appears to be a tug-of-war on a large and ancient scale. Scores of men on one side are doing their utmost to pull over exactly the same number of men on the other side, while the umpire, or whoever he may be, represented by a larger figure than the rest, is seen in the middle between the two contending parties, and sitting on the back of a turtle, whatever allegorical meaning that fact may contain. It is obvious, then, that the wish of each party is not only to pull over the other one, but also to turn the turtle. The expression to 'turn turtle' is generally understood as mere modern slang, but here it was exemplified since ancient days and cut into the stone.

On some other side, the bas-reliefs represent warriors fighting with shields, spears, bows and arrows, war-horses and war-chariots ; or perhaps a group of prisoners and slaves led captive by their conquerors ; and though I looked with care, I could not see any weapons so modern as even a mortar or a Brown Bess ; for these figures only represented the feats of the brave days of old, when there was man to man and steel to steel. The few representations of horses were particularly good, as if drawn from quite a different stamp from the samples of the equine species that exist in the country nowadays.

While saying this about the equine species of Indo-China at the present period, I know I am going against the generally received opinion that the ponies of this country are a very fine breed. The mistake has arisen from seeing an occasional fine pony in places like Saigon and Bangkok. These fine ponies, however, are the pick of hundreds, while most of them are very small. As a class they may practically be considered as a second-rate edition of the Pegu ponies of Burmah, which latter may be counted as the best of this particular variety of horseflesh.

But perhaps the most interesting of all these sculptures is the one to be seen in the middle of the east side of this same wall. This piece is a few feet from the ground, and is about four or five feet high, and somewhat more in a horizontal direction. It consists of engraved writing which is still fairly distinct, and which we were told had never yet been satisfactorily deciphered. If the inscription could be read aright it might throw some real side-lights alike on the building and the builders.

The first half of the double line leading from the main entrance, and marked (3) in the figure, represents a flight of stone steps leading up to the second platform; and all the other double lines represent roofed corridors (8), (9), and (10), between pillars on the outer sides and walls on the inner ones. The central square, surrounded and crossed in a crucial way by roofed corridors (10), is reached from the west by a very steep and long flight of stone steps, and both at the corners and in the middle are similar flights of steps, as represented in the figure, the flights at the corners leading in two different directions, as duly laid down in the diagram. This, as will be seen, is an exact square, approximately 189 feet on each side along the inner wall of the corridor; and each of the four angles of the square is surmounted by a tower (5) of big stones, while in the very centre is the biggest tower (6) of all, beneath which is a very large figure of Buddha, in profound contemplation as usual, as well as with the flat feet and orthodox toes already commented on in these pages.

The guide was anxious to bring us to see what he called the *bomb-bomb*. This was a small room only a few feet wide along the side of the second platform, and its virtue consisted of the fact that it gave out a peculiar echo. And yet it was scarcely an echo either, as the surrounding walls were too near the speaker for that purpose. When speaking, the voice sounded as if the person were speaking into the mouth of a very great boiler, with a very narrow neck; and on tapping the breast smartly with the closed hand, the chest emitted a sound, as if it were quite empty, without any lungs at all, and to which physicians apply the term 'emphysematous.' The guide was very proud of his *bomb-bomb*, as he called it, but I did not think much of it. The sound must be the merest accident, without any previous design whatever on the part of the ancient architects. A very marked echo was once pointed out to me in a narrow passage in the mausoleum of the famous Chinese emperor Yungló, who, with several other Chinese emperors of the

Ming dynasty, is buried some twenty-five or thirty miles to the north of Pekin. But this echo, also, is probably an accident, and not at all the result of profound forethought.

On the first platform, halfway between the north-west corner of it and that of the second platform of Angkor-Wát, there are the ruins of a largish temple (11), and a similar one is to be seen between the south-west corners of these platforms respectively The same process (12) is repeated on a smaller scale between the same angles of the second and third platforms. We looked for the same kind of temples to the north-east and south-east corners of these platforms, but the temples were never represented on the east side at all.

The amount of earth required to fill in these platforms must have been enormous, as may be seen at a glance at the length of the sides of the first platform, roughly calculated at 705 feet by 588 feet, and of the second platform, 405 feet by 345 feet. As the general run of the country is quite flat about Angkor-Wát, this vast accumulation of earth leads one to the conclusion that the great moat, which converts the locality into an island, must really be mostly artificial, and that the earth taken out of it must have been used to fill in these separate platforms during the progress of the building.

Otherwise the building is entirely composed of stones, including walls, floors, roofs, windows, doorposts, and what not. The windows are formed of round upright columns of stone, worked in a way that makes them look as if they had been fashioned in a turning lathe. And it is between the intervals of these ornamental stone bars that the light of heaven is admitted from the outside.

The size of the stones varies according to the purpose which they serve; but they may generally be described as distinctly ponderous. Sometimes a single stone or two forms the side of a door or one of the numberless pillars supporting the roofs of the extensive corridors. But who carried them, or how their great ponderosity ever got there, is a question not easily answered.

The quality of the stones seems to vary greatly, from the hardness of granite to that of freestone, sandstone, or even laterite. The building seems to have been very much used before being finally deserted, and the worn condition of some of the flights of steps bears ample testimony to the countless priests who must have trod on them during the past ages. These steps reveal a lateritious formation, even to the casual observer, whereas the great heavy stones in the walls would give one the idea of being composed of a much denser and more enduring material.

Sculptures are to be met almost everywhere throughout the ruins, those in sheltered situations being, of course, much better preserved than those more exposed to the elements, as many of them are. The building altogether is more remarkable for its great extent and elaborate sculptures than for its height, and the central tower, which is the highest part of the building, is probably not much more than two hundred feet high, if even quite so much. On this account the first view of Angkor-Wát, when walking towards the main entrance, is not particularly imposing, as it nowhere presents a bold, prominent front to the observer; and it is only after looking well over it that the visitor is struck with its magnitude and original grandeur.

There are several other ruins scattered here and there throughout the jungles of this country; and next to Angkor-Wát the largest is Angkor-Thóm, sometimes called Nakkon-Luang by the Siamese. It is only three or four miles to the north of Angkor-Wát, and is surrounded by the same kind of extensive wall noted in connection with Angkor-Wát, but said to be still more extensive, and to enclose scores and even hundreds of acres. Angkor-Thóm and the other ruins in that portion of the country are supposed to represent the remains of the capital town of ancient Kumēr.

The path from Siäm-Réäp to Angkor-Wát, and especially that from Angkor-Wát to Angkor-Thóm, passes through a very magnificent forest with some very large trees, conspicuous among which may be seen the splendid Dammer-pine, from which the dammer of commerce is obtained. Though the trees that supply the dammer are called pines, yet they do not appear to be pines at all, or perhaps the resin known as dammer may be obtained from different kinds of trees. Among other purposes, the natives themselves use this dammer for making torches, as well as for making their boats watertight, just in the same way that we use the pitch obtained from the pitch-pine; and their water vessels are also invariably made by close-fitting wickerwork of bamboo slips, soaked and seasoned in this resinous dammer till they get as watertight as the skin of a whale, besides being extremely light to carry. They extract the resin from these big trees by chopping a gap into the side of it near the ground and placing smouldering embers in the hollow so chopped out. The resin then oozes down and gradually accumulates in this hollow till taken away by the owner. We saw several of these great trees scorched in this way during the journey from Angkor-Wát to Angkor-Thóm, and in the hollow cleft of one of them there still remained a quantity of the brown dammer resin not yet taken away.

During this trip, as during the previous one to Angkor-Wát, both Sancho the interpreter and myself were gaily riding on fiery steeds. As we approached the main gate of the vast, park-like enclosure, we found the floor of the gateway raised a few feet from the ground by a large number of big stones, some of which were not in such regular order as they doubtless were when originally laid down. Sancho, who was a very light squire, got over it on his Dapple easily enough, and I hoped that my Rozinante would rise to the occasion also; but he came down in the effort with me still sitting on his back. I expected to be violently shaken off when he struggled on to his legs again, but the poor little beast never did struggle, but laid quietly there till I came off at leisure. This was only our second mount on the whole journey, and did not encourage us to make much further use of these small creatures in the future.

Angkor-Thóm is much more in ruins than Angkor-Wát, and is also probably less extensive, though equally massive in its architecture, if not even more so. It is also on a different plan from Angkor-Wát, and is less easily traced, on account of its completely tumble-down condition. What remains of Angkor-Thóm now would rather point to some great private residence than to a monastery like Angkor-Wát; but it need not be described in detail, as it is so completely in ruins. Several other less extensive ruins are scattered about, but require no particular mention here, as I was not able to visit them; and none of them are so extensive as either Angkor-Wát or Angkor-Thóm.

And now, gentle reader, have you been able to follow the description of Angkor-Wát? Well, if you have, I am very glad to hear it, as I have scarcely been able to follow it myself when writing it. But let us return to lighter themes.

Nobody, as I said, knows with any certainty who built Angkor-Wát, or at what period of the world's history the work was originally constructed. It cannot possibly be the remains of the Tower of Babel (!), for the fable about Angkor-Wát is that it was built by angels, which would at once do away with the Tower-of-Babel theory, for the builders of it could not be angels, anyway, or they would not have been dispersed as they were.

The fable proceeds that there was once a king of the country called Prakét-Maláia, and this king of Kumēr was the son of an angel, and this son of an angel was very pious and good to the destitute; in fact, he was a real *Gharib-purwar* (friend of the poor), as they say in Hindustan. And the kind angels his half-brothers and sisters, and his cousins and his aunts, were all anxious to do the good king a good turn for his piety and goodness. And so one fine morning the good king woke, and beheld Angkor-Wát! There it was, built during the night by his angelic relatives, and ready for the good king to occupy. And the good king was so very, very good, and so humble and self-denying, that he did not like to live in such a splendid palace, and he asked the consent of the angels. And the angels, they gave their consent. And when the angels had given their consent, the good king handed over the beautiful building to the *phras*, the pious monks, and he himself lived ever after in abstraction and retirement.

Such is the fable about the building of Angkor-Wát. Some of the large stones have a round shallow hole in them, almost exactly like that driven into stones before blasting, but our trusty guide said that this was the place where the angels caught the stones when placing them in position. Only the very largest stones have this peculiar mark at all, and there is generally one hole only in each stone, so that the angels that built Angkor-Wát must have had one finger only, or at most one finger and a thumb. Something of the same kind of story, but not actually the same, was told me when visiting the famous shrine of Borobodo in the island of Java some years ago ('Toil and Travel,' p. 136). But in that case it was only men who built the shrine, and they took only three days to do it by the great favour of the Buddha, and without the noise of maul or hammer.

Both Angkor-Wát and Borobodo are doubtlessly Buddhist ruins, and as the Buddhist religion is only some 550 years older than the Christian one, it follows that neither of these buildings can be quite 2,500 years old. But whether the one or the other of them was built by angels it is very difficult to say. Neither of these magnificent buildings, however, is probably older than the sixth century of the Christian era. Sir Stamford Raffles, who was Governor of Java during the British occupation of that lovely island, speaks of Borobodo as probably the finest ancient monument in the world, and in his 'History of Java,' as quoted by Russel Wallace, concludes in this fashion about it :—

> The amount of human labour and skill expended in the great pyramids of Egypt sinks into insignificance when compared to that required to complete this sculptured hill-temple in the interior of Java.

If Sir Stamford Raffles had seen Angkor-Wát he would give it the preference over Borobodo, large and massive though it is. But at the time of Sir Stamford Raffles—which is not very long ago either, the ancient ruins of Angkor-Wát had probably never been seen by a European. The style of the buildings is essentially different, of course, Angkor-Wát being a monastery, while Borobodo is a solid structure without any interior. In short, it is a cairn on a gigantic scale, and belongs to a class of structure technically known under the name of *stupa*. Yet the labour expended over Angkor-Wát has probably been much greater than that expended over even the Borobodo, as, I think, most people would admit who happened to see the two ruins.

As I had previously seen the Borobodo in Java, as well as Angkor-Wát in the kingdom of Kumēr, I took the opportunity of visiting the Pyramids of Egypt on my way home. The Pyramids, though more massive, are not so elaborate in workmanship as either Borobodo or Angkor-Wát. If all these ruins, the most magnificent of ancient times, were discovered recently, and nobody knew anything about them, Angkor-Wát, in the opinion of most people, would take the first place, with the great Pyramid of Cheops third. It must, however, be admitted that the Pyramids are far older and of more scientific importance than either of the others.

It is strange that so shrewd an observer as Sir Stamford Raffles should ascribe the monuments of Java to the Hindoo religion ; and in this opinion he is apparently followed by Dr. Russel Wallace, who, however, says that he did not see the best of them himself. But neither Dr. Wallace nor Sir Stamford Raffles was probably familiar with the monuments of India, the original home of both Hinduism and Buddhism alike. And there is scarcely any monument, even in India itself, to be compared in their own way with the two monuments under observation ; for the monuments even of Agra and Delhi are of comparatively modern origin when compared with these ancient ruins.

Not because India is not so old as either Java or Kumēr, but because the ancient Indians, both Buddhists and Hindoos, went in more for artificial underground caves, such as the well-known Elephanta caves in a small island in the Bombay harbour, and the Ellora caves, a couple of hundred miles north-east of Bombay, which are the largest artificial caves to be found anywhere. But whatever some of the other monuments of Java may be, Borobodo certainly had never anything to do with the Hindoo religion. It is in fact a solid stupa, typical of the Buddhist religion, and by far the most magnificent of its kind in existence, just the same as Angkor-Wát is the most magnificent old monastery in connection with that faith, or with any other.

The stupa form is probably the most ancient memorial of Buddhist worship, from which the modern white and gilded pagoda has been latterly developed ; and the oldest of them all is the stupa known under the name of Sarnāth, four or five miles away on the outskirts of Benares, where Gotauma Buddha is said to have first begun to preach his doctrines. But that stupa is a mere cairn compared with Borobodo ; for though Buddha was born in India, and first promulgated his religion there, yet Buddhism seems never to have prevailed over India itself to the same extent as it did in Ceylon, Java, and Further Asia. And, as if to confirm the belief that Borobodo is a Buddhist shrine, we once came across a very small temple in Java, not far from Borobodo, with a large image of Buddha, as typical and complete as any to be seen in Burmah or Japan, even to the length of his finger nails.[1]

It is probable, then, that most, if not all the ancient monuments of Java, are of Buddhist and not of Hindoo origin. It must not be forgotten that the styles of sculpture, and other peculiarities of the two religions, are not always distinct in every detail, but that they sometimes encroach upon, and overlap one another. The occurrence, for instance, of an image of the Hindoo goddess Dûrga among the ruins of Java would by no means prove the same ruins to be of Hindoo origin. And with regard to the caves of India itself, for another example, it is generally admitted by antiquaries that it was the Buddhists who were the first cave-diggers in this ancient country. Yet in the Ellora caves, the largest in India, sculptures symbolical of Hinduism and Buddhism are to be found in different portions of the same caves. And indeed it is not in architecture and sculpture alone that different religions overlap one another. For it is so with even the tenets of religions (a much more important matter), as may easily be seen from the remnants of Druidical paganism that still remain among ourselves, after fourteen or fifteen centuries of Christianity.

As the Borobodo, in short, is the king of solid structures, so is Angkor-Wát the king of monasteries—only more so. The Buddhists have a weakness in building their monasteries in a rectangular fashion, with courtyards inside, even to this day; and I was at one time living in the monastery connected with the Arrakān Pagoda near

---

[1] I have left these paragraphs as they stood in my manuscript, which was written far away from a good library. But while thus venturing to disagree with the supposed authority of Sir Stamford Raffles, on the authority of my own personal observations in various Eastern lands, I am very pleased to find that I was unconsciously confirming it. For on reaching once again Britannia's rugged shores, I took the opportunity of consulting Sir Stamford's 'History of Java,' and in vol. ii. p. 66, found the following conclusive passage: 'With respect to the remains of architectural grandeur and sculptural beauty which I have noticed, I shall simply observe that it seems to be the general opinion of those most versed in Indian antiquities, that the large temple of Borobodo (a corruption perhaps of Bará Buddha or Great Budh) and several others, were sacred to the worship of Budh.'

Mandalay, which was built on this very principle. We were in fact living in the rooms from which the priests had just been ousted as a temporary measure. But though bearing some resemblance in its rectangular mode of construction, this monastery was no more to be compared to Angkor-Wát than the Sarnáth near Benares could be compared with the Borobodo of Java. All the temples in Benares, the holiest city in India, could in fact be accommodated in the vast park-like enclosure I have already mentioned in connection with Angkor-Wát.

Putting aside the angelic theory, it is curious to know how Angkor-Wát was really built. It is a long, long distance away from the sea, and no stone or quarry of the kind contained in it can be discovered at all within a reasonable distance, as almost all this particular portion of the country is composed of alluvial deposit only.

And then as to who built it. The present inhabitants of Kumēr, without being mere degraded savages, are certainly as simple and non-inventive as most people; and the whole of their brains put together (and well shaken up) could not execute so excellent a design as the ruins of Angkor-Wát, to save their very souls. Is this, then, the same kind of people as lived in Kumēr in ancient times? The same remark applies equally well to Java, when its ancient ruins and present population are compared and considered. Are, therefore, the present inhabitants of Java and Kumēr the descendants of more civilised ancestors, or are they a different people altogether from those who devised and built the mysterious monuments to be found in these countries? Sir John Lubbock is probably too bold when he writes on this subject :—

'That existing savages are not the descendants of civilised ancestors. That the primitive condition of man was one of utter barbarism.'

But the terms 'savagery' and 'civilisation' themselves are of such wide and vague significance, as not at all easy to be properly defined; and, like religion, people might argue indefinitely about them without coming to any satisfactory conclusion. Many people will think that if all restraint and example were withdrawn, it would only be too easy for human nature to relapse, if not into utter barbarism, at least dangerously near it.

Sir John Lubbock is apparently an out-and-out evolutionist. But one hesitates to abandon 'the grand old gardener and his wife,' till at any rate he gets something equally good to put in their place, and this is scarcely supplied by the oyster, the jelly-fish, or even that funny little crystal that the funny little German philosopher is keeping up his sleeve. When Dean Swift said that it was a bold man who first ate an oyster, he ought really to have said that it was a bad as well as a bold man who first did so; for by the modern theory of evolution (which, by the way, had not been evolved in Swift's time), he was really a most loathsome cannibal, eating and devouring one of the 'Ancient House' from which he himself was lineally descended.

But neither Darwin nor even his antagonists seem ever to have conceived the idea that whatever involves a hypothesis may also involve an antithesis. Granted for argument's sake, that the story of the original horticultural couple is not true, how do these philosophers know but that man was the first organism created, and that all the other forms of life may have literally descended and degenerated from him, instead of ascending towards him? This theory seems never to have entered the heads of the wise men; and I give it them therefore for what it is worth, as a sop for the next meeting of the British Association, and with the hope that they will call it the theory of De-volution, as opposed to E-volution; or, if they like—The MacGregor Theory!

It must always be remembered that progress, in whatever sphere, is the result of an effort, while degeneracy is but the result of mere negation. To keep the engine going, whether mental, physical, or vital, you must needs feed it with the food convenient for it. To let it play itself out, you have simply to do nothing. Restrain your hand from feeding the helpless infant, and you need not do anything more, for the infant decays and dies as a matter of course. Only take away the spark of life, and the body naturally crumbles into the dust whence it came. Should God but withdraw His mysterious hand from this beautiful universe, Cosmos would at once become Chaos. Why has the Perpetual Motion never been discovered? Because it presumes to go eternally of its own free will, without any effort—without a feeding-bottle, so to speak. And this, I fancy, it can never, never do, for it can't get on without it.

But let us resume our march to Síäm-Réäp, for now we must direct our course southwards towards modern Cambodia and Cochin-China. After staying at Síäm-Réäp one more night on our way, we duly proceeded to Lake Telé-Sáp, which literally means 'The Great Lake,' as it is really one of the largest lakes in Further Asia, though comparatively so little known. For Asia, though abounding in lofty mountains and noble rivers, is wonderfully deficient in large lakes, as compared with America, or even with Africa. After tramping seven or eight miles, we met the boats that were intended to take us through the whole length of Telé-Sáp, for they could not get up to Síäm-Réäp itself, as there was not enough water in the river at this season.

The two boats were the 'Roderick Dhu' and the 'Lady of the Lake.' The 'Roderick Dhu' was the larger and heavier of the two boats, and had a complement of four oarsmen, whereas the 'Lady of the Lake,' being lighter and more graceful, had only three. West, Välloo, and the Kumēr guide went into the larger one, as well as most of the luggage; while the little bird 'Jimmy' and myself stayed in the smaller and handier craft. Though only eleven persons all told, we were of diverse tongues. There was English, which West and I spoke, and nobody else; there was Hindustani, which Välloo and I spoke (very badly), and nobody else; there was Siamese, which West and the new guide spoke, and nobody else; and, finally, there was the Kumēr language, which the guide and crew spoke among themselves—and nobody else. And thus it happened that it was through the tedious process of percolation that we were able to communicate at all with one another; and thus we floundered and blundered along.

Roughly speaking, each of the boats would be twenty to twenty-five feet long, and six or seven feet wide in the middle, where it was covered with a kind of matting hood as a protection from the sun by day and the dews by night, while the fore and after parts were left exposed for the purposes of rowing. Neither of the boats had any masts or sails, as at this time of the year the wind was expected to blow against us all the way—and so, indeed, it did. The 'Roderick Dhu' was more complex in its interior, but that of the 'Lady of the Lake' could be covered over with several separate pieces of bamboo framework that served the purpose of hatches, and when these pieces were placed in position, the 'Lady of the Lake' presented a flush deck, so to speak, from stem to stern. It was therefore entirely open to the breeze coming from either of these directions, though the hood in the middle obstructed the breeze from either side. And so it was across the middle of the boat, under this canopy, and over this bamboo so-called deck, that I stretched my mattress, and spent the next eight days to come.

CHAPTER XVIII

> There's a lady on land and a lady at sea,
> To make a man happy as happy can be.
> But the 'Lady of the Lake' is the lady for me.
> *Trifles in Triplets.*

Mirage Village—Wife 'o'er the Border'—An afternoon Visit—Kampong-Khām—Native fishing-nets—A rough day's work—Tyndall and the sound of falling Waters—Relapsing into utter Barbarism—*Charab*, the Chatterer—Reach region of Modern Cambodia—Preäm-Préstong—Fishing *à la mode* with the Boat's Tiller—Trawling and other Methods—Pelicans and 'The Ancient Mariner'—*Charab*, the Jingo—Cast away at Night-time—Mode of Mooring Boats—It's all Specific Gravity.

WHEN we had got everything on board, we found that both the boats had taken the ground, and required a deal of yelling and shouting before we got them off again; and then we floated down the river in our little light canoes, like the nigger minstrels from old Kentucky's shore. A little later on we reached the lake, and there at last was the great Telé-Sáp in front of us, in all its muddy glory. In the distance, a mile or two from the shore, we could see a real village that looked very odd so far away from land, and assumed the appearance of a mirage on the surface of the water.

This being another Saturday, we got the boats moored at this amphibious-looking village, and there stayed the whole of next day, before making our first start across the treacherous waves. The house near which we moored the boats belonged to the principal amphibian, who was a Chinaman, and was in fact a fish-curer, who bought the fish from the Kumēr fishermen. We got quite accustomed to these queer villages later on, but none of them looked so queer as this one, on account of its novelty on first presentation. These villages are all only temporary structures of the most flimsy character, built of bamboos, and supported on piles firmly driven into the muddy bottom, and roofed with the usual palm-leaves.

Our visit happened to be at the very height of the fishing season. For it is only when the water is comparatively low that the fishing is carried on, and in less than a month after this the rain would come, the lake would rise and swell, and the very village itself would be deep, deep beneath the surface of the waves; so that it would be nothing more than a mere name without a habitation. No great damage would be done, however, as the houses are practically worth nothing, except the supporting piles, which would remain till the water would subside again, and then the wattle houses would easily be built on the top of them, and the fishing and everything else would go on as merrily as before.

West, who spoke Chinese, was made very welcome by this Chinese fish-curer, and lived with the family during our brief stay. The Chinaman made us all welcome, but as I could not speak the lingo, I preferred to remain on board the 'Lady of the Lake,' and climb up from it now and again to have a chat under difficulties through the interpreter. There were two or three other fish-curers at this village, all of them Chinese, but this was the principal of them all. He, too, had a Kumēr wife and family, as well as a Chinese wife and family 'o'er the Border,' the same as the Chinee we previously met at Kallán. In this case also the wives were not a bit jealous of one another, and I did not care to ask the Kumēr wife, lest it might cause domestic broils after I left the locality.

He was curing, he said, eight different kinds of fish, which he did by drying them in the sun on the ample bamboo terrace around his bamboo house. And the reason, of course, that these queer villages exist at all is the extreme shallowness of the lake towards the shore, preventing boats coming near it when loaded with fish.

In the darkening twilight I withdrew my boat from the houses into the open, so as to let her swing to the breeze. Soon afterwards there was far too much of a breeze, as it began to blow so strong that I could not trust the rickety moorings, and as I slept alone in the boat, I had to get them strengthened lest it might be blown

LAKE DWELLING ON TELÉ-SÁP.

To face page 180.

across the lake during the silent watches. And as it turned out afterwards, I did get blown away in this manner on a future occasion, though not at the present one, for we found this lake rather squally during our passage through it.

These squalls surprised me at first, as there are no mountains at all near the lake in this region, the general aspect of the ground being as flat as possible ; and I can only conclude that the squalls occur here as on the plains of hot countries generally, by the heating of the soil during the scorching hot season, which was here at its very hottest ; and that the squalls extend over the lake for some distance from the shore, if not right across it. The Chinaman said that these squalls became more and more frequent till the very bursting of the periodic rains, exactly the same as takes place over the arid plains of India, and gives rise to those whirlwinds and sand-storms familiarly known in that country under the expressive name of '*devils*.'

Next afternoon we went in a small dug-out to visit the houses of some of the fishermen a little way off, and found them primitive enough. They were arranged in rows, and each house in a given row communicated with its neighbour over stretches of creaking and bending bamboos, across which only an expert could travel with safety, and worse even than the frail Dyak bridges of Borneo. After trying this mode of progression, we very soon got tired of it, and were glad enough to get back to the boats again, with the dug-out half-full of water, as the weather got so squally while we were away, that the waves splashed into it. The 'Lady of the Lake' had also been tumbling about on her own account, resulting in the breaking of one of the lamps, a matter of no great importance on ordinary occasions, but quite a different affair in our wanderings, when we could not get another to replace it.

As it was very hot, even though squally, I resorted to a bath in the lake that same day. But the water was only waist deep, and was so muddy, and the bottom so soft, that I thought I should not bathe in the Telé-Sáp in a hurry again. Yet I did bathe in it frequently afterwards, sometimes as often as three times a day, just for the sake of having something to do ; and fortunately, though there were more than plenty fish to nibble at one's legs, there were no voracious crocodiles to devour people altogether.

The water of the lake at this village of Chongkaneät was very filthy, as all sorts of abominations found their way into it. We asked the Chinaman whether they ever attempted to purify it in any way before drinking it, when he replied that they did not, that the water was very good, as the fish about the village ate up everything. And so they ate the dirty fish, with as much relish as King Norōdom of Cambodia swigged his magnums of champagne.

The dawn of Monday morning appeared at last, and soon after we unloosed our moorings, waved good-bye to the Chinaman, and sailed on our first lake journey. And so we rowed away, passing interminable fishing stakes between us and the shore, which we kept two or three miles to our left. The lake seemed actually swarming with fish, and in the early morning one of them jumped into the 'Lady of the Lake' to wish us good luck; and so we cooked him for breakfast for his kind good wishes.

That night we reached the floating and fishing village of Kampong-Khām without any occurrence worthy of remark. The village, though not so large, was a replica of Changkaneät, that we had left in the morning. It was dark when we got there, but on getting up next morning, we saw some fishing nets hanging to dry on the bamboo railings that stretched between the houses, and went over to see what they were like. They were composed of tanned twine, with meshes of about the same size as those used for sea trout along our own coast, and were seven or eight feet deep. Their length, of course, would vary at pleasure, and we then saw that the most usual system of fishing on the lake was by trawling, as I shall describe more in detail when I shall have gone in for the business myself.

Our next day's trip was a very trying one, and it began to blow and thunder and rain in a very pronounced manner. Two or three times were we compelled to moor the boats, and thrice did we try to make progress again. We had to give it up at last, without being able to make a fair day's journey. For though we tried hard to reach the shelter of the next fishing village, we were quite unable to do so, and had at last to moor the boats two or three miles away from land, and take our chance for the morrow. The squalls would not last very long. They seldom do. And soon after, the weather would be as calm and serene as before. But as long as they did last, the boats, being flat-bottomed, tumbled about like tubs on the waves. The lake also being very shallow, only a few feet even out here, and the water being fresh water, the waves would rise rapidly with the wind, and as rapidly subside again when the wind was over.

I watched some of these heavy rain-pours in the lake with some little interest, for they were as heavy as almost any raindrops I had previously seen. Professor Tyndall had died not long before I left India, and in one of his obituary notices I had read that he was the first to point out that the noise made by falling waters was due to the minute air-globules contained in the same. No doubt raindrops in their descent take up air both in solution and suspension, but, watching these great liquid blobs flopping in millions in the lake around us, and making their peculiar blobby sound, I thought that the mere impact of the water-blobs themselves would be quite enough to account for the blobbery, if Tyndall had not said otherwise.

A little bird apparently got blown from the land by the squalls this day, and settled down on the boat's head, but flew away when we tried to catch him. By the time that the night shades had fallen, the wind was quite calm again, and the water without a ripple. We asked the Kumēr guide if this was the beginning of the rainy season. But it was not, and would not be yet for nearly a month. This was a dreary enough night, as everybody got drenched to the skin with the rain, and looked very miserable. Besides, I had just run out of my tobacco, and of the flour with which the gallant Vālloo used to cook my bannocks. No wonder, then, that we felt miserable. In fact, we were rapidly relapsing into utter barbarism, eh, Sir John Lubbock?

The new Kumēr guide that we brought with us to Angkor-Wát and through the lake was rather interesting in his way, and full of superstition, like most others of his kind. At night the boats were usually moored only a few feet from one another, and, whenever the shades fell, he and West kept up a continuous noisy chatter, every philosophic opinion of West being clinched with the words *charab, charab* by his new companion. The words *charab, charab* began to ring in my ears at last, and I asked what they meant, when West said the English word for *charab* was the word 'good'; that, in fact, it was used in conversation as we use the words 'very good, very good'—as an expression of consent to the speaker. The meaning of the word *charab* in Hindustani is 'bad,' just the very opposite of its meaning in Siamese; and so we nicknamed the new guide with the name of *Charab* during the rest of the voyage; and, as the oarsmen took it up, it has probably stuck to him ever since. There is much efficacy in a good nickname judiciously chosen. For here was this Kumēr guide rejoicing in the name of *Charab*, because the word meant 'good,' while a Hindoo would be highly offended by it, because the very identical word meant 'bad' in his vocabulary.

We had now actually left behind us the southern boundary of that portion of Kumēr, or ancient Cambodia, that now belongs to Siam, and were steering our way through the portion of the lake within the limits of modern Cambodia, of which the puppet king is still alive. Among the crew of the 'Lady of the Lake' was a young Kumēr lad, who could not be more than sixteen or seventeen years old. He was a gay, cheerful little fellow, but his incessant labour at the oar must often have tired him out; and he had been taken on board by the rest of the crew because he was an orphan boy who had lost father and mother when a mere child. I therefore frequently took a spell at this young lad's oar, in the mornings and evenings, when the sun would not be too overpoweringly hot, so as to relieve the young lad from the weariness of doing too much, and myself from that of doing too little.

The men rowed in the open sun in the space before and behind the hood in the middle of the boat, and, of course, no European would row in such a position in the heat of the day, if he could possibly help it. The Cambodians row like the Siamese, and they all do so standing up and looking forwards, like a Venetian gondolier. This style of rowing, though looking difficult at first, is not really hard to learn, and, after a few trials, I could row fairly well for a short spell, but could not stick to the business like the crew, who kept on jogging at it with exemplary perseverance.

On Wednesday afternoon we reached Préäm-Préstong, on the west side of the lake, for here the two sides of it approach one another within six or seven miles in a kind of hour-glass constriction, after which the lake broadens away again in a south and south-easterly direction. We arrived early at this village, and were fortunately in good time to see the people trawling for fish. A net like the one I have described, and some one or two hundred yards long, passed, but was not stretched, between two boats. The boats kept moving slowly onward, keeping their distance from one another, and dragging the net after them. The slack of the net naturally bulged away behind, and in the middle of this bulging portion was a kind of cul-de-sac, or big, narrow-necked bag of the same network material.

In the hollow formed by the bulging out of the net behind, a couple of men walked in the shallow water in front of the nets, as they were being slowly dragged through the water by the boats, and each of them was armed with a thickish stick. Whenever any of the fish, which appeared to be pretty abundant, got caught in the meshes of the net, it immediately began to splash vigorously, when one of the men hurried over to get a hold of it while still entangled; and then, after catching it, he dealt it two or three smart blows on the head with the stick, and so killed the fish, and placed it in the receptacle just noted. Fish must have very weak heads, as they are so easily killed by smart blows on their empty skulls.

This was rare fun, we thought, and on the principle of doing in Cambodia as the Cambodians do, I went over the side of the boat, nearly as nude as the natives themselves; and, arming myself with the tiller of the 'Lady of the Lake,' began to help the fishermen in their work of slaughter. And so did West, the valiant Vālloo, and the chattering 'Charab.' And there I smote the fish on the head with great precision, as if I had been brought up to the business, much to the amusement of the rustic natives. We enjoyed ourselves immensely this evening, after being kept inactive so long in the boats, and we got as much fish as we wanted for our trouble.

Most of the fish were about the size of a sea bream and not at all unlike it, but thinner and deeper in shape. In this same place, a little later on in the evening, we also saw some people setting fishing lines, and waded over to see what they were like. In general idea they were like what is known as small-lines in the north of Scotland, but with snoods only six or seven inches long, and with rather rude hooks. But then I suppose the fish in lake Telé-Sáp are not so canny (!) as the Scotch fish, and are silly enough to be imposed upon by anything. The bait on all the hooks that we looked at consisted of fids of fish, which is probably the only bait available along the muddy shores of the tideless Telé-Sáp.

It is evident then that the fish is caught in several ways, by hooks, by nets, by fishing stakes, and by spearing, which last practice is mostly confined to the rivers that flow into the Telé-Sáp towards the north, and to the largest of which I have already referred, as passing through Arrānh and Sisophon, and finally falling into the north-west of the lake below Battambong.

So wonderfully abundant, indeed, is the fish in this lake, that when the latter retires after its usual annual flood, the fish is frequently left high and dry on land during the process, and in sufficient quantity to serve as manure for the soil, which, however, one would think is rich enough without it.

There were any number of fish-eating birds in this neighbourhood, and, indeed, all over the lake, including large flocks of pelicans, flamingoes, and other birds that I had never seen before; for the lake throughout must be a grand feeding-ground for all fish-eating birds. At this place we also saw large numbers of porpoises gambolling about. Once or twice on the journey I tried to shoot one of the pelicans. But I killed none, as they generally kept too far away, and the boat bobbed about too much in the water.

'Charab,' who was delightfully officious, deprecated very much my trying to shoot the pelicans, and said that if I did so a storm was sure to follow. Such are the superstitions of various lands about the shooting or killing of certain birds and animals; for this was only another version of the story of the albatross, and yet it is very doubtful if 'Charab' had ever heard of the 'Ancient Mariner,' or the misfortunes that befell him after shooting that bird of evil omen.

'Charab' was a bit of a Jingo, and seemed very easily alarmed. But whether he was really so, or only pretending, in order to enhance his own business and personal importance, I am unable to say. He was also such an incessant talker, that, as his mouth was always full of the abominable *pansupari*, his intonation was none of the clearest. This inveterate habit of Indians and other Eastern races to chew their betel-nut and leaves is a very vile one, and leaves their mouths so sloppy and foul when chewing this favourite condiment of theirs. But neither among the Indians, nor yet among the Burmese, is this habit carried to such an extent as it is in Siam and the other parts we were now travelling through.

'Charab' was very anxious that we should not stay at Preäm-Préstong during the night, as he said this part of the country was infested with Chinese robbers; and that a little while ago a boat belonging to a friend of his had been plundered in this locality, and that the crew had to abandon the boat to save their lives, and let the Cantonese robbers carry off everything of value in the boat. West, who alone could speak to him, seemed to give credence to 'Charab's' story, and, under the circumstances, there was no use being too punctilious. However, it was too late to leave our moorings, as it was now getting quite dark, and we were two or three miles away from land.

During the first portion of the journey I was generally armed, and seldom slept without a loaded revolver beside my pillow, as a precaution against treachery on the part of the natives. But the latter had almost invariably received me with such unfailing goodwill, that I had lately dropped this practice as being too much of the Captain Bobadil style. This night, however, at the importunity of both West and 'Charab,' I gave them my shot-gun and a few rounds of cartridges into their boat, in order to give a warm welcome to the Chinese raiders, and also kept myself prepared for any surprise. Nothing happened. But it is only right to say that the great majority of these accidents occur when people are off their guard, without taking any precautions for their personal safety. Yet though the robbers did not come to attack 'Charab,' another accident happened which might have proved equally inconvenient.

At night-time everybody went on board the 'Roderick Dhu,' leaving me alone to my private cogitations in the 'Lady of the Lake.' When starting on this part of the trip, West was invited to put up at night in the same boat as myself, if he liked to do so. He preferred, however, to stay in his own boat, and he certainly had a more pleasant time of it there, as he and 'Charab' were always busy laying down the law on some important subject, for 'Charab' seemed a real prince among chatterers, in spite of the quids of *pansupari* that so frequently bulged out his cheeks and marred his eloquence.

This particular night the wind began to blow hard, and what did it do at last but drive my boat off her moorings, when I was alone in her, and fast asleep. They did not seem to keep a very good look-out on the other boat, in spite of their dread of the Chinese robbers, and so none of the men saw my boat driven away in the dark. Fortunately one of them woke up by the tossing of their own boat, and on looking about he missed mine. They immediately gave chase and recovered my boat at last, while I was still as sound asleep as Jonah. It would scarcely have been a pleasant sensation on waking in the morning to find myself alone, alone, all, all alone; alone on this wild, wild lake, perhaps out of sight of any shore; and with neither food nor fire, as everything of that sort was aboard the other boat. Thus the accident of being cast away, which I considered as a possible contingency on my first night at Telé-Sáp, at last took place, and it was fortunate for me that it ended so harmlessly.

The wind subsided after a while, and the boats were brought back to their former mooring ground after some little trouble, during which the 'Roderick Dhu' injured her stern. Having been so ruthlessly awakened I could sleep no more that night, but sat up till daybreak, watching the clouds scudding across the moon, which was then on the wane, and had only risen a short while before. I did not wonder much at the boat drifting away from her moorings. The wonder was, I thought, that she did not do so oftener, for the moorings of these boats are of the most primitive character. They simply consist in driving into the soft muddy bottom one or two long poles, which each boat carries for that purpose. This alone shows at once how shallow the greater portion of the lake is at this season, when we could moor in this fashion two or three miles from land.

It was curious to note the easy way in which one of these comparatively light men could drive these poles a couple of feet or more into the muddy soil by only laying their own weights upon the upper end of them from the gunwale of the boat. And yet when they went overboard themselves, as they sometimes did, they did not appear to sink so deeply into the mud after all. But experience teaches fools, and much more so men of ordinary common sense. I used to notice when I went myself to bathe in the lake that, when the water was shallow, I invariably sank into the muddy bottom more than when the water was deep, and came up, perhaps, to my shoulders; and when I thought about the matter the reason was not far to seek. When the water was shallow the soft, deep mud had to bear all my weight above the water-line, and I therefore sank deeply; whereas, when the water was deep enough to come up to my shoulders, the greater part of my weight was already nearly buoyed and balanced by the water itself, and I tripped along the muddy bottom with a light, fantastic toe. 'Eureka!' said I. 'I have found it. Why, it's the old, old tale of specific gravity after all.' And so, when these rough piles got driven into the slimy ooze, they held their grip tenaciously, especially when two were driven together in slightly different directions. And, as a matter of fact, the boat on this night got cast away, not by the poles losing their hold, but by the rest of the gear breaking. So much, then, for the crude but serviceable method of mooring boats on the remote inland lake of Telé-Sáp.

CHAPTER XIX

> ' Let me,' he cried, ' once more again,
> Go tread my Mother Earth,
> For there be perils on the main,
> And oh, by Jove, that berth
> Is cramped enough to make one roar
> With pangs and pains—let's go ashore.
> 							*The Landlubber's Lullaby.*

Landing at Chunnok-Tréän—Chinese praying paper—Why do devils wear shoes?—Outlets of Telé-Sáp—General remarks on ditto—Telé-Sáp's future prospects—The Giantess and the Pig—A truant husband—Floating down the river—Reach Kampong-Chenáng—A French frontier village—Reception by the French—Where, where was Captain Bertuzzi now?—Mispronunciation—' Mussoo, Mussoo Docteur'—Steam launch 'Cambodge'—Arrival at Penhom-Penh—English the coming Volapuk—But Gaelic shall never die.

AFTER duly repairing the stern of the 'Roderick Dhu,' which detained us some little time, we at length proceeded on our way, coming in sight of a few hills in the distance to the south. The lake, indeed, though generally known as Telé-Sáp throughout, is yet divided by the natives into three different portions, known under three different names, namely, Telé-Sap (proper), comprising the portion to the north of the constriction noted at Preäm-Préstong; Telé-Chamuá, the portion widening to the south-east; and Telé-Pókh, the portion more directly to the south, and at this low-water season a good deal separated from the other two portions by a series of islands, which are all covered over during the rains.

On Friday we stayed for an hour or two at a place called Chunnok-Tréän, and were able to go ashore for the first time since leaving Síäm-Réäp, for this village was really a *terra-firma*, and not a couple of miles away like most of the other villages. In this fishing village there were any number of Chinese, who apparently formed the greater portion of the people. This also was the last of the fishing villages of any considerable size. The lake all through simply swarms with fish of different kinds, and it is doubtful if any other two rivers in the world excel the Menam and Mekong rivers, as well as lake Telé-Sáp, in their abundance of the finny tribes.

We rambled among the bazaars whenever we got ashore, and got a packet of Chinese praying paper, very cheap. You don't know what a Chinese praying paper is? Well, at a certain time of the year, these valuable papers are burnt by the pious Chinese of the interior as an offering to the 'devils.' That was the interpretation I got from West. On the particular praying paper in my hand were imprinted various designs of what the 'devils' (*sic*) would receive when these papers were burnt.

West had already puzzled me in his usage of the word 'devil' in connection with his ghost stories, and it was not till this occasion that I discovered the meaning which he attached to it. I noticed on the paper in my hands various representations of useful articles, such as a chair, a candlestick, a pigtail, and various articles of clothing. But what struck me most was the figure of a pair of shoes. I remonstrated with West why they should be offering anything to devils, as they were very wicked, and deserved no offering or goodwill of any kind. I could, however, see the use of a candlestick, and even of a candle, if the devils could get them by burning these papers on which they were depicted, as they are supposed to be in a dark place. But I could not see the use of the articles of clothing shown on the paper, and as for the shoes, they were simply preposterous. 'Why,' cried I, in a burst of righteous indignation, 'why do they offer anything to devils, for they are the enemies of mankind, and never do any good; and why the shoes—for surely they are in a hot enough place not to require them?' Then West explained that the 'devils,' as he called them, were the souls or ghosts of departed relatives, and this also explained why he used the same term to the Penteānas that ran after him on a previous occasion.

We left Chunnok-Treān later on in the day, and that night moored near two small islands. There was some difficulty on this occasion for the first time in getting good, soft enough ground to stick the poles in ; so the mud, like everything else, has its own special uses, of which the casual observer is not always aware. The lake widened again beyond these islands, and after crossing this portion a few miles wide, we entered the largest effluent of the great lake Telé-Sáp after a fairly good trip, taking it all round ; though it must frankly be confessed that the memories of things done are more pleasing than the doing of them.

The water flows out of Telé-Sáp by various channels, to join the great Mekong river, of which newspaper readers have been reading so much not long ago, in connection with the Franco-Siamese troubles. The whole of this portion of the country is traversed by quite a network of water-channels, that divide and subdivide, and then join again in every possible manner, the same as the Menam does in the latitude of Ayouthia, only on a more extensive scale.

We followed the largest of these channels which debouches into the Mekong at Penhom-Penh, the capital town of the kingdom of Cambodia. As the word 'Menam' means *Mother of Waters*, so the word 'Mekong' means the *Boundary Water*, though at this time of day it is rather difficult to know how it originally acquired that name, as it really at present, or till very recently, forms no boundary of any country whatever, but on the contrary flows successively through South-west China, North-east Burmah, and then through Siam, Cambodia, and Cochin-China, where it finally falls into the China Sea.

It was through this principal outlet from Telé-Sáp that the 'Roderick Dhu' and the 'Lady of the Lake' proceeded. It varied much in its progress, according as it received tributaries or gave out some to the water channels ; and many of these channels are of course obliterated as such during the rainy season, when the lake rises and covers a large amount of area that was island and dry land when we were passing through.

A peculiar feature about these communications between lake Telé-Sáp and the great Mekong river is the fact that, in the slack or dry season, the water flows from the lake to the river, and at the height of the rainy season, from the river to the lake in the opposite direction. This is a strange fact, if it is a fact, and I believe it is. Roughly speaking, the lake will be a hundred or a hundred and twenty miles long at this time of year, but of course varies greatly according to the season. During the rains it covers a far greater area, flooding a large extent of country, more especially in a westerly direction.

The extremely muddy water of this lake (even at this time, when the inpour from the tributary rivers is at its lowest), as well as its very shallow character and general flatness of the surrounding land, naturally suggests to one that this portion of the country is of very recent geological formation; consisting, as it does, for the most part of simple alluvial deposits brought down from the Eastern Himalayas during comparatively recent geological ages. The greater portion of Siam south of the Laös mountains, along the southern border of which we crossed the country, and the greater portion of Cambodia also, consist of this recent soil, rich in rice, swamps, forests, and fevers.

And doubtless at a comparatively early future geological period the great lake Telé-Sáp will be sapped out, and be mostly dry soil filled in by the continuous *débris*; and then, except during the periods of inundation, its place will only be represented by river communication only. And while thus anticipating the future physical aspects of this portion of the country, one cannot help casting a glance behind, and picturing to himself the past history of the same.

In this retrospect it requires no great stretch of the imagination to fancy that when those wonderful ruins of Angkor-Wát and Angkor-Thóm were built, the locality may not have been nearly so far from the seaside as it is at present. Nay more, granted that things go on gradually as they now do, without any serious telluric disturbance, it is even possible to predict that the time will come when the greater part of the Gulf of Siam itself will be dry land by this same process of gradual deposition. For even already, this great gulf, one of the largest in the world, is so absolutely shallow, that any ship with ordinary length of cable can actually anchor in almost any part of it all the way from Singapore to Bangkok, a distance of something like a thousand miles.

The deltas formed at the mouth of the Menam and the neighbouring rivers of Tachim and Meklong (not Mekong,

o

please observe), are rapidly and perceptibly gaining on the narrow northern portion of the Gulf of Siam from year to year. And so recent is the geological formation on which Bangkok itself stands, that the shells of the most common shell-fishes have been found buried as much as twenty feet below the surface. Indeed, the greater part of this south-eastern corner of Asia may be called a mere modern country in the geological signification of the word.

But we had now left the great lake behind us, and were holding our course to Kampong-Chenáng. On the way we came in sight of a couple of hills a few hundred feet high; and hills being so rare hereabouts a fable was invented to account for their origin. They were not, however, created by angels like Angkor-Wát, but by a giantess and—a pig! 'Charab,' indeed, was not quite sure whether the giantess was an angel or not, but she was at any rate a little above the common standard, though she had the frail weakness of mere ordinary folk, namely, the weakness of falling in love. Her affections were misplaced too, like those of many others who are neither angels nor giantesses; for her choice fell upon a mere ordinary man quite unworthy of her.

For shortly after the honeymoon this wicked man appears to have grown tired of his unwieldy partner, and at last he ran away from her, as if he were a mere ordinary person of mere modern times. The giantess was cut to the quick by the conduct of her unfaithful husband, and started after him mounted on her favourite pig. But her husband had started on a pony, and, having got the lead, kept it. It would be highly amusing to watch the giantess pressing the pig, and to listen to the musical falsetto squeals of the latter. Yet all the efforts of the giantess and piggy-wiggy were of no avail, for on reaching the left bank of this river, the pony with the truant husband had already swum across it. And there the giantess with a true lover's sigh, and the pig with a true piggy-wiggy groan, laid themselves down and died. And there they still lie, and no mistake, in the form of the two hills mentioned. This story of the chattering 'Charab' must of course be quite true, for the hills are still there to testify to its truthfulness; and what else on earth could they possibly be but a giantess and a pig?

That evening we reached Kampong-Chenáng, where some Europeans were said to reside, because Kampong-Chenáng is the frontier village, occupied by the French in this part of Cambodia. The boatmen had worked hard to be sure to reach the village before dark, and as we found ourselves in ample time for that purpose, they dropped their oars to have their rice, while the two boats glided gently along with the current. At last we could make out a larger house than the rest in the middle of the village, near the bank of the river, and we naturally concluded that this was the house of the Europeans, and so it was.

There we let the boats float along. When we reached near enough, and while I was standing in front of the hood of my boat, we could make out three or four Europeans spying the two boats, and evidently wondering who in the world could we be. Whenever we landed I took with me West and Vālloo, and hurried to meet the strangers who were still standing on the verandah of the big house, and I broke the ice by expressing a hope that they spoke English. But they apparently could not, and so the conversation got more puzzling than ever. In this remote Eastern corner, to see white people exactly like one another, and yet requiring to speak to one another through the interpretation of Asiatics, was very edifying—especially to the Asiatics. And so the conversation went on from French to Cambodian, from Cambodian to Siamese, and from Siamese to indifferent English, or *vice versâ*. And then I began to think of Captain Bertuzzi, whom I had left a prisoner at Bangkok, and who would have been very useful on this occasion.

When landing from the boat I had forgotten the French passport, which I had taken the precaution of getting at Bangkok, in case I should pass through French territory. When thus conversing with difficulty, I understood one of the officials to be directing another to telegraph to the French authorities at Penhom-Penh the sudden arrival of a perfidious Briton from the far north. I then remembered about my credentials, and detaining the official for a moment, sent West to get the passport out of my cash-box. They were then apparently satisfied, and I understood them to agree among themselves that there was no necessity for telegraphing. Yet they did telegraph after all, as I found out not long afterwards.

They kindly asked me to have pot-luck with them at dinner, and I was glad to do so, in spite of our incompatibility of tongues; and after a little while we got on wonderfully well, for one of them in particular spoke some little English, though it was very difficult to understand him from the way he was pronouncing it, as he had evidently learnt it from books.

The senior of the three belonged to the city of Lyons, where President Carnot was assassinated not long afterwards, while another of them belonged to Ajaccio in the island of Corsica in the Mediterranean, and was really an Italian by extraction. Suspecting that I did not know where Ajaccio was, they brought over a small atlas to point it out to me. 'Oh yes,' I said, 'Ajaccio is in Corsica, where Napoleon was born.' They seemed to brighten up at the mention of Napoleon, who threw such a lustre over their country not a hundred years ago.

My casual hosts, as I said, knew a lot of English words, but it was the pronunciation that caused the trouble. For they had learnt them from books; and books, though very useful in their way, are quite incapable of imparting the niceties of pronunciation of any language whatever. Nor need we wonder at this. For it is only the other day that the English have found out the proper way of pronouncing Latin, which they have been mispronouncing for the last thousand years or thereabouts; that is to say, since first the Northerners came to know anything about that classic language at all. They brought over a biggish book written by somebody named Saunderson, who had evidently emigrated to France for his own if not for his own country's good; and his book was intended to smooth for Frenchmen the thorny way of learning English. The first sentence one of them read was, 'The locksmith was very ill, but was cured by the doctor,' and it would require a very 'cute doctor indeed to understand what the sentence meant as pronounced by the speaker.

I glanced hurriedly over certain pages of this book, but though it was doubtless a good book of its kind, it was far from being infallible. In a series of English words arranged in vertical lines on a certain page, their phonetic French pronunciation was given opposite them. In the same series were the words 'four' and 'for,' the one at the top, the other at the bottom of the line, and I saw that they were both phonetically spelt in French by the letters *f-o-r-e*. Now, no educated Englishman pronounces the words 'four' and 'for' in exactly the same way, nor either of them phonetically as *f-o-r-e*. To while away the time and say something, I pronounced these words for them as they ought to be pronounced, and in order to show further how difficult it is to pronounce English from the mere spelling alone, I took up the word 'four' again, and successively pronounced the words 'four,' 'pour,' 'sour,' and 'tour,' rolling my r's into chariot-wheels, to bring out their true Scotch flavour, and explaining how all these words are differently pronounced, though identical in both vowels and final consonants. The Frenchmen gaped, and perhaps thought to themselves what an excellent schoolmaster I should make to teach Frenchmen English, oblivious of the fact that I should first have to learn French myself.

And so the night passed, till I thought it was high time for me to be thinking of retiring. They cordially offered to put me up, but as people in outlandish places like Kampong-Chenáng have to rough it a good deal themselves, and have seldom much spare comfort, I preferred sleeping in the 'Lady of the Lake,' which had now become a kind of home to me. 'Charab,' the Jingo, was always afraid of robbers, and partly on his suggestion, we hauled the boats some fifty yards out into the stream, in order to swing clear to the breeze and current.

By this time I had got some tobacco, to prevent relapsing into utter babarism, &c.; and after hauling out into the stream, I was having a quiet last pipe sitting in the stern of the boat before withdrawing under my hood. I was not long sitting there when I saw all my quondam companions coming down the wooden staircase of the house, with lanterns in their hands, and walking to the river's edge. When they reached this spot, one of them began to wave a piece of paper over his head, and to shout across the water, 'Sir, Sir, Mussoo, Mussoo Docteur, telegramme, telegramme (waving the paper) Governeur, Cambodia, Penhom-Penh, steamer, steamboat, come to-morrow, bring Mussoo to Penhom-Penh;' and with the last word he made a sweep with his hand down the river in the direction indicated.

I could not make out at first what on earth he could

be driving at, and I called West in the other boat with his superior gift of tongues. At last, and after several repetitions, we concluded that they must have telegraphed to Penhom-Penh after all, and that they had received a reply that the Governor of Cambodia was sending a steamer up the river to bring me down to Penhom-Penh. I thanked my courteous hosts with all the '*mercies*' I could muster, and withdrew beneath my hood, not feeling quite sure that I quite comprehended the conversation.

But when I woke in the morning and peeped out of my shell, there, sure enough, was the pretty steam-launch the 'Cambodge' waiting to bring me down to Penhom-Penh, having arrived at Kampong-Chenáng in the course of the night. I went ashore for a short while, to say good-bye to the kind French officials, and to have a hurried look round the place. Kampong-Chenáng certainly did not seem a very enviable place to spend one's days in; and little do comfortable people at home realise the monotony and weariness of living in places like this one.

Kampong-Chenáng was quite a large village, on the bank of the river. The latter would be rising shortly, and then the site on which the French wooden house was then placed would be covered with water. They had already prepared for this by having the open under portion of the house packed full of large bamboos, which are always very buoyant, of course. And so when the river would rise and the water would come, the house, like another Ark, would float on the top of these buoyant bamboos. It would then be taken into a small creek in the vicinity and anchored there like a ship till the rain would begin to abate down again. As one of the strangers showed me this contrivance, and comically shrugged his shoulders, and contracted his eyebrows *à la France*, I began to think that Kampong-Chenáng was a particularly fine place to live out of.

But the good launch 'Cambodge' had got up her steam, and it was time for me to get on board. There was now no further use for either the 'Roderick Dhu' or the 'Lady of the Lake.' Nor was there for the chattering 'Charab' and his doughty crews; for they had done their duty and might now turn home again. And as the 'Cambodge

The "Lady of the Lake."

To face page 198.

steamed along the two humble boats before turning round, and 'Charab' and the boatmen asumed the usual attitude of palming their hands in front of their faces, in saying good-bye, I felt a kind of sorrow in parting with them. 'Poor children of nature,' thought I to myself, 'perhaps you are more innocent and faithful than people who lay claim to greater pretensions.' But the 'Cambodge' soon turned her nose down the current, and Kampong-Chenáng and all connected with it rapidly faded out of sight for ever.

We left Kampong-Chenáng at about eight o'clock in the morning, and reached Penhom-Penh about four o'clock in the evening. Supposing the 'Cambodge' to have steamed ten knots an hour down the current, this would give the distance by river between Kampong-Chenáng and Penhom-Penh at about eighty miles. Penhom-Penh itself, the capital town of Cambodia, is situated on the Telé-Sáp tributary as it falls into the main body of the great Mekong river, and this is the largest tributary that the Mekong receives in this region. Most of the town, including the King's Palace, is on the right bank of the Telé-Sáp branch, but numbers of houses are also on the left bank, above the angle formed by the junction of this branch and the main river.

The house of the French Governor was quite near the landing-place, and when I went to thank him for sending the 'Cambodge' up river for me, we found that we could not understand one another. This, however, did not prevent him from putting me up during the three days that I stayed at Penhom-Penh. Like many another capital town in the East, Penhom-Penh is not the old capital of the country, but Udong, a dilapidated place further up this branch, and which we passed on our way down. And it is here that the mother of the present king lives to this day.

M. Marquant, the French Governor, was an old bachelor, and the only person who lived with him then was his private secretary, or *secrétaire peculier*, as they say in France. Neither of them was proficient in English, and I felt a little awkward at my inability of conversing intelligently with them. My only excuse was the consoling reflection that it is simply impossible for any traveller to know the language of every people he may meet in his wanderings, and that the French had as much right to learn English as I had to learn French, though I *am* going to learn French some day.

Indeed, the French are quite the worst linguists in Europe, worse even than the English. Not because Frenchmen cannot become linguists, but because they don't care to take the bother. French till very recently was the most prevalent of all the European languages, and is so still on the continent of Europe. So that Frenchmen hitherto had not the same incentive to learn foreign languages, for it is of comparatively recent years that the country has taken to colonisation on anything like a large scale.

English, on the other hand, has lately been taking the wind out of the sails of all the other European languages, by this very process of colonisation. We neither know nor appreciate the debt due in this respect to the random rover, nor how much the language, as well as the general prosperity of the nation at large, owes to commerce and private enterprise. These wanderers do not always bring the most classical English to the lands they visit. That would be superfluous, for the populace of any country do not learn a foreign language with strict observance to grammatical rules. They sometimes do not know their own grammar, and their British interlocutors do not always know theirs. But yet it is the bargainings and dealings of Englishmen with natives of far-away countries, that help on the English tongue more than anything else This is quite a mercenary view to take of the business, but it is the true one. The natives comprehend that it is for their advantage to learn English, and many of them do learn a smattering of it in one way or another on that account.

The Chinese, the most conservative of nations, speak more English in port-towns than they do of any other language except their own. True, it is 'pigeon' English, by no means easily understood by the stranger. But there it is, and it spreads and improves as it goes along. Yet the number of people in the world who speak English at present is not nearly so large as the number of people who speak, say, Chinese or perhaps Hindustani. But English has now got such a lot of widely-spread and separate focuses, that it is quite within the sphere of possibilities for it to become the universal language, and real international volapuk of nations. This does not mean, however, that all other languages must die a sudden death on that account, for languages take a very long time to die. It is doubtful, for instance, if the Gaelic of the Highlands of Scotland was ever spoken by a couple of millions at any one given time. Yet it has continued to live on and on since the beginning of the world, and will probably do so till the end of it.

CHAPTER XX

There once was a woman who lived in a shoe,
With plenty of money and nothing to do,
And how to expend it I'm blest if she knew.
. . . .
She asked of the prophet, she bothered the priest,
Her rapture of soul having nobly increased,
Then built a pagoda—and slowly deceased.
Eastern Anecdotes.

Description of Penhom-Penh—What is a pagoda?—A work of merit—Promotion to Nirvana—Effects of pagodas on scenery—The great pagoda of Penhom-Penh—French Governor of the Kingdom of Cambodia—Atenuse, my *secrétaire peculier*—Royal palace of Penhom-Penh—*Kohn-Chik* again—King Norōdom the Second—His habits of life—Unable to visit him—Luang-Prabang—View of the Buffer State.

THE capital town of Penhom-Penh is not a very large one, nor is it particularly beautiful or romantic. It is said to contain fifty thousand inhabitants, though the visitor would scarcely think so, and it has lately been greatly improved by the French authorities. The town, they say, receives its name from an old woman named Penh, who spent all her wealth in building a pagoda here. The word 'Penhom' means a 'hill' in this language, and enters into the names of some other places that we travelled through, such as Penhom-Sok, the village that we visited when we went astray. Penhom-Penh, then, means 'Mother Penh's Hill.' It is not a hilly place by any means, according to our ideas of hills, but there is a small mound on the outskirts of the town, about as big as the grave of a fairly-sized giant; and it is on this hill that Mother Penh built the beautiful pagoda. But she, poor woman, went the way of all flesh, and till the French took the country over, the pagoda was getting sadly out of repair.

Some readers may not know what a pagoda really means

and I don't know that I understand all about it myself. But it may be roughly described as a monumental cairn, built to the honour and glory of Buddha, the chief character in the Buddhist religion. The building of a pagoda is what the Buddhists call a 'work of merit,' because it goes further than any other good work towards expediting the builder to the attainment of Nirvana or personal extinction—that sound, sound sleep from which there is no awaking.

The pagodas vary immensely in size, from the simple white conical cairn on the top of a hillock, to the great Shway-Dagon Pagoda at Rangoon, one of the largest shrines in the world. Monasteries are sometimes connected with the very largest pagodas, as with the Arracan Pagoda near Mandalay, where I once occupied the room of one of the priests. But by far the largest number of them are solid structures only, without any interior, and of no use on earth save the toil and trouble of building them.

It is comparatively few of them that contain an image of the Buddha, or are resorted to for religious purposes. They are simply 'works of merit,' great and small, that make smooth and rapid the way to the utter annihilation of the builders, surely neither a noble nor devout consummation to be prayed for by aspiring humanity. Yet it is the principal ingredient in the Buddhist religion all the same. Again, though there is great merit in building a pagoda, there is none whatever in repairing one after the builder's death. It is his work of merit alone, and nobody else has got anything to do with it, either then or thereafter.

It would only be reasonable to suppose, when a fine pagoda had been built, and the builder had died, that his surviving bosom friends would naturally like to keep his memory green by repairing his pagoda. But it is not so; and except in the case of the very largest pagodas, which become more or less public State property, the pagodas are allowed to decay with the death of the builders. If you wish then to reach the utter extinction of Nirvana in a hurry, you must build a pagoda for yourself, for the mere repairing of your friend's will avail for nothing to either his shade or yours, when you start on your mysterious journey. It may not be absolutely necessary for a Buddhist to build a pagoda to attain Nirvana in the long, long run, but the building of one, and especially a big one, will do much to hurry on the expedition. Hence the rich presumably require fewer incarnations and transmigrations than the poor in arriving at the final silent shore.

The effects of this belief lead to an enormous number of these pagodas being scattered broadcast over these lands, and the country certainly seems more pleasing on account of them. Burmah, however, in this respect surpasses all other countries, for it is pre-eminently the country of pagodas. The deserted town of Pagān alone, on the left bank of the Irrawaddy, is said to contain not less than ten thousand of these crumbling monuments; and when seen from the deck of one of the river steamers, when the river is up, the whole place looks like a great cemetery covered with conspicuous whited sepulchres.

The pagoda of Penham-Penh is one of the very finest. It is not entirely a solid cairn, like most of the smaller ones, but has got rooms, niches, and recesses in it; and it is deemed extremely sacred by the inhabitants. On this account, one of its rooms, I was told, was used as a native court, as the inhabitants have got such superstitious fear and veneration for it, that none of them within its precincts dare deviate from telling the truth. Wonderful pagoda! Would that there were more of your kind, that would make people at all times to tell the truth. Old Mother Penh, therefore, has done a good work of merit, and has probably achieved annihilation long ago on account of it.

Her swell pagoda, though, was rapidly passing away into its own Nirvana, or extinction, when the French came on the scene; and they, good Catholic Christians that they are, restored the pagoda thoroughly, without probably ever thinking that by doing so they would sooner reach Nirvana or not. And now the Penhom-Penh pagoda is the principal spectacle of Penhom-Penh.

Next perhaps in interest is the King's Palace, which, however, is nothing very much of a show, as compared with the Palace at Bangkok, or the Golden Palace of Mandalay, even before the latter was desecrated, and converted into mere Government offices.

Before arriving at Penhom-Penh we were told that there was an Englishman living there, but the Englishman turned out to be a German, who kept a store up there,

and who spoke English very well. The first evening of
our visit to Penhom-Penh, I understood that next morning
they would get an interpreter for me during my stay.
This was a large-boned native of Martinique, nearly as
dark as an African, but with joyous good nature beaming
through his nearly sable features. Next evening I drove
down to the Palace along with the private secretary, with
Atenuse, the Martinikan, acting the part of interpreter
between us.

Atenuse spoke English rather well, and said, I think,
that he was a born British subject, though he was then an
ardent Frenchman, and a clerk in the Penhom-Penh
High Court. At the Palace itself we met even a Cambodian
who spoke English. He had been sent to Singapore by the
last king, to be educated there, and was now the chief
man at the treasury of Penhom-Penh. He had not spoken
English for years, he said, and that I was the first Englishman he had ever seen at Penhom-Penh. By-and-by he
may see plenty of them, passing through Penhom-Penh on
their way to Angkor-Wát.

The Palace, taken as a whole, is too modern to interest
the traveller much, for the most prominent part of it has
been built mostly in European fashion by the French
themselves. And though this doubtless does not diminish
the comfort of the same, yet it lacks the charm of quaintness. I was very keen on paying a visit to the King; but
though the Governor, I believe, wrote him for that purpose, I was not able to see His Majesty, on the plea that
he was not well. His Majesty, King Norōdom the Second,
they say, is seldom seen by anyone, as he confines himself
to the Palace, and spends most of his time in his harem,
smoking, and drinking magnum-bonums of champagne.

Till recent years the kingdom of Cambodia owed more
or less suzerainty to the larger kingdom of Siam. But
the courts of the two kingdoms did not pull well together,
and when the French came on the scene, the new king
of Cambodia threw himself into the arms of France, and
thereby cut off his own nose to spite his own face. King
Norōdom, the present king, has the honour, if honour it
may be called, of being the last king of Cambodia, for he
is to be succeeded by no successor; and it may be emphatically said of him that he reigns but does not govern.

He is a mere puppet, who used to get a thousand dollars a day from the French in exchange for his kingdom; and whatever his kingdom may be worth, this is far too high a price for His Majesty Norōdom the Second.

During my short stay at Penhom-Penh Atenuse, the Martinikan, was always at my disposal, and in fact became my *secretary peculiar!* I paid a visit with him to the King's bathing-house on the side of the river, which was much out of repair, as I fancy that His Majesty and his harem seldom bathe there now. We also revisited the Palace when they were going to perform the inevitable ceremony of Kohn-chúk on one of King Norōdom's sons, who had just come of age for that function of haircutting. Quite a crowd of natives thronged about the gate and thoroughfare, along which the procession was to pass; but after staying in vain for a little while, I could not wait any longer for fear of losing my dinner. The ceremony of Kohn-chúk must be going on pretty frequently in the palaces of Siam and Cambodia. Yet His Majesty King Norōdom the Second is not nearly so prolific as some of the kings mentioned on a previous page, as he has only eleven sons and nineteen daughters—quite a small quiverful in comparison.

Near the Mekong, a good deal further north than Penhom-Penh, was the scene of Phra Yott's feat of arms, that had landed him in such trouble at the time I left Bangkok, and near the same is the portion of country that is the present subject of dispute between Siam, France, and Great Britain. I should have wished very much to have visited this identical locality, but unluckily I was not able to do so. The means of communication up in that direction were extremely slow at this time of year, and anything but extremely sure. Besides, alas! my time was not my own, and I feared that my leave from India would expire when I should perhaps be locked up in these remote regions. I had, therefore, reluctantly to abandon this project.

Suffice it to say here, then, that in that latitude the British possession of Upper Burmah extends in an easterly direction across the Mekong, in a belt of land seventy or eighty miles across from north to south. It is between this belt of land and the French Indo-Chinese province of

Tonkin, that it seems so desirable to place some neutral zone, to act as a buffer to both countries. And it is therefore the particular corner of the country that has lately contributed to acquire for the whole of Siam the *sobriquet* of the Buffer State, after which this narrative receives its appropriate designation. The original intention was to place this strip of ground under the dominion of the Celestial Empire, but at the moment of writing, John Chinaman is getting such a drubbing from the dapper little Japs, that I am afraid this arrangement will fall through, as the Son of the Heaven has at present quite enough to do to look after his own wide and loosely-jointed dominions.

The day before I was going to leave Penhom-Penh the Governor gave an entertainment to some of the French residents of the place, and here I was fortunate enough to come across one or two people who spoke English, and with whom I was therefore able to chat more freely than with the others.

CHAPTER XXI

> You'd make me a citizen; well, to be sure,
> 'Tis more than I ever could hope to procure;
> But why for the boon do you force me to pay?
> An honour is none that is bought in that way.
> *The Ready Response.*

Farewell to Penhom-Penh—In England they drink scandal and tea—In France, coffee and brandy—The 'Nam-vian'—The Irrawaddy and the Mekong compared—Shallow coast of Cochin-China—Reach Saigon—The Café Anglais—Noor Khan the Mohammedan—The steamship 'Schwalbe'—Commercial interests of Great Britain and France in Siam—Progressive character of the Siamese—What to do with the servants—Vālloo turns trump—Becomes a Frenchman—A peculiar advocate—The town of Saigon—British bunkum.

It was now high time to say good-bye to M. Marquant, the Governor of the kingdom of Cambodia, who had taken me down from Kampong-Chenáng, and entertained me during my short stay at Penhom-Penh. For the steamer 'Nam-vian' was out there in the confluence of the two rivers, and was sailing away to Saigon that early morning.

The Mekong is already a large river before receiving the Telé-Sáp tributary at Penhom-Penh. It then, however, becomes a much larger one. But it soon afterwards splits into two, and the confluence arising from the two rivers coming from the north, before splitting into the two rivers flowing to the south, is known to the French under the name of 'Quatre Bras.' It is next to impossible to judge of the size of a river by sailing through a portion of it only. At New Orleans, for instance, near where the mighty Mississippi debouches into the Gulf of Mexico, nobody would think that it is the longest and the second largest river in the world; and comparatively small rivers, during certain stretches of their course, put on an appearance as if they were really the mighty mothers of waters.

I was familiar enough at one time with the Irrawaddy, the beautiful river that flows through Burmah from one end to the other, and was with the first expedition that ever ascended so far up as Mougoung, some ten or eleven hundred miles by river from the sea, and till then never visited by Europeans. And over the greater portion of it I sailed several times. But judging of the Mekong at Penhom-Penh, I should think it is fully as large, or even larger than the Irrawaddy, while no one knows precisely how long either of them may be, as the remote sources of both alike are hidden among the mists and mysteries of the mountains of Thibet, flowing and tumbling among those undiscovered glens and gullies, from whose bourne no European traveller has as yet returned.

But while giving the Mekong the credit of being probably larger, it is neither so straight nor so navigable as the Irrawaddy. There are twists and turns in both of them, of course, as in every other river in the world, but those in the Irrawaddy are comparatively few, while the navigation of the Mekong is also much marred by the rapids that occur further up in its course. The Irrawaddy, too, splits and squanders less than the Mekong, and keeps pretty well together till quite near the Bay of Bengal, whereas the Mekong splits nearly as high up as Penhom-Penh itself. This point, however, is in favour of the Mekong, for even after giving off this large and navigable offshoot, it still remains a large river itself, and navigable to deep-draught vessels all the way to the above-mentioned city. Indeed, the captain of the 'Nam-vian' said that the ship drew sixteen feet of water, and there is no steamer of the Irrawaddy Flotilla Company with anything near this draught. But the whole of this portion of the country, like the greater portion of Lower Siam, is entirely rich alluvial soil, amply supplied with natural waterways, being cut up in every direction with quite a network of intercommunication.

The 'Nam-vian' was comfortable enough, and had none of those unwieldy 'flats' on either side of her that so seriously impede one's speed up the Irrawaddy, or at any rate that used to do so once upon a time. The captain of her also spoke English, which was another point in the

P

ship's favour.[1] I had always thought that we were a much less temperate nation than the French; but there was the real state of matters on the authority of a French copybook! How I pitied the poor Frenchmen, swigging away at their brandy and coffee, while we were going in for scandal and tea only.

We called at several places on the way down the Mekong, which require no particular mention here, and reached Mytho about two o'clock in the morning. This river port is connected with Saigon by rail, which, with the exception of a small piece in Tonquin, is the only railway hitherto in all French Indo-China. Nearly all the passengers left the ship here, and went to Saigon by rail, while I stayed with the ship so as to go round the coast, as there was nothing to be seen in going on to Saigon by land at night-time. The only incident of note that occurred during the short trip was in the case of a Chinaman, who was being brought to Saigon as a prisoner for trial, and who, though handcuffed, jumped overboard during the night, and was probably drowned.

Every river has its bar as every Jack his Jill, and so has the Mekong. And, therefore, when we reached towards the mouth of the river, we had to wait an hour or two for the return of the tide, before we should be able to cross the bar. And then we sailed into the open China Sea for some considerable distance, as the coast along here is very shallow for a long way out. There is sometimes a heavy swell on this coast, and the 'Nam-vian' required all her deep draught to get through it all. The coast is also so sandy and shifty that it requires careful watching, and the ship this time was actually guided by buoys and stakes, when ten or twelve miles away from the land. By-and-by we entered the comparatively small river on which Saigon is placed, the most twisty of its kind; and that same afternoon I landed safely in the neat little town of Saigon, the capital town of all the French possessions in the Far East.

I had been told at Penhom-Penh that there was a café

---

[1] Here I met Saunderson's exercises again, but in manuscript this time; Exercise No. 9 particularly amused me: *En Angleterre on aime le thé avec du pain et du beurre; en France on prefere le coffee et la l'eau de vie*—In England they like tea with some bread and butter; in France they prefer coffee and brandy. On reading this sentence my heart bounded with joy.

at Saigon where they spoke English, and which was called the Café Anglais on that account. And as Atenuse, my *secretary peculiar* up there, had telegraphed to this café, I found someone from it waiting at the pier when the ship arrived, and to the Café Anglais I repaired in due course.

It was kept by a man named Noor Khan, one of the purest and best of Mohammedan names; and I was a little surprised to find the name so far away East, though people of all creeds and colours wander largely about nowadays. If there is one tenet better than another in the Mussulman faith, that tenet is—'Thou shalt not drink,' otherwise it is essentially a sensual religion, whose very paradise is full of carnal pleasures and black-eyed Susans. The principal Mohammedan precept then is, 'Ye may kiss yer lass, but ye maun na drink yer glass, and ye may aye whastle on the Sawbath.'

On coming downstairs the next morning I met Noor Khan in tow with two officers from ships in the harbour, and swigging away at beer with keen appreciation. Noor Khan spoke English well, and invited me to join them. But beer had always a too fattening effect on my flesh and a too flattening effect on my spirits; and, besides, it was too early in the morning to take anything. Nay more, I was shocked to see a Mohammedan with the thorough name of Noor Khan drinking away like a mere ordinary Christian. 'You, Noor Khan,' I said, 'an ancient Mohammedan, and swigging away at beer; I'm ashamed of you.' And then Noor Khan immediately laid out to abuse Mohammed and all his belongings. I had a shrewd suspicion, however, that Noor Khan was no more a convert from Mohammedanism than I was, for the simple reason that he never was a Mohammedan. He was a middle-aged man, of a rich olive complexion and good features—but he was no Mohammedan. He had probably adopted the name as rather an aristocratic one, and I have a shrewd suspicion that Noor Khan was an Indian Portuguese, who had originally started from Goa, near Bombay, and whose real name might possibly be Piedro Desouza.

When sailing up the river on the day of arrival, we passed a small German ship called the 'Schwalbe,' lying at the river-side. It has already been described how the little ship 'John B. Say' was sunk by the Ocean-butterfly Fort, while guiding the French men-o'-war on their way to Bangkok. This small ship of one hundred and fifty tons was then the only regular ship plying between Bangkok and Saigon, and she made the round voyage once every four or five weeks. When she was sunk and disabled, there was no French ship to take her place, and this same 'Schwalbe' was chartered for a season by the French Government from a German company, in order to carry the mails between the two cities.

We were, therefore, glad to see the 'Schwalbe,' as she would be leaving for Bangkok in two or three days at the latest. My agreement with West and Välloo was that they should have full pay and passage paid, till such time as they would reach Bangkok back again. But, behold, on making inquiries, we found that the charter of the 'Schwalbe' had just expired, that she was no longer on the run between Saigon and Bangkok, and that, in fact, there was no direct communication at all by sea between the two places at this time.

The 'Schwalbe' would be eight or nine hundred tons, and therefore a great improvement on the 'John Baptist' with her wretched one hundred and fifty tons only. One or other of them represented the whole regular tonnage plying between French Indo-China and Bangkok, the capital city of Siam; and after the 'Schwalbe' dropped, there was no communication whatever till a ship would arrive in the Far East, which was then being built on the Clyde. This state of matters contrasted very much with the prompt and efficient communication established between Bangkok and the British possessions of Singapore and Hong Kong. Instead of a monthly communication, as lately with Saigon, Bangkok has regular communication with Singapore at least twice a week by the Blue Funnel Line, besides any number of outside ships like the 'Independent,' in which I had sailed myself. And, again, there is a regular weekly communication with Hong Kong by the Scottish Oriental Line, possessing about a dozen ships with an average of a thousand tons, and the handsomest little vessels of their kind I have ever seen.

By far the greater portion of the industry of Siam is also in British hands, like the large railway they are at present constructing between Bangkok, Ayouthia, and Korāt, and which will be opened within a year or two. According to the last official Blue Book issued by the

British Government on the Franco-Siamese question, it was shown that 87 per cent. of exports and 97 per cent. of the import trade of Siam were with Great Britain.

This book does not wish particularly to dabble much in politics, as there are plenty of irresponsible babblers running about, who only too readily rush into those thorny paths where wise men fear to tread. Yet I cannot help saying here how deeply interested the British nation must necessarily be in the affairs of Siam, whose annexation by another European Power would be a serious blow at both the prestige and commerce of our country in the Far East. Besides, Siam—next to Japan—is by far the most progressive nation in the whole of the East; and it would be a pity, then, that such a promising child of civilisation should be smothered in its infancy.

It was very disappointing that the 'Schwalbe' had stopped plying to Bangkok, as this was the way I intended to send the servants back to where they started from, and the only way now open was to send them round by Singapore, and so on to Bangkok. The 'Schwalbe' was sailing for Singapore in a day or two, and would bring them on their journey so far. She was sailing a little too soon for myself, as I wanted to stay seven or eight days at Saigon; but the interpreter was anxious to go with the 'Schwalbe,' as he was like a fish out of water at Saigon from his ignorance of French, though he was glib enough in the Siamese and Chinese languages. Indeed, though he was a very small man, he had a very large head, that looked almost bigger than his body when the great helmet was on, and I should think that he had a special aptitude for languages, though hitherto imperfectly developed.

Their duties were practically finished when we came in touch with the French at Kampong-Chenáng, so that I had now no further use for them. Paying them up therefore till the probable date of their arrival in Bangkok, and for a few days more, in case of unforeseen detention, they were free to proceed with the 'Schwalbe,' if they liked. Válloo, however, had appeared to me such an ultra-foolish lad, that I took the precaution of giving all that was due to him to the interpreter, for handing it over to Válloo's wife on reaching Bangkok, leaving Válloo himself with only enough to take him along. To secure his interests still further, I took a receipt for the money from West, and gave it to Vālloo, so that he could lawfully claim his own when he reached his destination.

And thus we peaceably parted, as they were going with the 'Schwalbe' that day to Singapore, and I naturally thought I had seen the last of them. Later on that same evening, who suddenly burst into my room but the inevitable Vālloo! I was quite surprised, for I thought he should be gaily steaming down the river by this time, and he was so excited that I could not make out what was up with him, as he tossed his long lanky arms about in a very edifying fashion. Whatever else was wrong with him, it was evident that Vālloo had been paying court in the bazaar to his friend Lord Shumshoo, for that was certain. He held a slip of paper in his hand, which he gave me, and though it was written in French, a language with which I am not very conversant, as the reader already knows, I concluded from it that Vālloo had become a French citizen —which he had!

The image of his poor little wife came at once to my memory; for the day we started from Bangkok she came to the pier with a tiny little infant in her arms, to say good-bye to her husband; and thinking even then that Vālloo had not done the best with the advance bounty, the very last act of grace I did before stepping on board the launch was to give her a few *ticāls*, and tell her not to be afraid, and that her husband would come back again all right. Was Vālloo then going to forsake his little wife and to live at Saigon?

He was so excited that I could not well make out what he was driving at, nor was I at all sure that he was telling the truth. I concluded, therefore, that he was purposely forsaking his wife; and though she might be no beauty, still she was his. In real righteous indignation I got hold of him by the arm, gently pushed him outside the door of the room, and earnestly prayed him never to see my face again. And so Vālloo, poor beggar, went away crest-fallen enough.

The door of my room was nearly over the bar of the café, and being then open, I heard people in the bar talking English, and on leaning over the banister, I concluded they were talking about Vālloo, though they did not of course know his name. I went down to inquire. A marine engineer had just landed at Saigon, and had seen

that Vālloo had not been permitted to go with the
'Schwalbe,' as he was a native, and had no proper document to leave the colony, while West was allowed to
proceed without him. Nay more, he had seen Vālloo being
converted into a French citizen very much against Vālloo's
will ; and that the French officials had taken not less than
seven and a half dollars of his pocket money in exchange
for that proud privilege, which was duly certified by the
slip of paper that Vālloo had given me.

I did not know whether to laugh or cry, to see Vālloo's
citizenship so eagerly sought after. But though Vālloo
was by no means an ideal servant on a journey like this,
yet I never disliked him, as I thought he was only a little
'daft,' and people are seldom unkind to poor daft bodies.
I called Vālloo back again, as he was still lingering about
the café, and I then became his real *ma-bap*, or his mother
and father, as they say in Hindustan, for I was duty bound
to protect him in his distress.

I tried hard to get back for him the seven and a half
dollars of which he had been unjustly deprived, but without
success. They were nominally worth thirty shillings to
him, quite a large sum for a person of his means.

I went to the British Consulate to get his wrongs
righted, but the Consul was not in. But I saw him the
next day, and he sent his first assistant with me to the
French Emigration Office to get back the almighty dollars
for Vālloo. I soon saw that in the Consul's assistant,
Vālloo had a very poor advocate to plead his cause ; for
he was always consenting with his confounded ' *wee, wee*,'
to whatever the French official would say. I got so
disgusted at last that I took Vālloo away, recouped him
for his loss myself, and was done with the business.

A few days afterwards I drove out with the British
Consul to a sort of summer-house he had five or six miles
out of Saigon. On returning to his house in the evening,
who was there waiting for him but the chief assistant,
accompanied by his wife and sister-in-law, neither of whom
could speak English. And during the conversation I
discovered, though the Consul's assistant possessed the
good old Irish name of O'Connell, that he was born at
Pondicherry, a small French possession on the Coromandel
coast of India, that his wife was French—and that he was

a Frenchman himself! No wonder then that Vālloo had so poor an advocate, and that he had lost his dollars, or that I had vicariously lost them in his place.

I had been in Saigon some years before this time, and though the town in the interval had not grown remarkably in size, it had done so in beauty. The trees that line so many of the thoroughfares had grown apace, and had converted not a few of them into beautiful avenues. A large creek that during my previous visit passed from the river through a portion of the town, and seriously obstructed the passenger traffic, had now been entirely filled in, and actually formed the principal boulevard of the whole place, at the top of which one of the military bands played twice a week.

There is not a military station in the whole of British India to which Saigon would yield the palm in regularity, cleanliness, and artificial beauty. This is saying a great deal, for military stations in India are particularly well looked after. As regards natural beauty, however, Saigon does not profess to possess any. It is situated on the right bank of the Saigon river, some fifty miles by river from the sea, and is built on a swampy and feverish patch of ground nearly overflooded in the rainy season, and all of it is as flat as ditch-water. The idea of the town is planned on a most magnificent and extensive scale, and Government House is one of the very finest European residencies in the whole East.

But the houses throughout the planned-out town do not rise so rapidly as might be wished to fill in the vacant spaces, and there are empty gaps here and there, especially toward the outskirts, that give the town a vacant and incomplete appearance. British towns in the East rise so much more rapidly. So I have heard it so often and often said; for in this respect, at any rate, we need not pray God to give us a good conceit of ourselves. And so, though the statement is true in general terms, yet we are so accustomed to vaunt about our own honourable selves that it is only right to say that some of them *don't* rise so rapidly after all. Is Madras growing by leaps and bounds? And what of the ancient city of Malacca, once the greatest emporium in Orient lands? But I shall reach Malacca by-and-by, and tell you all about it.

CHAPTER XXII

The Baron, the Baron, he tore his hair,
The Baron was wrathful beyond compare.
. . . .
And why was the Baron so wild with rage,
That nothing on earth could his wrath assuage?
. . . .
I'll tell you the reason, the why, and the what,
'Twas only because—they had stolen his hat!
The Bouncing Baron.

Välloo converted against his will—Bite of a mad dog—Välloo again in trouble—Could not possibly part with Välloo, my Arab steed—Cape St. James and Poulo-Condor—The s.s. 'Tibre'—Her French captain—'Oh, yes, yes'—Indian conjurers—Robbery of my gold watch—Conjurers confined in cells—The Baron and his jewels—The guilty thief—Sentenced to two years' imprisonment—Välloo becomes the Old Man of the Sea.

SAIGON is the largest French military station in the Far East, but as a military station it is not so large as some military stations in India, none of which, however, is very large, when viewed from a European point of view. From the civil and commercial view, it may be looked upon as part of the much larger native town of Chalon, which is only four or five miles away, and with which it is connected both by water and by a narrow railway. Viewed in this light, Saigon is more important than it really looks in itself.

It has got beautiful shady drives in and out of the town, fine Zoological and Botanic Gardens, and a nice theatre, better than any in India, and the companies of which are subsidised by the French Government. What would the British Mrs. Grundy say if we began to subsidise theatres from public funds? After these, the most characteristic things about the town are its open-air *cafés* and its fine shops. Though Buonaparte called us a nation of shopkeepers, the French are just as shoppy.

Indeed, commercial enterprise, shops or no shops, and that restless love of adventure, have conduced to Britain's greatness quite as much as the mere vanity of military glory ; for our country, without being so military as some other countries, is as martial as any of them, which is the proper thing to be. There are many wheels within wheels in a great community, and though the man best at making money may not, perhaps, be the best to make a hero, yet a great nation must comprise both, as well as fools, knaves, clowns, and philosophers.

The only Englishman who lived at the Café Anglais was Mr. W——, a marine engineer, who first told me of Valloo's involuntary naturalisation. The poor fellow was down enough on his luck himself, as he had lately been bitten by a mad dog, or a dog supposed to be mad ; and he had gone all the way from the British island of Penang to be treated in French Saigon after the Pasteur method. It took him something like a fortnight to go through the whole process of rabbit-brain inoculation, and he was still staying at Saigon when I left that place. I shall tell later on how the life of this engineer was probably saved by his trip to Indo-China, apart altogether from the Pasteur cure.

Having now done all I wanted to do in Saigon, I prepared to depart in a small ship called the 'Tibre,' belonging to the Messageries Maritimes Company, the largest French Marine Company, and perhaps the largest shipping company in the world. This little ship 'Tibre' leaves Saigon for Singapore and *vice versâ* every fortnight, alternating in this respect with one of the great ocean liners of the same company, and establishing a weekly communication between Singapore and Saigon in each direction east and west.

By sailing eastwards by this local mail from Singapore to Saigon, the traveller would have a week's stay at Saigon and surroundings, and could then sail by one of the Messageries Maritime's ocean liners on to Hong Kong, China, and Japan. In the opposite direction westwards, the traveller would land from Hong Kong at Saigon from one of the said ocean liners, stay a week there as before, and then proceed to Singapore by this local mail. This trip is well worth doing, as a change from the beaten tracks ; and if the traveller goes to put up at the Café Anglais, please give my respects to that arch-Mohammedan, Mr. Noor Khan, and tell him I am very well.

The 'Tibre' was by no means a very small ship, nearly a thousand tons, and she was this time lying out in the river, a short distance from shore. And so Välloo and myself got a shore-boat, put our luggage into it, and went gaily on board the 'Tibre' on a certain early morning. When getting my luggage arranged in one of the cabins of the ship, I learnt that they were taking Välloo on shore again! That fatal slip of paper they had given him against his will, and for which he had to pay seven and a half dollars, also against his will, was now becoming a veritable thorn in the flesh of poor Välloo. If he had been my private servant (which he was), without this crass piece of paper, there would be no obstacle in his way at all. But by this unfortunate document he had practically become a Frenchman, and as a native, he could not leave the colony without a fresh passport.

This was a fine kettle of fish that we were in now. The official, who pressed for taking Välloo on shore, knew that I had taken him across the wilds, knew that he had been made a Frenchman by mistake and against his will, but yet he said that he could do nothing, as he had to carry out the port regulations. The ship was just going to start with the mails, and there was no time to go to the Emigration Office, even if it were open so early. And so I was at last to be parted with Välloo, my mettled Arab horse—my beautiful, my brave!

But not a bit of it. For when it came to the very pitch, I told the official that I could on no condition part with my servant, and that they must return my luggage to the boat again, as I would not go with the ship without him. The official was taken aback by this announcement, and probably thought that it was carrying officialism too far to prevent a servant going with his master, because they had made him a fellow citizen against his will. At last he said that as he was sure he was my *bonâ fide* private servant, he would permit Välloo to go with me, although that fatal slip of paper made him a French citizen, till exchanged for the usual passport. And so the valiant Välloo at last was free. I don't blame the French officials for this, as of course they were only carrying out the letter of the law, and I only mention the incident as a part of the comedy of errors that were always following in poor Vālloo's footsteps; for I shall once again have to take him on the platform at Singapore, and then dismiss him for ever.

There appear to be several ways of approaching Saigon from the sea, as this portion of the country is so much traversed by water channels. The route by which we entered from the sea by the 'Nam-vian' was not the same throughout as that by which we reached the sea by the 'Tibre.' For the 'Tibre' reached the sea near Cape St. James, where the French have a sanatorium, as well as large telegraph offices, and it communicated with Saigon by land through a trunk road forty-seven miles long, though the direct distance is only twenty-five miles. We stayed in the offing for a short time, and it is a pretty little place as seen from the sea, with a rough background of low hills behind it. But it is so exposed during the south-west monsoon that ships are not able to call there during that season.

Early next morning we called at a small French military outpost called Poulo-Condor, which is also exposed to the south-west monsoon, but not so badly as Cape St. James, as there is an island (or *poulo*) in the offing that shelters the harbour to a certain extent. Three French officers and the wife of one of them were going to this outpost, and went ashore that early morning, and so I was left alone in my glory with the captain of the ship.

The enormity of a crime must mainly depend upon motive. I sincerely hope so. For I was often and often guilty of the lie confirmative during that short voyage. The captain of the ship was the only one who dined in the saloon, and as I was alone with him for the next three days, I am sure it would make a cat purr with pleasure to see our ludicrous attempts at conversing with one another. The numberless times that I repeated the trite expression of 'Oh, yes, yes,' when never understanding a word of what the captain was saying, will not, I hope, be counted against me. Nor was the gallant captain himself to be outdone in politeness, with his frequent '*Wee, wee, Mussoo, wee, wee, Mussoo,*' when equally ignorant of what I was trying to say. But we got fine weather, and landed at Singapore in due course.

On the way between Borneo and Bangkok, though the 'Rajah Brooke' called at Singapore, I did not go ashore there at all. Nor did I wish to do so, even if I could. For at that particular time I had a real Macpherson-'gainst-Mactavish kind of feud against Singapore and all its belongings; and I shall tell you the reason why. The episode, indeed, should really form the first chapter of this narrative, but that I did not like to begin my story with a record of robbery, though I am sorry to say I shall be compelled to conclude it with one.

On the way down from Calcutta to Singapore at the beginning of this journey, a young traveller came on board our ship at Penang, who had been ill there for some time, and was still so on coming on board the ship. The day we landed at Singapore he came into my room at Raffles' Hotel to have a chat, and who turned up at the same time but a set of Indian conjurers, anxious to show off their skill in legerdemain. Indian conjurers were no novelty to me, but as the traveller was a stranger in the East, I allowed the conjurers to come into the room and exhibit their talents, instead of showing them off in the verandah, as is the usual custom.

They went through the performance, including the 'basket trick,' creditably; and, after being rewarded for their sleight of hand cleverness, they went their way. And so did the stranger, saying he would come back in the evening, so as to have a drive out together. But when I began to dress for the occasion, behold my braw gold watch, which had been placed on the dressing-table, was gone. There could be no doubt, I thought, as to who the thieves were. My watch must have been spirited away by the black art of the conjurers. We telephoned at once to the police head-quarters, and had the conjurers followed up and promptly arrested.

This was Saturday evening. The stranger got very excited over the business, and seemed sorrier than I did myself about the loss of the watch; for he knew that it was for his amusement, more than for my own, that I had allowed the conjurers to come into my room. We both went at once to the police-office, where I made a declaration about the loss of my property, while my companion was ready to swear black and blue that he saw the watch lying on the dressing-table when he was in the room.

And the end of it all was that the conjurers, consisting of two men and one woman, were all locked up in the police-office cells that same night; for who *could* have committed the crime but they? The only other possible person, we thought, would be the room servant, whose movements, as a privileged person, would not be observed in and out of the room. Detectives were sent on the trail of the watch at once, but without success.

Communications between Singapore and Borneo were so few and far between, that I could not afford to miss the 'Rajah Brooke,' which was going to sail on Tuesday evening. I returned to the police-office on Monday forenoon, to confirm the statement that I had made on the previous Saturday, and there met the conjurers, who had been brought out of the cells for identification. But the evidence was not strong enough to convict them, for none could swear positively that any individual one of them stole the watch, though we were, we thought, morally certain that one of them *must* have stolen it. The conjurers were again remanded to their cells, but as I was bound to go with the 'Rajah Brooke,' and could not personally stay to follow up the prosecution, they were released a day or two afterwards.

The robbery being duly reported in the Straits newspapers, it became known in the locality, and the upshot of it all was that the conjurers got hounded out of Singapore, and probably found their way back to their native town of Madras once again. But by that time I was far away in Borneo.

I was particularly sorry to lose the watch, for it had been given me as a keepsake by a Dutch lady, for services rendered in a moment of emergency, after she had fallen into a boiling quagmire in the wilds of New Zealand, when travelling there with the writer some years before. I would naturally, therefore, not part with it for a great deal more than its intrinsic value. But it was gone like decayed love, never to return again. This is why I had the Macpherson-'gainst-Mactavish feud against Singapore, and the reader will doubtless say that I had very good reason! . ..

A still more serious robbery took place in this same hotel two or three months afterwards, and, strange to say, it occurred in the very same set of rooms that I then occupied. Baron Something, the Austrian Ambassador to the court of Japan, was on his way east to take up his new appointment, and occupied these rooms (No. 41, avoid them !) during his few days' stay at Singapore.

And when the Baron woke one fine morning he found that not only his gold watch was gone, but also other trinkets of some considerable value. And when the Baron missed his property, he raged furiously and tore his hair as only barons can do. And when the Baron had torn his hair so frantically, as only barons can do, there was a great hue and cry through the hotel to catch the thief and recover the Baron's property. And the hotel people began to think of the conjurers, who had stolen my watch, but they were not to be found, for they were in another land. And when the conjurers could not be found, they made search among those who could be found, namely, the servants of the hotel. And when they made this search, where did they find the Baron's property but in possession of the Chinese *malee*, or gardener of the hotel, whom nobody at all suspected. And so the Baron recovered his property and his temper, his hair grew again, and he went on his way rejoicing, while the gardener got rigorous imprisonment with hard labour, for a period of two long years !

Now could this same thievish gardener have also stolen my watch from the very same rooms (No. 41, avoid them !) ? He could have easily come in through the back room without being observed, as he did on the other occasion. And the poor conjurers, who were hounded out of the place, were they innocent after all ? Who knows ? But whether they were or not, the coincidence clearly shows how liable to error our very shrewdest suspicions may be, and how careful we should always be in forming our opinions, and in drawing our conclusions, for the conjurers may have been innocent after all.

The first thing I looked for after arriving at Singapore this time was for a ship to take Vālloo to Bangkok back again ; and I was not long kept waiting, as there was a ship leaving for that port the very next day. I got a ticket for Vălloo in the agent's office, and engaged a surf boat to land Vălloo safely on board his ship, which was lying out in the harbour. The chief officer was in charge, and the ship was sailing in an hour or two; but he said that though the ticket was all that he would require, the emigrant agent, when he came on board, would not let my servant go unless he had the necessary paper for doing so. Why, this was Saigon over again, and yet this was a free colony of the much vaunted Land of Liberty.

These restrictions on the movements of the natives may perhaps be necessary, but they must be very irksome to these poor people, who can scarcely call their souls their own. I hope, therefore, that they believe in the doctrine of Fore-ordination, for the poor beggars can scarcely be expected to believe in the doctrine of Free-will. By this time indeed poor Vălloo was becoming a veritable Old Man of the Sea on my back, and I could not get rid of him. There was no use of waiting till the emigrant functionary came on board, to plead Vălloo's cause, for I had had enough of that at Saigon. The only thing to do was to take Vălloo ashore again in a hurry, which I did. And after going to the wrong office once or twice, we finally got hold of the right one. Here I procured the necessary pass for Vălloo, returned with him back to the ship again, and she was shortly afterwards sailing gaily out of the harbour with Vălloo on board.

And so I saw the last of the valiant Vălloo, who sometimes made me very angry and sometimes made me laugh. During the time he was with me, though he had no chance of becoming either a Rooshian or a Prooshian, he might easily have become a Frenchman; but yet he remained an English-*man*, much to the honour and glory of the British Lion. And long before these pages can appear in print, he will probably have talked over and over again to his little wife (and the baby) about his wonderful adventures with the white stranger, from whom he ran away in the wilds of Láös, but who proved his true friend in the hour of his need.

VĀLLOO, THE DARK DELINQUENT.
Though "Vālloo, Vālloo" oft we cried,
Yet Vālloo never once replied.

CHAPTER XXIII

> She sits on a rock, and the wind through her hair
> Eternally sings from the fragrant sea,
> And now and anon she repeats in despair:
> 'My true love returns not again to me;
> My lover returns not to me again,
> From over the waves of the raging sea,
> Oh, *why* don't the steeds with the foaming mane
> Return not my true-love again to me?'
> *The Sighing Maiden.*

The country mouse—Saigon and Singapore contrasted—Singapore the City of Rickshaws—Steam no match to two-legged ponies—Mrs. Bumble and the Rickshaws—Reasonable inquiries—The fate of Captain Bertuzzi and of Phra Yott—The French and Chantaboon—His Highness the Sultan of Johore—An 'At Home' with His Highness—The recent breach of promise case—General opinions—The sighing Penelope and lost Ulysses—Parting with *Jimmy*—His varied accomplishments—Thoughts of becoming a Mahdi.

BEING essentially a country mouse, I prefer the country to the town, and one glimpse of Nature to an age of Art. But when I go to the town, I like to see the little rodents, the town mice, gnawing and sawing away at their various pursuits; some of them gnawing at wood and some at iron, but all hoarding the gold, when they can get it. In this way Singapore was satisfactory enough, as everyone looked in such a suspicious hurry, as if fearing that everyone else was going to steal his gold watch and jewels from him. It contrasted wonderfully with Saigon that I had only left a few days before. And it made me think that there must be something attractive in business, besides the mere hoarding of gold. There were the gallant ships out in the harbour, and here on shore were the busy, busy town mice that supplied them with their merchandise.

Singapore, indeed, is a pretty sight, not so much the town itself, the business part of which is too cramped, but the beautiful broad harbour, with such a lot of ships in it every day in the year. But what particularly distinguishes Singapore is its jinrickshaws. Various cities in the East receive nicknames from certain predominant peculiarities. Thus Calcutta is nicknamed the 'City of Palaces,' Bombay, the 'City of Ducks' (that is to say, Bombay Ducks), while Madras is the 'Benighted City.' On the same principle Singapore is the 'City of Rickshaws.' There is probably no other place with the same number of rickshaws, and generally speaking they are very good ones too. Not in Hong Kong, not in Shanghai, and not even in Japan itself, I think, has the institution of rickshaws grown so great. I was riding in one of them some day, and noticed that the number of another one going on in front of me was considerably over 6,000, though the population of Singapore is considerably under 100,000 inhabitants. This surprised me, but I was afterwards told that nearly 8,000 rickshaws run daily on the streets of this tropical city.

Not very long ago an enterprising syndicate who believed in the blessings of steam started extensive steam-cars over the city. But they had to shut up shop shortly after. For the two-footed ponies in the jinrickshaws actually worked the iron horse off his legs. Nay more, jinrickshaws have become quite fashionable. Only the other day, and if you suggested a ride in a jinrickshaw to a woman of quality in Singapore, the woman of quality would turn up her nose at you. But all that is changed now. The governor of Singapore was away at this time, but I was told that his wife had lately taken to riding in a jinrickshaw and keeping a private stud of Chinese two-legged ponies for that purpose, just for fun. Mrs. Bumble, the woman of quality, immediately followed suit, and if you now suggest a ride in a jinrickshaw to Mrs. Bumble, far from turning up her nose, she makes it look quite archaic (that is to say, with an arch) with the happy pleasure of anticipation. Such are the freaks of fashion.

But to speak in earnest, a good jinrickshaw is really a pretty little carriage, with its elegant wheels and its brass shiny mountings; and there is no reason why any one should turn up his predominant feature at it. As a rule they will cover the ground nearly as fast as four-wheelers, such as the four-wheelers one meets at Singapore. The two-legged ponies are almost invariably Chinamen all over the

Far East, with the single exception of Japan, the country from which the jinrickshaws originally sprang. They are generally strong sturdy men, but yet perspire a little too freely in such sultry climates. By constant exercise the calves of their legs get so developed, and their hips so plump, that they move between the shafts with all the ease and elegance of sturdy little Highland ponies.

When I reached Singapore I turned up the back numbers of several papers, to make up for lost time, and see what had occurred when I was in the wilderness. There were two persons that I wished particularly to know about, and these two distinguished people were Captain Bertuzzi and Phra Yott: both of whom I had left in the clutches of the law on my leaving Bangkok. As regards Captain Bertuzzi, I am glad to say that he stood his trial and was honourably acquitted, the verdict being (1) that there was not sufficient evidence that it was he who killed the native, and (2) that he was at any rate only acting in self-defence when attacked by two natives, one of whom got fatally stabbed in the scrimmage. I was glad to see this, as I could scarcely believe that my would-be interpreter across the country was a hardened criminal. Indeed, the short article I read about his case exonerated him so completely, and dwelt so much on the supposed dangerous condition of the country at this particular time that I cut it out, intending to give it verbatim here. But unfortunately I lost my cash-box afterwards with this slip of paper, and many others in it, as will be duly recorded in the proper place.

And what of Phra Yott? His fate was very different. When I left Bangkok, the general impression there was that the seven Siamese judges would sacrifice him to appease France. But the judges did nothing of the kind. Prince Bitchit and his fellow judges acquitted Phra Yott on every count of the indictment. France was neither pleased nor appeased by this. She got Phra Yott tried again by a mixed court, and this tribunal sentenced poor Phra Yott to twenty years' penal servitude.

Poor Phra Yott! perhaps you are a patriot. If you are, and if you only knew it, you should try and comfort yourself with the reflection that some of the best and bravest patriots have suffered for their country even a worse fate than yours before now; although it must be confessed that twenty years are a long time wherein to chew the cud of bitter fancy.

The Siamese town of Chantaboon, something like a hundred miles south of Bangkok, and, next to Bangkok itself, the most important port in the kingdom, was occupied by French troops when I was in the country, and they are still there at the time of penning these pages. The ostensible reason for occupying the town at all was Phra Yott's action, and it was held out that when Phra Yott's case would be finished, so would be finished the French occupation of Chantaboon. But there they still are sitting—still are sitting—like Edgar Allan Poe's raven, although Phra Yott has been sentenced to imprisonment with hard labour, probably for life. The story goes the round that the French will not leave Chantaboon till Phra Yott has served his twenty years' penal servitude, as the full measure of his crime will only then be wiped out. This story, of course, is too ingenious to be true. But it may be safely said for one thing, that if the French will not vacate Chantaboon for the next twenty years, they will not do so till the Greek Kalends, and that if they don't do so within a reasonable period, the question of Chantaboon is likely to become quite as important as that further north, because Chantaboon is comparatively speaking within a stone's throw of Bangkok itself, and the river, of which it is the principal port, is the natural outlet of both the provinces of Angkor and Battambong, already alluded to.

There was comparatively little for me to see at Singapore this time, as I had been there several times before. There was, however, one notable exception, and that was His Highness the Sultan of Johore. Some years ago I went over to his capital of Johore itself, from which he takes his designation, but he was then in Europe, for he dearly loves the North, like many other people. Johore is at the extreme southern point of the long and narrow Malayan Peninsula, and is practically the furthest south point of the whole vast continent of Asia. It is separated from the small island of Singapore by a sound only a mile or so wide, and the drive across the island from the town of Singapore to Granji Pier opposite Johore is under twenty miles, and is a particularly pleasant one.

I intended to go over this time once again, as the Sultan

was at home. But while staying at Singapore there was an announcement that His Highness was going to have an 'At Home' at his town residence, on the outskirts of Singapore itself. This would do away with the necessity of going over to Johore, as I would attend the 'At Home' instead. I wished to see His Highness, partly because he was a very interesting person in himself, and partly because he was very much before the public when I started from India, on account of his very amusing breach of promise case.

The Chinese two-footed ponies in the rickshaws are obtuse enough in their intellect—all ponies are ; but the drivers of the four-wheeled 'groaners' are vastly worse. If you told them that you were going to Jericho, they would instantly take upon themselves to drive you there. But they are extremely bad at reaching their destination if you do not know the way yourself, especially if you cannot speak the 'pigeon.' Our driver on the evening of the Sultan's 'At Home' was particularly dull of comprehension ; but by patient perseverance we reached the Sultan's palace at last, probably among the very last arrivals.

Mrs. Brown-Potter, the once famous American beauty, had already sung her song, for she was then at Singapore with a company of strolling players, and was acting for the time being at the Town Hall, and the function of presentation had also been already over. I was sorry I was so late, as I wished to be presented to His Highness, which, however, I afterwards managed through the English aide-de-camp attached to His Highness's person. The Sultan appeared affable and simple enough, as he moved to and fro among his guests. I did not expect to see any ladies at this function, as I was afraid His Highness would be unpopular with the fair sex, on account of his having so recently jilted an English lady. But not at all : His Highness was very popular in Singapore, and all the beauty, as well as the chivalry of the place, were there in all their bravery.

His Highness was a man considerably over sixty years of age, of a light olive complexion, and so gentle and mild in his manners that no one would expect him to play the part of a wicked Lothario in breaking women's hearts. He would be considered small of stature for a European, but quite the average height of the race to which he belongs, as he is a pure Malay by blood, and very few of this roving race are of anything like tall stature. And they are also far more uniform in height than Europeans, as they seldom differ from one another in this respect for more than two or three inches at the most.

His Highness, who was very popular in Singapore, spoke English thoroughly well, and was quite European in everything except the red fez on the top of his head, as became a true and faithful follower of the Prophet. He gave these 'At Homes' now and again, and they were immensely popular when they came off. But the mere occurrence of this 'At Home' naturally gave rise to gossip about His Highness; and his recent jilting affair would have revived again, even if it had died out, which it had not at this time.

Like many another personage of exalted rank, he delighted occasionally to drop his greatness and his rank, and go about *incognito*, under an assumed name, as if he were mere ordinary flesh and blood like other people. And nothing could show both the humility and fascination of His Highness better than the way in which he stormed the citadel of Miss M——'s heart, for he was then living under the very ordinary name of Mr. Albert Baker, an English name that bore a convenient resemblance to his own real Malay name of Abu Bakhur.

The Sultan had a large revenue, but his heart was larger still. And he was, therefore, very expensive in his mode of living, especially when he went among his friends in the North, where he spent a considerable portion of both his time and fortune. The natural consequence followed. His Highness was in debt. Many people regretted the late breach of promise case, more for the sake of the Sultan than for the broken-hearted one, who suffered so grievously by the conduct of her truant lover, Mr. Albert Baker, of that ilk. The trial of the case lately in England will still be in the memory of many readers, and it will also be remembered that it elicited one important fact, namely, that though the Johore territory is under British protection, yet that the Sultan thereof is practically an independent prince, over whom the British law-courts have no jurisdiction whatever.

This fact, though gratifying to the Sultan in a way,

(From Photo by Herr Nache.)
HIS HIGHNESS THE LATE SULTAN OF JOHARE.

To face page 231.

has yet done him some harm. His lavish expenditure having, as I said, depleted his treasury, His Highness wished to raise a loan of 100,000*l*., as his friend John Bull has had to do on more than one occasion before now. But when the wary capitalists came to know by this breach of promise case that they would have no legal claim against him, if he refused to pay up, they closely tied their purse-strings, and would not advance him the money he wanted. This was a pity; for it put a check on the large-heartedness of His Highness. If he had married the broken-hearted one, they say, this fact of non-liability to pay would never have come out, the capitalists would have gladly lent him the loan, the sighing one would be comforted, and would, after all, be only one more or less in his already extensive harem; and, in short, the world would go on merrily as before. But all that is changed now. The lone one is sighing on the shores of England, and whispering to the breezes, 'Will ye nae come back again?' for her lost Ulysses; while Ulysses himself, poor fellow, is stranded on the Calypso of Singapore. So much for love.[1]

But I must now descend from sultans to chickens. For I had now to part with Jimmy, my jolly little bird with four legs, mentioned on a page before. I refrained from mentioning him much in this narrative, as I wanted to give him a page of peroration all to himself. This was the callow bird without any feathers, but with four legs, that I caught at the remote village of Kallán, and that proved a valuable pastime to me during a portion of the journey, as he very soon turned out the most pettable of pets. During my trip on the great lake Telé-Sáp, time hung heavily on my hands, and the ogre of weariness peeped at me through her spectacles now and again. I could not always be reading, for my eyes would grow tired, nor could I always be writing, as the 'Lady of the Lake,' notwithstanding her pretty name, was not at all well adapted to clerical purposes. And though I jotted down the little incidents of the journey, these took up very little time, while this book, 'Through the Buffer State,' was then in the womb of futurity.

[1] This genial Malay prince died shortly after this chapter was written, but as nothing ill-natured has been said about His Highness, the text is allowed to stand.

In short, I was suffering from having too little to do, a very irksome complaint, which is much more common than is generally supposed, even by the sufferers. Under these circumstances I occasionally amused myself by making a pet of Jimmy, who was seldom in his cage, except during the night, or when the raging winds would blow. By far the greater portion of my time was spent lying on my back, on a folding cork mattress stretched across the boat, under the shade of the hood, and almost my only occupation was reading the few books I had brought with me on the journey, some of which I read twice over. Jimmy was never happier than when perching on one of my knees, which was generally raised above the other one when lying down. Failing that, my breast was the next best perch he could think of, and his continual purr of pleasure, like that of a cat, was quite edifying to hear.

His only aversion was my eyeglasses, at which he would peck fiercely to take them away. But on these occasions he was remanded to his cage for punishment, as bad boys are sent into corners when they misbehave themselves. If I happened to walk from one end of the boat to the other, poor Jimmy was sure to follow, and when the wind would blow a little too hard for him, he would nestle in the calmest nook he could find by my side, like a sensible little puppy.

But the best thing of all that he did was to pick rice seeds out of my ears. Mahomed's pigeon that was supposed to personify the Holy Ghost, by whispering wisdom in the ears of the prophet, when he was only picking millet seeds out of them, was really nothing to Jimmy. Had he four legs, for instance? No. Then he wasn't like Jimmy. And Jimmy could pick out seeds quite as well, though I am not prepared to say that he was always whispering wisdom in my ears, for he was too intent on the seeds to be then whispering anything. I was always intending to take a photograph of the odd-looking Jimmy. But he was so ugly that I was waiting till he got a little bigger and handsomer, and got a few more feathers on his back. And the result of it was that I forgot about it in the end altogether. Nor did it matter, as almost all the photographs turned out an utter failure.

Indeed, Jimmy was so queer and so docile a bird, that

I was seriously thinking of setting myself up as a new Mahdi, with Jimmy to whisper wisdom into my ears, the same as Mahomed's dove did in his. But on further reflection, I came to the conclusion that, however dignified it would sound to be a Mahdi, yet it had its drawbacks. For life would be too tedious to be always playing the rôle of a false prophet. And so I gave up that idea, and now I was going to give up even Jimmy himself. He had grown apace when he was with me, having plenty to eat, plenty to drink, and nothing to do ; and having nothing to do probably agrees with chickens.

He was a callow being almost entirely featherless when I got him. But the feathers eventually began to grow, and so did his supernumerary legs. What have Darwinians to say on the effects of so-called 'sport' in the establishment of permanent species ? For the variations of species depend on ornament as well as on utility ; and some hens might really think Jimmy both beautiful and ornamental on account of his odd lanky legs. Or had all chickens originally four legs, and was Jimmy only reverting to the original type ? Was his case in short one of Evolution or Devolution ? Some one may be able to solve this conundrum, though I cannot.

But Jimmy was rather backward in some things, for by the time I parted with him he had not yet declared his sex, so that I am quite unable to say whether his name was really Jimmy or Jinny.

Everybody liked Jimmy, and when the Frenchmen at the outpost of Kampong-Chenáng first saw him, they raised their hands in wonder, shrugged their shoulders, and exclaimed, '*Phenomenon, phenomenon!*' But alas, I had to part with Jimmy. As I then expected to be going home at once, my first intentions were to take Jimmy with me, and hand it over as a curiosity to the Zoological Gardens, or some similar institution. But here I had to change my mind.

The valiant Vălloo, daft though he was, was very fond of Jimmy ; but now that he had left me, who would look after the bird ? For I had enough to look after myself, as I was now going to be without servants till I reached India back again, and I had some rough travelling in front of me still. For Jimmy's own sake, then, I gave him as a gift to the Singapore Zoological Gardens, where Jimmy is at this moment, perhaps, crowing on some nice little dung-hill of his own. Mr. Riddley, the curator of the Gardens, promised that he would be looked well after ; and if his new master will be as fond of him as his old one, poor little Jimmy will have no reason to complain. Good-bye Singapore ; farewell Jimmy and Vālloo !

CHAPTER XXIV

> 'Tis melancholy sure to see
>   The sites and scenes of old renown,
> The roofless halls that wont to be
>   The glory of some ancient town;
> Now fallen to such low degree,
>   And unto dust slow crumbling down,
> But yet possessing still to me
>   Romance and beauty all their own.
> *The Hand of Time.*

Old Malacca—Its change of hands—St. Xavier's curse—The town's decay and its cause—Malacca the 'Blighted City'—Malacca and Madras compared—Its equable climate—Its shallow anchorage—Ancient and modern Argosies—Cities struggling for existence.

AND now to all intents and purposes I was homeward bound, though considerably delayed on the way by known and unknown causes. Though the time at my disposal did not permit me to visit Luang-Prabang in the north of Siam, yet my rapid journey down the Mekong from Kampong-Chenáng to Penhom-Penh, and from Penhom-Penh to Saigon saved me a good deal of time, of which I was now anxious to make the best possible use in another direction. And how could I do this better than working my way back along the Malayan Peninsula, and visiting among other things the historical city of Malacca, at one time the most important city of the East under European control, but now a mere wreck of ruin and decay?

It was when the Portuguese ruled the waves that Malacca first came into fame and prominence as the great mart and emporium in the Far East. Then the Dutch, in their day of grandeur, took it from the Portuguese in 1641; and, last of all, in 1793, we in our turn took it from the Dutch, in our day of grandeur, which has been waxing stronger and stronger ever since, and will do so till the end of the world. It was in this city of Malacca that the celebrated

Portuguese missionary, St. Xavier, laboured for many years, but found it so hard to convert the natives (as many a devout missionary has found since) that he is said to have left it, after literally shaking its soil off his sandals, and cursing it as a God-forsaken and wicked place.

He then went to Goa, at that time the headquarters of Portuguese India, and still at this fag end of the nineteenth century remaining a Portuguese possession, while the greater portion of the rest of India has passed away into other hands. If St. Xavier really cursed Malacca in this old apostolic manner, his curse would certainly appear to have had some effect, judging from the dilapidated condition of the place at present. The stranger visiting it now will find it hard to believe that it ever was a very important commercial centre; yet there is no doubt that it was so once.

The city that has now dwindled down to less than 20,000 inhabitants is situated on the open sea face, without even the slightest bit of a creek or bay, let alone a harbour, for shelter. The want of a good harbour seems to be a great drawback to the growth, and especially to the stability of cities, and it is the main cause why Madras, for instance, has lately allowed herself to be so much outstripped both by Calcutta and Bombay in the race for progress. For, like Malacca, it is situated on an unbroken sandy coast, the coast of Coromandel, on which the long rollers of the Indian Ocean eternally roll and comb and break with an everceaseless roar. So that as Madras is called the 'Benighted City,' Malacca may aptly be called the 'Blighted City,' seeing that the curse of St. Xavier has had such terrible effects on its future career.

One advantage Malacca has over Madras is the fact that it is situated in a part of the world in which raging winds scarcely ever blow, and in which the ocean seldom or never roars. It is a very different case with Madras, for it is not at all infrequently the scene of storms and tempests of a very violent character. The present writer was there ten years ago, waiting for a passage to Rangoon, when a cyclone was expected by the meteorologists to burst over the city, and the ships were duly warned and actually sailed out of the anchorage for safety, as they would have a better chance in fighting the element in the open sea, than when riding at anchor in the so-called Madras Roads. The storm came on sure enough, and from the verandah of Lipport's Hotel I was even able to watch one or two of these ships fighting the gale, only a few miles from the land.

But not only that storms do not blow in this region, but the island of Sumatra, stretching away to the north, though invisible from Malacca itself, effectually shelters it from the long ocean rollers to which Madras is so exposed. What strikes the stranger most, however, is the extreme shallowness of the Malacca anchorage. Why, it's as shallow, if not so muddy, as lake Telé-Sáp itself. The small coasting-ship 'Neera,' with which I went there, had to anchor a mile or two from the land; and the water is so shallow all the way out, that a fine long bridge stretches direct from the shore for more than half a mile into the shallow sea. European residents in Malacca will tell you that the coast must have been much deeper at one time, and that the bottom must have silted up during later ages. This view cannot be the correct one, for granted that no particular convulsion followed the curse of St. Xavier, there is nothing about the harbour to fill it up to any appreciable degree, for the small river on which the town is placed could never have been of any material importance in bringing *débris* down with it, as is the case with larger rivers like the Mekong or Menam, for instance.

The reason is really to be found in the fact that Malacca, though important enough in its day, would not at its best be called a very great city in ours, and in the other fact that in those olden days, the ships were really very small and very probably beached on the sandy shore when waiting for cargo, as is done with mere fishing smacks at the present period. People scarcely realise the vast difference in size between ocean-going ships in those days as compared with these.

Some twenty years ago the author happened to be the surgeon of the Peninsular and Oriental steamship 'Australia,' then the queen of the Peninsular and Oriental fleet, and said to be the finest ship that had ever gone to India at that time. But she was only 3,600 tons. While writing these pages, only a score of years afterwards, the 'Caledonia,' the new queen of the same fleet, is 7,500 tons, or somewhat over double the size of the 'Australia.' Nay more, he was on board the 'City of Paris,' when that great ship nearly foundered in the Atlantic in 1890. She was 10,500 tons; and though the biggest and fastest ship then in the world, she has since been eclipsed both in size and speed by the 'Campania,' as well as by the 'Lucania,' all of them built on the Clyde except the 'City of Paris.' I only mention these facts in order to show the vast strides that are being made in shipbuilding of recent years. Why, Columbus crossed the Atlantic in the 'Santa Maria,' a caravel of a hundred and fifty tons; and no ocean-liner, however big and however fast, will ever again achieve so splendid a victory.

Malacca is the oldest of our present possessions in the Far East, being a British dependency for almost exactly a hundred years at the time of writing this narrative; and it has never made much progress since the Portuguese had it, or perhaps since St. Xavier shook his sandal shoon at it in execration. When the pretty little island of Poulo Penang was first occupied, the town of Penang immediately began to cut out the town of Malacca, as it was a more convenient port of call for ships to and from the further East. And when we acquired the island of Singapore, the go-ahead town of that name rapidly began to cut out both Penang and Malacca. Such is the fate of cities as of men; they have their entrances and their exits, and have to struggle on the stage of existence on the principle of the survival of the fittest, like everything else in the world.

The town of Malacca is familiarly known in the Straits Settlements under the nickname of 'Sleepy Hollow,' on account of the absolute dulness of itself and all its surroundings; yet this 'Sleepy Hollow' will always remain an interesting place, for it has not only given its name to the Straits, which are the key to the Far East, but even to the whole peninsula on which it stands, which is generally known to foreigners as the Malacca Peninsula. But let us go ashore and see what Malacca is like.

CHAPTER XXV

> Come, show me the mines where the yellow gold
> Was wont to be gathered in days of old,
> The gold of old *Ophir* that decked the Queen
> In garments resplendent with sparkling sheen,
> That fringed the rich robes that Queen Sheba wore,
> When Solomon reigned in the days of yore.
>
> *Queen Sheba.*

Untravelled travellers—Uncomfortable passages—Malacca Rest-house—Ancient Cathedral—'Upper Crust Club'—Mount Ophir—Its Scripture basis—Khlang and Qualo-Lumpor—The coffee and tin industries—The future of John Chinaman.

THOUGH there are several small steamers running up and down this coast, there are seldom more than four or five Europeans on board any of them for crews, and they scarcely ever dream of going ashore at Malacca, which is so far away from the anchorage, and with nothing to do when people get there. I have always been fond of sailors, and think them the bravest people in the world. Yet I cannot help saying here that, taken as a class, they are the most untravelled travellers on the face of the earth. With some few exceptions, they seldom see anything at all of the countries they visit, except the harbour and its more immediate surroundings. Most of them will tell you that they hate the sea, yet they get so accustomed to be on board their ship that she becomes their home, and they seldom leave her.

A captain of an American ship was travelling with me once across the Pacific as a distressed seaman, sent home by the American consul at Hong Kong, after losing his ship on one of the Caroline Islands. His ship was not a big one, he said, something under a thousand tons, but he was sorry to lose her, as he had steadily risen in her from an ordinary sailor to be master of her. Did he not feel the time long at sea? Yes, he did. But all the same, when chief mate of this same fated vessel, he had been over two whole years trading from port to port, without ever taking the trouble to go on shore. And yet how many gallant and romantic young lads run away to sea—*to see the world!*

Though the master of the 'Neera' was by no means familiar with 'Sleepy Hollow,' as he called it, yet he was aware that there was a rest-house there, and there I went. The rest-house alone went to show that lodgings ought to be had cheap in the town of Malacca, for in its time it would have been quite a fine big residence, looking out on the ever-melancholy sea, though few people resided there now. These rest-houses in the Malayan peninsula are kept up in exactly the same way as what is known as Traveller's Bungalows in India, and are entirely the property of their government. This one was looked after by a Madrassee who spoke Hindustani; but had visitors so seldom that he was also a subordinate in some Government office, which did not at all tend to improve his catering for his occasional visitors; and I was rather out of it now, as I was without any servants of my own.

The only other person living in the rest-house at this time was Mr. B——, the Assistant Resident of the Malacca province, who had just come to Malacca, and was waiting for his own house to be got ready. The rest-house not only contained accommodation for occasional, very occasional wanderers, but also contained the station library, with a fair assortment of books and papers of various kinds. The rest-house was a fair example of many other houses in Malacca, solidly and well built in former days, but now with a great many apartments to let, and without any immediate prospect of being crowded with lodgers.

The most conspicuous object from the sea, and in fact the most interesting object in the whole place, is a fine old ruined cathedral, built during the palmy days of Portuguese occupation, on an elevated plot of ground not far from the long pier and the landing-place, and now surely though slowly crumbling down into dust and ashes. On going to visit this ancient ruin, I came across many flat grave-stones on the floor of the cathedral, with inscriptions on them, and no doubt covering the bones of some who were distinguished in their day.

The one, however, that attracted my attention most, referring as it did to the most distinguished of them all, was a slab on the wall, of comparatively recent origin. This tablet stated that St. Xavier, the celebrated Portuguese missionary already mentioned, had died, and that his body had been placed there (apparently in a niche), in the year 1553—nearly three hundred and fifty years ago. This statement on the slab does not tally with the story that he shook his sandal shoon at the place when he went to India. But, perhaps he afterwards regretted and returned again to remove the curse, but couldn't. I think the general impression is that this famous divine died in Goa, and in the bookless place where I am now writing I am unable to find out which is the correct version of the story. But there in Malacca, at any rate, is the slab to his memory, according to which his body was laid there in 1553.[1]

This ancient and interesting cathedral has no roof now, and is no longer used for the purpose of piloting to the world to come. Yet strange to say, a portion of it is still used for pilotage of a more sublunary nature; for this portion now constitutes the Malacca lighthouse, that guides the ships of the present day into the Malacca roadstead during the dark hours of night.

One evening I went with one or two others to have a look round the place. We first visited the Malacca Club, where some half a dozen people were congregated, smoking, drinking, or playing billiards. After it got dark we went into another place, up a couple of flights of narrow, dark stairs. 'Hullo,' I said, 'is this another club?' 'Yes,' said one of my companions with a cynical smile, this is the 'Upper Crust Club.' There are only between thirty and forty pure Europeans throughout the whole of the Malacca Province, and certainly not more than twelve or fifteen in the ancient town itself; and yet Malacca had two clubs. Could the petty differences of rank be drawn out to finer issues? and what ridi-

---

[1] So far as I could afterwards find out, the true facts of the case are, that St. Xavier died and was first buried in China, and was buried afterwards in this cathedral at Malacca, and finally that his body was taken away and buried for the third time in Goa, on the Malabar coast of India, where his ashes remain for the present. Query: How much of St. Xavier's ashes ever reached Goa?

R

culous vanity life must be to require such artificial means to maintain its importance! This Upper Crust Club consists of the Resident, Assistant Resident, Residency surgeon, chaplain, government engineer, and a practising barrister; and that's all. However, we played pool that evening, and I was delighted to win a whole live almighty Mexican dollar from the Upper Crust Club of Malacca.

During my short stay at the rest-house, almost the only European planter in the province happened to come to Malacca on business; and having put up at the rest-house, he kindly invited me to visit his plantation in the interior of the country. He lived some twenty-five or thirty miles straight inland in a due easterly direction, and I was only too pleased to go with him. There he had a tapioca plantation and factory, which I went over with some curiosity, as I had never seen a tapioca factory before. Mr. S—— had only recently bought this estate, and was going to make a fortune out of it—which I hope he will. The great size of the tapioca tubers must exhaust the ground very rapidly, but there is plenty of virgin soil in this locality to be cultivated in endless succession.

The mere planting of tapioca is simple enough. But it is only a small portion of the business, from the time that the cuttings are first planted in the ground, till the tapioca is turned out in the factory, and separated into its different varieties according to the qualities of each. Few people know the varied and often complex processes of labour required to produce some of the simplest articles of daily use, and I have already confessed that I did not know myself that sago consisted of the pith of a palm till I went over to Borneo to gain that piece of knowledge; for the maxim of 'live and learn' is a very wise and useful one. It was Mr. S—— who kept in a cistern a supply of the mudfish that looked so ugly and tasted so sweet, when I was crossing the wilds of Laös, as already recorded in a previous chapter.

The whole of the Malayan Peninsula is fairly mountainous, with the ranges generally extending from north to south, and more or less in line with the coast on either side. Some ten or twelve miles from the residence of Mr. S—— is a conspicuous mountain, possessing the very biblical name of Mount Ophir, and supposed by some to be the

Mount Ophir from which King Solomon got his gold when building the Temple at Jerusalem. This supposition cannot be true. In those ancient days of limited navigation, it was a far cry from Palestine to Malacca; and the name, indeed, is more likely to have been given to the mountain by the first Portuguese, who may perhaps have discovered gold in its vicinity.

But further than this, the Bible does not use the word mount or mountain at all in connexion with Ophir. The only passages in sacred scripture, so far as I know, that refer at all to Ophir are the following:—

1 Kings xxii. 48: 'Jehoshaphat made ships of Tharshish to go to Ophir for gold: but they went not; for the ships were broken at Ezion-geber;' 2 Chronicles, viii. 18: 'And Huram sent him by the hands of his servants ships, and servants that had knowledge of the sea; and they went with the servants of Solomon to Ophir, and took thence four hundred and fifty talents of gold, and brought them to King Solomon;' also ix. 10: 'And the servants also of Huram, and the servants of Solomon, which brought gold from Ophir, brought algum trees and precious stones;' the book of Job xxii. 24: 'Then shalt thou lay up gold as dust, and the gold of Ophir as the stones of the brooks;' and last of all, but far from least, the beautiful forty-fifth psalm, and ninth verse:—

> Among thy women honourable,
> Kings' daughters were at hand;
> Upon thy right hand did the queen
> In gold of Ophir stand.

It will be observed that none of these passages (and there may be more), mention that Ophir was a mountain; nor, indeed, does any of them mention what it was. Sailing up the coast northwards, this Mount Ophir is very conspicuous and very deceptive in its appearance; for by the time you reach Malacca you fancy you have left it far behind you to the south. The reason of this is that ordinary small atlases give one the idea that the west coast of the Malayan Peninsula is almost due north and south, which, indeed, it nearly is in its general bearings, but is far from being so in several individual places. When sailing up the coast to Malacca, the course is pretty nearly north-west. So, when you travel to Jazin, where I went on this occasion almost directly on the way of Mount Ophir, you fancy you are going south again, whereas you are really going almost due east.

I was nearly tempted to climb this mountain, and should certainly have done so if I thought there was anything romantic or Biblical about it. But as I knew that there wasn't, and as I had already reached within three or four thousand feet of the highest climb on record, it was scarcely worth my while to scale the paltry 4,000 odd feet of Mount Ophir for the sake of 'doing' it. I would much prefer to go on the principle of 'Excelsior,' or go one better, so to speak.

And thus I left Malacca and the Upper Crust Club. The construction of a railway had just then been sanctioned by the British Government, to connect Malacca and the general railway system that is being so rapidly pushed on through the entire length of the Malayan Peninsula, and which will eventually extend from Moulmain, in the south of Burmah, all along this long peninsula to Johore, the southern extremity alike of the Malayan Peninsula and of the great Continent of Asia itself. The Malaccians hope that Malacca will then begin to flourish again, and I can only hope that their hopes may be realised.

We proceeded then to Port Dickson, farther up the coast, and later on to Khlang. The steamers along this coast are very wretched, with the exception of one or two. I was in four of them, and they were all uncomfortable, and two of them were not intended to carry European passengers at all. However, the traveller is bound to put up with these discomforts if he wishes to travel as he ought, for he cannot be always luxuriating in buns and pancakes when roughing it in this way.

When wandering through the Malay Peninsula, as was my usual custom when passing through other places, I began to learn a few words of the language of the country, to be of course forgotten almost at once when the journey was over. Like many other languages, I found that the Malay language abounded in slang, just the same as our own. We all know how such words as burke, boycott, &c., became common English words. And I found almost an exact parallel to the latter term in the Malay tongue. For instance, according to a Malay vocabulary in the possession of one of the skippers with whom I sailed, when a man was transported or put in Coventry for any crime, he was said to be 'bombayed.'

Under this funny word 'bombaia' was attached a note of explanation, saying that the word originated from the former custom of transporting criminals from Malacca to Bombay, when the criminal was said to be 'bombayed,' just as we might use the term 'botany-bayed' in our own country not very long ago. I do not know myself that prisoners ever were transported from Malacca to Bombay, and I rather incline to the opinion that the reverse was the case, namely, that prisoners from Bombay were often transported to the Malay Peninsula, as they are to this day to the Andaman Islands, in that same direction.

It is interesting to notice how certain words of certain languages travel, and take root here and there in distant soils. I have already alluded to the word 'Farrang' all over Further Asia as meaning a European stranger, though it originally meant a Frenchman only. The same may be said of the Portuguese word 'companha,' a courtyard or enclosure, long ago introduced into the East during the Portuguese predominance there, and still existing in British India under the form of 'compound,' the enclosure round a bungalow, as well as in Further Asia, where, in the form of 'kampong,' it has come to mean a village—as, for instance, Kampong-Chenáng, where I first met the Frenchmen in far-away Cambodia, and which means the village of Chenang. The Bengali word 'syce,' a groom, is understood from Afghanistan to Yokohama, in Japan. Many other instances of the same kind might be quoted, and I shall therefore only mention the English word 'boy,' which is understood almost all over the East to mean a native servant, who may be far indeed from being a boy.

I reached Khlang at last, a name hitherto quite unknown in my geographical vocabulary; and so was Quala-lumpor—a much more important place, as it is the principal town in the province of Selangor, over which there is a sultan, but which is practically under British rule. Both Selangor as a province, and Quala-lumpor as a town, are much the most flourishing places on the mainland of the Malayan Peninsula. Khlang is but the port of Quala-lumpor, and is comparatively a small place, twelve miles farther down the small river than the principal town, with which it is connected by rail, a commodity of which there is a good deal in this province, either building or built.

At this time Selangor, more especially the neighbourhood of Khlang, was very much before the public as the coming country for the coffee industry. Coffee at the present moment is the real paying concern, though not very long ago it could hardly pay the cost of producing it. But times have changed. I wonder what the world would do if times did *not* change now and again. And the great cause of change here has been the abolition of slavery in the empire of Brazil, aggravated by the late political troubles in that same country. This condition of affairs, combined with the insecurity of property consequent on the recent civil wars, has caused the coffee industry to languish in Brazil, at least for the present. A few years ago and Brazil produced three-fourths of the coffee of the world, but now it produces scarcely any at all.

It has also been lately discovered that coffee does not require the cloudy hillsides which were at one time deemed an absolute necessity for its production. This is particularly the case with Liberian coffee, which is by no means a highland plant, and even prefers the rich, muddy loam of the lowland plains. And a richer or loamier soil than that around Khlang would be hard to find anywhere. Hence the rush in Selangor at this time for coffee allotments, to which even old Ceylon planters were eagerly turning their attention. The recent rush for coffee-planting is, of course, only a temporary one that will gradually calm down. For the supply in due time will adapt itself to the demand, and prices will naturally fall in consequence. But for those who have coffee concerns in good working order it must be one of the most paying of industries just for the time being.

While I was at Khlang, a price of twenty or twenty-one dollars per picul would give a handsome profit; but the price of coffee at Singapore then was over forty dollars per picul, and went up to forty-four since. So coffee, coffee, is at present the magic word for making money, though how long it will last I am not able to say.

Quala-lumpor is finely situated among hills and hollows, but otherwise savours very much of a busy mining town.

The houses of the few Europeans are placed on pretty knolls and hillocks here and there, with good scenery around them, while the Residency occupies the best coign of vantage among them all. A scenery devoid of sea, lake, or river is always to me wanting in something, and Quala-lumpor is wanting in all these, except the tiny river that flows on to Khlang ; but otherwise the locality is very pleasing.

The great industry of the province is tin, tin, tin ; and tin, indeed, is the most important industry throughout the whole peninsula, though gold and other metals are also found here and there. This metal, tin, is found in Selangor in the form of black oxide, distributed in coarse, heavy grains in the clayey soil near the surface, so that the vicinity of Quala-lumpor is quite covered with these shallow excavations in search of this precious ore, which is easily reduced to the metallic state and ready for export.

The labour is all done by the Chinese, who also own a great deal of the wealth and property of the place. Indeed, the Chinese are a wonderful race. They swarm through the whole of Siam, where they form a far more important commercial element than the Siamese themselves. They force their way through the mountain passes between their own country and Upper Burmah, and eat away the poor Burmans out of the land of their ancestors. In Australia, if their immigration had not been timeously checked, they would have multiplied till they and the rabbits only would have been left in possession of the land. They are, in short, a veritable plague of locusts, before whom the other nations of the East cannot possibly hold their own from an economic point of view.

As a rule, they are a quiet, thrifty people, and I hope they will excuse me for saying that they are occasionally the vilest of thieves. Many people at home think that in these foreign possessions of ours all the riches belong to our own countrymen, while the natives are never anything but hewers of wood and drawers of water. Let them go to Singapore or Penang, and there they will find that by far the greater portion of the wealth of these towns belongs to the Chinese population, who are as much foreigners in these places as we are ourselves. Let the heathen Chinese be abused as they may, yet they form a very important item among the puzzling problems and premonitions of the future ages.

CHAPTER XXVI

> Oh, Death, how searchless are thy ways,
>   Thy laws how secret and profound!
> Thou sparest one for many days,
>   And for his sake another's drowned;
> But bear in mind, capricious elf,
>   Against whose shafts there's no safe shield,
> That even thou must *die thyself*,
>   And unto Life thy spoil must yield.
> *Life and Death.*

The Orang-Bukits—A primitive people—Their poisoned darts—The effects of clairvoyance—Their Æolian harps—Loathsome leprosy—Visit to general hospital—Foundering of steamship 'Setthi'—Saved by the bite of a mad dog—The durian and mangosteen.

WHEN putting up at the rest-house at Khlang, I accidentally came across a brother of Mr. S——, who had put me up at Jazin in the Malacca Province. He was going in extensively for both pepper and coffee plantations, and lived only a few miles away from Khlang, on the opposite side of the little river. I went to see him one day, and he gave me to understand that there was a small village a few miles off, the people of which were Orang-Bukits, the primitive aborigines of the Malayan Peninsula, and he was also good enough to accompany me there for the purpose of interpreting for me. These people generally roam about the forest without any fixed or permanent abode, and the more advanced Malays in former years used to hunt them down like the beasts of the field.

Except a small portion belonging to the kingdom of Siam, the whole of the Malayan Peninsula is now under British rule and protection. Since that happy day the Orang-Bukits are allowed to live in peace and quietness, and they are gradually getting to settle down in little villages like the one we were visiting, which consisted of only a few houses on the top of a low, flattish hill. From a cursory view of those I saw, it would be folly to attempt a description of these aborigines, who are scattered here and there over the whole length and breadth of the land, receiving different names in different localities, but all essentially the same race.

They are generally supposed to be among the most primitive of all races ; but as regards the few of them that I saw, I could not well make out any marked ethnological differences between them and other odds and ends of humanity that I had previously come across. They were said to be very truthful and honest by Mr. S.——, who had some of them occasionally working on his plantation, and that they were very accommodating in the way of food, as nothing came amiss to them, from rats and snakes to roots and leaves.

They have got some idea of music, too, to calm their savage breasts, and they stick up in the open parts of the forest long hollow pieces of bamboo, with slits cut in them here and there ; and these bamboos act the part of real Æolian harps as the wind blows over them. I have seen some of these bamboos sticking up, and have listened to their music ; but during the two days that I went in that direction, the wind was altogether too calm to bring much music out of even an Æolian harp itself.

Various written descriptions have been given of the many, many uses to which bamboos are put by uncivilised races in tropical climates, but I don't remember ever seeing any mention of them in connection with musical instruments. Yet here it was. Nay more, small hard slips of bamboo comprise the very sounding-boards of the musical instrument called ranàt, alluded to on a previous page, but a description of which I cannot wait to give here.

Like the Dyaks of Borneo, they shoot their game with poisoned darts, which they throw from peculiar hollow tubes, or blowpipes, generally known under the name of sámpatans. When we went to the house of the chief of the little tribe, I tried hard to wheedle him out of one or two of these sámpatans, but nothing at first would prevail on him to part with them, as the Orang-Bukits have scarcely risen yet to a due appreciation of the almighty dollar. At last, after a good deal of clairvoyance, and telling him all sorts of nonsense through Mr. S.——, who translated, I was able to coax him out of a couple of his best sámpatans for a consideration.

He had only a few of the poisoned darts with him, and as I wished to see how quickly the poison killed, I wanted him to shoot with one of the darts an innocent hen that was quietly scraping away for her livelihood. But this the savage would not do—and perhaps he was right. His son gave me into the bargain a few poisoned darts, and in a few days afterwards prepared for me a fresh supply of darts and of the poison they use on the tip of them. This poison they prepare from an extract made from the root of one tree, *aca-epoh*, and the leaves of another, *tunik*. These sámpatans and upas poison, or whatever it is, are still in my possession, but I have never been able to throw the darts myself from these blowpipes, which these savages were able to do easily to a considerable distance.

We then adjourned to one of the other houses, and here we met an object of the deepest misery, in the person of a young girl under twenty years of age, of this same tribe, lying on the floor and actually dying from leprosy. It was a most pitiful sight to see this young girl, with her legs and arms partly shrivelled away, and deformed and cramped by this most loathsome of all diseases. How countless are the ways of human suffering; and how little comparatively has human skill accomplished yet to put an end to them!

A day or two afterwards I met Dr. W——, the principal Medical Officer of the Selangor State. He was then, with only one other European surgeon, looking after a large State hospital of something like 500 beds, and with every requisite apparatus. He had several cases of leprosy on hand, which is rather common among the Chinese tin-miners; and he said that leprosy, above all other complaints, was pre-eminently the scourge of Selangor and the peninsula throughout; and moreover, that there was a village farther down the sea-coast to the south where lepers married and were given in marriage, with the result that almost everybody in the village was a leper. Many eminent physicians have puzzled their heads in vain to find out *the* true cause of leprosy. But they are apparently as far from it as ever.

When I landed at Penang from the German ship Teutonia,' I inquired after the steamship 'Setthi,' as I wanted to pay a visit to the great pearl fisheries of the Mergui Archipelago ; and the route of this ship was between Rangoon and Penang, calling at one or more of these islands on her voyages to and fro. Mr. W——, whom I left under treatment at Saigon for the bite of a mad dog, was the European engineer of this little ship, which belonged to a firm of Chinese merchants. And I promised him, when leaving Saigon, that I would try and take a passage in his ship, if I could hit her off when I reached Penang, for she left Penang only once in every three weeks.

Mr. W—— reached Penang before me, duly cured, I hope, if he required a cure, which I very much doubted. But on the particular voyage of the 'Setthi' from Rangoon to Penang where he was to join her, she was caught in a cyclone near Rangoon, and foundered with a loss of over fifty human lives. If Mr. W—— had not gone to Saigon on account of the dog's bite, he would to a certainty have been on board his ship, and would have been drowned. And thus the life of Mr. Woodworth of that ilk, chief engineer of the steamship 'Setthi,' is probably unique in history, as having been saved from a watery grave by the bite of a mad dog !

There was one curiosity I was able to gratify on this journey, and which I often wished to gratify before, but in vain—and this was the desire to be somewhere about the Straits Settlements when certain fruits peculiar to the Straits were in season. It looked as if I were going to miss the opportunity this time again. But, luckily, by the time I reached Penang on my way back the fruits in question had already ripened. Among others, there are two fruits in particular that grow in the Straits Settlements and surrounding, and nowhere else.

There is a general notion that the climate of these Straits Settlements is like that of India, or that of any other tropical hot place. This is far from being the case. Generally speaking, the greater portion of India, except during the monsoon, has got a very dry climate, where month passes after month without speck or cloud in the burnished sky. The Straits Settlements, on the other hand, has got a very cloudy, moist, and even rainy atmosphere almost all the year round, while the heat never rises so high as in most parts of India during the hot season.

The *mangosteen* and *durian*, the two fruits in question, love a moist, shady climate, and are actually frizzled out of existence in climates where the atmosphere is not almost invariably humid. They therefore refuse to grow in India, or almost anywhere else except in the doldrums near the Equator. These two fruits are far less known to the ordinary traveller than is generally supposed; and that was the reason why I wanted to see them at their best, and why I write about them at all here, for they come into season at a time when the traveller who values his comfort is well out of the tropics, and the same may be said of the mango of India and elsewhere, which is never seen by the visitor in the pleasant cool season.

Among those who have tasted it, there is no fruit about which tastes differ so much as about the *durian*. It is a large fruit, not very unlike a pineapple when at a little distance, but it is nearly round, and not elongated like the latter, and the outer surface is armed with hard, blunt spines, instead of the soft outer texture of the pineapple. The rind is also so hard, and the fruit so large and heavy, that, as it happens to grow high up on large forest trees, it has been known before now to cause death by falling from the tree on the bald pate of some unfortunate native pedestrian walking quietly down below, though I am not sure if any of them ever happened to kill a European.

When this hard rind is properly cut open, the interior is seen to consist of four or more compartments each compartment filled with three or four seeds of about the size of a chestnut, imbedded separately in a thick, viscid substance of about the same consistency and appearance as very thick yellow cream. This latter pulp is the edible portion of the fruit, having each lump covered with a thin, gauzy white film that serves to separate each compartment from its fellows. It is as to the value of this cream-like pulp that opinions so vastly differ that some Europeans who pass their best days in the Straits never taste it, or only taste it once, but never again; while others, on the other hand, consider it the real jam-jam and manna of the wilderness.

It is confessed, however, even by its devotees, that it is

a fruit that requires a little time to be appreciated, and that grows on one only by acquaintance. I was not long enough in its company to put this last quality to the test, but I could quite see that one requires to be educated up to it, for it is by no means a real relish on first trial. Every offensive smell in the dictionary, from garlic and onions to sulphuretted hydrogen and rotten eggs, has been hurled at the head of this unfortunate fruit, and it cannot be denied that occasional whiffs float sometimes across the atmosphere of an undescribable and overpowering quality. These puffs blow when they list, and come and go at their own sweet pleasure, like the sighings of zephyrs turned upside down. They are like the incomplete blendings of several incompatible smells before being finally amalgamated. So powerful is this smell to the upturned noses of over-sensitive people, that the presence of the fruit in the same room with them is as unbearable as the presence of a cat to some other peculiarly constituted individuals.

On the other hand, to the prominent organs of other chosen people this fruit smells like real perfume and tastes as rich and luscious as ambrosia itself. To some people it occupies a medium position between these two extremes, for though they find the flavour certainly high, yet they can both smell and eat it without any great compunctions of conscience, and gradually get fond of it. Personally, I was not long enough acquainted with the durian to bring about this happy state of matters. But that it is esteemed a valuable fruit is shown by the high price paid for it, more especially by the rich natives; for when I was in Penang then, the fruit was just beginning to come into the market, and you could not get a good ripe one much under half a dollar, or, say, a shilling or so.

The character of the mangosteen, the other localised fruit of the Straits, is different, for everybody likes it; and many people who can't endure the durian near them think the mangosteen the finest fruit of any. I was not quite such an utter stranger to the mangosteen as to the durian, for we had met before on more than one occasion; but this was when the mangosteen had got a little old, for there is scarcely any other fruit so delicate and perishable as this one.

It is about the size of a small mandarin orange, with a darker and much tougher rind, which, however, cuts fairly easily to the knife, and exposes the interior fruit from which the rind, when it is ripe, is quite free. This inner fruit is almost exactly the size of a golf ball (so much in fashion when I pen these lines), of a pearly, clear whiteness, and divided into four or more segments, after the manner of an orange and other fruits of the kind. Sometimes the segments are five, six, or even more, in number, and if you wish to know how many segments the interior fruit contains before opening the rind, you have only to look at the top of the unopened fruit, and there you will see the remains of the original flower-cup, or calyx, divided into parts that correspond with the number of segments of the fruit inside. Generally speaking, the fewer the segments the better the fruit, as the individual segments are likely to be larger.

Each of these segments may contain a seed, but when the mangosteens are very good, these seeds are almost entirely *cultivated* out of existence, so that scarcely anything remains but the pulp alone. And even when one or two seeds remain, they are so soft that they are generally eaten with the rest of the fruit, to which they impart no disagreeable flavour whatever, unless the mangosteens are bad and the seeds harder than they ought to be.

This, then, is the fruit that is esteemed by many even above the famous mango of India and other places, with which, however, it has nothing in common, except the more or less resemblance in name. But there is no fruit so variable in quality as a mango, from the ropy, turpentiny variety of dry up-country climates, with its hard, thick stone in the middle of it, to the truly luscious mangoes that grow where the soft zephyrs blow from the sea on the Malabar coast of India, with a seed as thin and flat as a pancake, inside a pulp too luscious to be described.

It would be as easy individually to pick out the beauty of beauties at a beauty show as to pick out to the satisfaction of everyone the fruit of fruits in an all-comprising fruit market. In the first place, fruits, just like beauties, possess various and often opposite kinds of virtues; and secondly, the tastes of the judges luckily differ immensely among themselves. I fancy, therefore, that a complete consensus of opinion about the fruit of fruits is as impossible as about the beauty of beauties in an all-comprising beauty show.

Notwithstanding the resemblance in names, the mangoes and the mangosteens, as I said, have but little in common. If one therefore gets a surfeit of mangosteens for a month, he would probably prefer a mango from the capricious love of change inherent in human nature ; and after a month of mangoes he would probably, for the same reason, prefer a mangosteen, a pear, or perhaps some other fruit. But taking one thing with another, as the cat said when he was licking up the cream, I think that a very good mango is the king of all fruits, though there are several people who can't abide it.

There are other curious fruits in the Straits with which I got supplied at this time for the sheer sake of novelty, such as the lansit, the ramputàn and the jack-fruit; but these are not so confined to the Straits Settlements, nor are their merits so often discussed by those who come in contact with them, as to require any special description here.

CHAPTER XXVII

Time passed, and I retraced again
  My steps to scenes of old,
And looked and looked, but looked in vain,
  For friends now dead and cold
  Beneath the silent mould;
While e'en the hills scarce seemed to me
The same as they were wont to be.
The Rover's Return.

Mandalay revisited—Scenes of lang syne—Changes of Mandalay and surroundings—'Britannia: a Dream'—The vile Kabyoo—The wounded Corydon—Two golden rules—Married on a wooden leg—The Woundouk of Bhamó—A real ruby ring—The Burmese crown jewels—Travelling hints on Burmah—Stranded on the Irrawaddy—Mr. Streeter and the Burmah Ruby Mines.

AND now we had left all the Straits Settlements behind, and were on our way back again to Rangoon in the British India steamer 'Nuddea,' the commander of which I had known long ago, but had not seen for twelve or thirteen long years. He had also enough mangosteens on board, which was another recommendation in his favour, so that we had plenty of opportunities of judging of their quality, as well as of the seeds and segments they contained. And there was plenty of room, too, on board the ship, for there were only two other passengers, one of them a Roman Catholic priest, and the other a mariner who had been nearly lost in the cyclone in which the ill-fated 'Setthi' went down. And thus I landed at Rangoon.

Having a short time still on hand, I could not think of returning to India without revisiting Upper Burmah (and Mandalay especially), where I had at one time spent nearly a couple of years of my life. Much had changed. Instead of going up and down by river, for instance, as on previous occasions, one is now able to reach Mandalay from Rangoon in about twenty-four hours by rail. Mandalay was not what it was. Poor King Theebaw's Golden Palace had been altogether converted into mere public offices and officers' quarters.

The monastery in connexion with the Arracan Pagoda, from which the Burmese priests, or *phoongies*, had been temporarily dispossessed, and where I lived on that occasion, was now in possession of the monks again.

The tank in its vicinity, from the steps of which we once used to feed the turtles swimming about, was just as it was before, and I fed the turtles once again, probably for the last time, and cooeyed to them to come to their banquet as on previous occasions. The pagoda itself was unchanged save for a fresh cover of paint, and of gold-leaf on the image of Buddha ; and there were the young Burmese maidens, or *minkalays*, some of them on their knees adoring Buddha, and some trying to sell their petty merchandise in the long passages, and all of them, as usual, in the best of good humour. And last of all there was the great image of Buddha himself, the most sacred image of Buddha in all Burmah, and lately decorated with fresh gold-leaf, and looking as fresh as paint, but as grave and thoughtful as ever, with the fingers and toes all of the same length, just as I had left them years ago.

But the Incomparable Pagoda, the largest pagoda in Upper Burmah, was gone, as it had been burnt down to the ground a few years before. And the large image of Buddha half-way up Mandalay Hill, had also been destroyed by fire in the prolonged interval. And there was no signal station on the top of the Hill any longer, for all these things had now been abandoned in these piping days of peace. The walled and moated royal city of King Theebaw had itself been all vacated by the Burmese populace, and with the exception of the Golden Palace, there was scarcely anything to be seen of the previous state of matters.

The extra-mural portion of the town, which was always the larger, was now larger still by reason of the addition to it of the former intra-mural inhabitants, and the otherwise greater growth of the capital city, following in the footsteps of peace and prosperity, with the many advantages that follow in their train. The streets in which pigs and pariah dogs used to wallow in dirt and mire, in search of what offal they could find, were now cleaned, gravelled, and some of them even macadamised, though a good deal of dust was still flying about at this broiling time of the year. And yet, with all these improvements, it was not like the former Mandalay, nor half so interesting, in a way, to me.

I wished very much to revisit Bhamó, on the inland borders of China, where I had once spent a good many days; but here again Father Time checked me, as he had previously done with regard to going to Luang-Prabang, in Siam. As my time was getting short, I could not depend on the certainty of communication on the Irrawaddy, as the steamers are always running on sandbanks at this season of the year, and sometimes remaining there for days. So my designs in the direction of Bhamó had to be abandoned.

At the very beginning of January 1886, I went up to Bhamó for the first time, in a notorious ill-steering stern-wheeler called the 'Kabyoo,' commanded by a Dane called Terndrop, and reputed to be the worst ship of the Irrawaddy Flotilla Company. Bhamó had just been occupied for the first time by British troops a few days before. The few other passengers who went with the 'Kabyoo' from Mandalay were dropped here and there at the small outposts that were then being established, while I alone was going up all the way to Bhamó.

It was shortly before then, in 1885, that the so-called 'Russian Scare' took place, and it was still fresh in my memory. For it was among the transport corps sending up commissariat supplies to oppose the Muscovite advance that the cholera broke out near Jacobabad, to which I have already cursorily alluded when speaking of that cholera camp as the greatest grilling I had previously endured. And it was from there I went to Burmah. I might be pardoned, therefore, for not being in the most friendly humour to Russia at this particular time. And so, as I was alone with only the master of the ship for the last two or three days of the trip, I wrote 'Britannia : a Dream,' just to while away the time. And as it has been lying dormant in my manuscript for the last nine years, I may as well repeat it here, if only as a change from bad prose to worse verse.

BRITANNIA:

(A DREAM IN ANAPESTS).

Behold, as I slept at the evening tide,
   I dreamt of Britannia's matron-like mould,
Her hand being extended away from her side,
   Above the fair heads of a triple of bold
Young rovers—the first with a *rope* in his hand,
   The second with *sword* at the point of présent,
The third being fully equally brilliant and grand,
   With *knowledge* displayed on each fair lineament.

Her brows were surrounded about with a wreath,
   Whence one brilliant diamond shone with a blaze
That rivalled the sun, as it flashed from its sheath,
   And dazzled the foe who should venture to gaze;
She held the brave flag of the Red, White, and Blue,
   And waved it with pride o'er her dutiful sons,
And viewed them as mothers are wonted to view
   The features and forms of their own little ones.

John Bull, with a smirk on his jovial face,
   Exactly the same as portrayed in *Punch*,
Was standing beside with commendable grace,
   And holding before him a ponderous bunch
Of all sorts of implements, silver and all,
   Which straightway he laid at Britannia's feet;
'Now take it, my dear,' he exclaimed, 'at your call
   I'd lay down my life and my service complete.'

A fierce-looking Lion and Unicorn stern,
   A Harp placed between them, sat silent in front,
And oh, by their aspect one well might discern
   How eager they were for the battle's red brunt!
Their tails were aye wagging affectionately,
   To those gallant lads that had made them such pets,
And judged by appearance and strength, you could see,
   'Twere not very safe to enrage them with threats.

Beside their big brothers were other brave boys,
   And promising yet to be mighty in deed,
To all the wild winds who had tossed their own toys,
   To stand by their side in the hour of their need;
Across the wide seas they had come from afar,
   Determined to stand for Britannia's right,
Each eager to join in the conflict of war,
   And all to be foremost and boldest in fight.

Amidst the proud scene stood a peace-loving sage,[1]
    Chief councillor he at Britannia's will,
A far-sighted Solon, whose wisdom and age
    Pronounced and proclaimed him a sage of great skill;
Though well-versed in classics and ancient lore,
    Yet well could he wend through the maze of finance,
For all kinds of talents combined in the store
    Of learning that shone from his noble old glance.

He looked to his front with complaisance the while,
    His hat in his hand and not far from his Queen,
His countenance lit with a genial smile,
    To witness the lads' imperturbable mien;
For well did he know, in event of a war,
    They'd fight long and hard for Britannia's sake,
And teach the aggressor, be 't Sultan or Czar,
    Before her bright presence to tremble and quake.

The angels looked down from their lofty abode,
    And fluttered their wings with approving delight,
Proclaiming their friendship, as sanctioned by God,
    And steadfastly sealed by Imperial right;
While skirting the clouds in their garments of snow,
    Saint Patrick, Saint George, and St. Andrew were seen
With hands joined in hands as they looked down below,
    On this very rare incompàrable scene.

Britannia thanked Mr. Bull for support,
    Approved the advice of her councillor hoar,
And blessed her brave boys in that genial sort
    Of tone that goes straight to the heart's inner core;
The lads stood attentive before their mamma,
    Each prompt to obey her maternal behest,
Her will being to them an inviolate law,
    For all to observe as the bravest and best.

Away in the distance a grisly old Bear,
    And other queer creatures were crouching low down,
Of dingy appearance and mangy, rough hair,
    Without any birthright to ancient renown;
They snarled at the pets, though afraid to advance,
    Excepting by stealth with their tails 'tween their feet,
Being sorely afraid they would lead them a dance,
    Before they were able to make their retreat.

The Bear was an envious beast of the field,
    And had a rough rabble of ragged recruits,
Irregular levies imperfectly ' wheeled,'
    And mean-looking knaves from the tail of the brutes.

---

[1] Mr. Gladstone was in power when this poem was written.

They envied Britannia's stately desmesne,
  And wanted to pounce on her progeny fair,
But oh, by their dastardly mien might be seen
  They ought to be cowering home in their lair.

With heart-winning smile and a toss of her head
  (And yet, gentle reader, no wanton was she),
Her locks in profusion were instantly spread
  Around her fair bosom, dishevelled and free ;
Down dropped from her tresses a beautiful flower,
  A mingling of Shamrock and Thistle and Rose,
And there on the ground in unconscious power,
  It lay for a time in its fragrant repose.

' The gauntlet is down,' she intently exclaimed,
  ' And woe to the caitiff who dares take it up.'
The Bear made a grab, though he looked very maimed,
  While all his vile horde made uproarious who-o-o-p.
I saw as the *sailor-lad* sprang to his spar,
  I saw as the *soldier* his sword girded on,
The *student* retired to prepare for the war
  Victorious forces from sources unknown.

A gay, gallant navy was sailing the sea,
  A proud-marshalled army was marching on land,
And there in their thousands the brave and the free
  Stood calmly awaiting the word of command ;
'Twas given, and then the loud roar of the guns,
  And clash of the sabres, were heard from afar,
And fierce in their onset, Britannia's sons
  Advanced to be foremost in order of war.

I saw till the clouds had surrounded them all,
  And foeman and friend had been mingled in one ;
But sure, when they lifted their death-screening pall,
  And darkness gave way to the rays of the sun,
That Albion's heroes the field would possess,
  As often their sires had possessed it of yore,
And stand on the ground in their stern loveliness,
  The foe at their feet by the far-distant shore.

Oh ! fierce was the struggle, and long was the strife,
  While war-horse and warrior rushed through the field,
And sadly appalling the carnage to life,
  Where blue-bonnets waved, unaccustomed to yield ;
The clouds rolled in this way and that way again,
  As swayed the battalions at times to and fro,
But never I doubted, though thousands were slain,
  Our troops in the end would discomfit the foe.

I listened, and heard the renowned British rush,
   So famous on many a death-stricken day,
When boldly our soldiers pressed forward to crush
   Whatever opposed their victorious sway;
The enemy now were commencing to reel,
   When order came forward to forge through the fight,
And then it was shown how the cold British steel,
   E'en now, as of yore, put the foemen to flight.

At last the loud roar of the cannon was still,
   And silence prevailed like the silence of night,
The clouds were uplifted away to the hill,
   And there stood Britannia's sons in their might;
No mirth marred their mien, as they gazed on the dead,
   Who never again would engage in a war,
While comrades were laid in their gory low bed,
   To sleep their long sleep from their hamlets afar.

I saw till the Bear was laid prostrate below,
   The Lion above in majestic disdain,
Awaiting the order of weal or of woe,
   To let him go free or to crunch out his brain;
Britannia suddenly stood on the ground,
   With bonnie blue eyes, and the flag in her hand,
While silent and stern stood her offspring around,
   To hear her next wish and obey her command.

I woke—and my ship was just dropping her chain
   In some unpronounceable port in the East,
And much did I marvel and wish to remain
   Asleep till the grand panorama had ceased.
Methinks I still see them bespattered with gore,
   The live and the dead in their dread panoply,
And lovely Britannia come to restore
   The peace that the Bear had declared to defy.

It was some years after writing the above verses that I went up to Siberian Russian myself for the first time, and liked the Russians very much. But then I could not like them half so much did I not love my own country more.

After we anchored by the river's side the night before we reached Bhamó, having finished these verses, I repeated them to the skipper, for want of anything else to do. He seemed to like them and asked if I would print them. I told him I would, and would send him a copy; which I now do forthwith, in order to show him how well I can keep my promise, though delayed for the quite appreciable period of ten long years!

In the evening, before it got quite dark, the two of us went on shore, and through a village whose name I now quite forget. There we picked up a young Burmese lad who had lately been shot right through the knee-joint. He himself belonged to Moulmein, in Lower Burmah, and was up in this high latitude cutting teakwood for his employers, when he was so dangerously wounded. We took him with us up to Bhamó, and I wanted to cut off his leg, as the only means of saving his life. But he wouldn't hear of this.

Among many others, there are two great rules in military surgery that came in on this occasion: (1) 'In penetrating gunshot wounds of joints, amputate;' and the sooner the better, as there is little or no chance of saving the limb. This is a very wise rule—a real golden one. (2) 'Never amputate without the consent of the patient.' This rule is not so golden, and may occasionally be a very foolish one. The first of these rules is based on the premises of Science, while the second is based on those of Morals, which are not always easy to define. But I am not here going to discuss the merits of them, as that would be out of the sphere of a descriptive narrative of this kind.

Shortly after occupying Bhamó the writer opened a civil hospital for the benefit of the poor ignorant natives, and invited the sick and the lame to come and see. Nothing conciliates the hostile natives more than the belief that you really desire to do them good, as I well knew from previous experience; and I had a certain amount of public funds placed at my disposal to help the more urgent cases.

The Burmese lad who stuck out against the amputation was dying by inches, and would have died long before but for his youthful frame and his cold-blood Asiatic constitution, which, as already mentioned, stands surgical injuries better than the hot, inflammatory constitutions of Europeans. However, the lad was at last reduced to a mere skeleton, when, almost saying he would ne'er consent, he consented to the amputation. The poor youth made an excellent recovery, and in a couple of months thereafter he was as fat and plump as a chicken.

His was one of the cases which required the kind of

monetary aid referred to. And so, after preparing for him a nice wooden leg that any warrior might feel proud of, he hobbled down to the river-side as proud as Punch, and duly went on board the steamer that was going to carry him on his journey. His case being rather a helpless one, on account of having only one leg, his passage was paid all the way, and a few rupees given him as pocket money in case of emergency. And so he left Bhamó, probably feeling very grateful.

But he had got so fit and fat, as I said, that with the exception of the leg he was better than ever. And so when he again reached the village from which we took him at first, who did he meet but the only girl that ever he loved. He had lost his leg in the wars; that was true enough, but he had also lost his heart to his sweetheart. And so he left the ship, forgot his friends and relatives in Moulmein, and lived at that remote village with the darling of his heart—for Love was still the lord of all! O woman! thou art the *real* lotus that makes men forget their country.

As this was the first amputation ever performed in remote Bhamó (for the Kachins had not yet begun to give trouble) the natives watched the progress of the case with curiosity, and apparently expected that the operator should not only be able to take off a leg, but even to make another leg grow in its stead. Such at any rate was the story sent from Bhamó to one of the Anglo-Indian papers, and which was gravely copied in part by no less serious or scientific a weekly than the *British Medical Journal*, which writes under date November 27, 1886, as follows :—

The repugnance with which Oriental races regard surgical operations is well known. The extent to which it prevails in parts of Burmah may be seen from a statement of a Bhamó correspondent of the *Pioneer*. From this it would appear that the majority of natives prefer to die rather than submit to the knife; and many suffering from severe gunshot wounds, or fractures of limbs necessitating amputation, have told the surgeons they prefer death to mutilation. This is not from religious scruples, but purely to distrust and aversion to the knife. At the same time, they will scar their bodies all over with the actual cautery, or wear holes into their flesh by the continual application of blistering fluids and mineral caustics. The results of these continual cauterizations, which are much used by the Shans as preventive and not remedial agents, are the formation of numbers of huge sores, ulcers, and warts of perfectly phenomena dimensions. With English medicines, the correspondent observes, they become familiarised comparatively soon; and after they have seen the beneficial effects of self-evident remedies, such as febrifuges and aperients, they run to the other extreme, and demand medicines to cure burns, scars, lame legs, and missing toes and fingers. Surgical science has not proved, from a Burman's point of view, sufficiently practical in its results to convince him of its efficacy.

It is related that the first surgical case Dr. MacGregor, then civil surgeon, had at Bhamó, was that of a gunshot wound through the knee. It being found impossible to save the leg, it was amputated and healed most successfully. On recovery the patient was provided with a wooden leg, and stumped about the bazaars paying visits to his friends, who of course had given him up as a dead man. The sight, however, was not encouraging to the Burmans, who said they had never seen a man with only one leg. They thought that perhaps it was better that the man's life had been saved, but at the same time, unless the English medical man could make a new leg grow in place of the missing one, he was not justified in cutting it off.

The present writer does not know who the writer of this statement could have been. Like many good stories, however, there is no foundation for it in fact, so far as he knows, as he never heard of these funny expectations till he read about them, not only in one but in several newspapers. But this was at the very beginning of affairs. Some time afterwards, when the Kachins began to rush down from their mountains, the Burmans might have plenty of opportunity of seeing surgical operations of various descriptions performed at this remote outpost of Bhamó.

One other anecdote from Bhamó, and I have done with it. People died in Burmah as everywhere else, even before the vile Ferringhi went up there with his curses of civilisation. And, shortly after going to Bhamó, we found that the Burmese *Woundouk* of the place was very ill— that he was, in fact, suffering from an advanced stage of the disease that is said to have killed the late Czar of Russia.

The case of the *Woundouk* was incurable, and, after due trial, he was recommended to go down to Mandalay for a change. The *Woundouks* were provincial governors under the old native *régime*, and there were only four of these magnates throughout the whole of the country altogether. This was the governor, then, of the North Province of Burmah, of which Bhamó was the centre. A few days, however, before he was to sail for Mandalay, I had to start on the Mougoung expedition. I went to see him in the evening before we were going to start, and had Captain Terndrop of the 'vile Kabyoo' for interpreter. And so, when I was taking my leave of the *Woundouk*, never to see him again, he gave me an apparently valuable ruby ring in token of past kindness and attention.

I was highly pleased with this real ruby ring from the *Woundouk* of Bhamo, the veritable 'last of the Mohicans' that was ever to hold sway there. The ring certainly looked very beautiful with its soft, twinkling ruby lustre, while on each side of the central ruby was a small, flashing diamond. The stone was certainly very valuable if it *was* a ruby, and who in the world could doubt that it was, seeing that it had been given me by the last *Woundouk* of Bhamó, and when he expressly said so?

But one fine day during the expedition curiosity, aided by evil counsellors, tempted me to take the stone out of its setting, which we did with some little trouble, and found that to the best of opinions the stone was only a garnet—which I believe it really was. How I hoped that the *Woundouk* of Bhamó would recover! And I still wonder whether he intentionally deceived me, or whether he had himself been imposed upon, and had given me a garnet under the impression that it was a real, valuable ruby. However, I still valued the ring as a memento and a curiosity.

Times soon began to get harder, and my Madrassee servant could not stand the hard work. He therefore got conveniently sick, and I had to send him back again to Madras at the first opportunity. Shortly afterwards I missed the *Woundouk's* ring, with the small diamonds still sticking in it, though the quasi-ruby had been removed, and I suspected that the slimy servant had taken it with him. One of the other servants knew where he lived in Madras, and I wrote him on the subject, and in due course received the audacious reply that he did take 'the ring with the two white little stones,' but that I had given it to him as a present. I answered that if he did not return the ring at once, I should report him to the Madras police. But there's many a mile between Bhamó and Madras, and as the false servant knew it, he did not even reply to my second letter. And such was the fate of the 'real ruby' ring presented to me long ago by the last *Woundouk* of Bhamó when he was sorely stricken, even unto death.

While staying at Mandalay this last time, the air was full of rumours about the ex-King Theebaw's lost regalia. It will be remembered that, on the taking of Mandalay in November 1885, the crown jewels were supposed to be stolen out of the Golden Palace, and it is not known to this day what has become of them. But, just at this time, there was great gossip about the confession in England of a discharged soldier of the Hampshire regiment, who confessed to have been on guard at the Palace during the first night of occupation, and to have stolen the crown jewels in company with a comrade who had since died. They buried the treasure under the ground, and a sentry box was soon afterwards raised over the identical spot; so that he and his comrade were consequently unable to recover the valuable prize which they had actually stolen when mounted on guard duty.

If true, it was a grave crime. But looting was said to be so common at this time, that, according to one source of information which I have seen in print, these men were not worse than others, and that the general and staff who first occupied the Palace, and the latter of whom were said to number exactly the figure forty, were known as 'Ali Baba and his Forty Thieves,' on account of the looting propensities of the staff, though not of the general himself. These rumours were probably unfounded or exaggerated.

But here was this corporal coming out to Burmah, with the permission of the home authorities, to recover the jewels that he and his now dead comrade had hidden in the earth, and of which he was himself to get ten per cent. *ad valorem*. This, it must be confessed, would be a funny method of rewarding burglary by a British soldier when on guard duty. He was even declared by some to have already come out, and to be actually staying in secret at the very hotel at which I was putting up myself. But the story died away like a baseless vision, and whether the discharged soldier made a confession or not, the crown jewels of Burmah have not been recovered up to date.

From the small and indifferent hotel accommodation at Mandalay, it is evident that pleasure-seeking tourists and travellers have not yet found out the beauties of Burmah. Yet it is a pretty country, and quite as interesting as India, to which such crowds resort during the cool season of the year there.

The best way to visit Burmah is to travel by rail from Rangoon to Mandalay, the whole journey now being made in about twenty-four hours. And then, if time permits, proceed to Bhamó by river steamer. If the famous Ruby-Mine Mountains are desired to be visited, the traveller should land at Khanyāt, and procure ponies there for the journey up the mountains, some of which are over six thousand feet high. But this is a long and hard trip at present, and the Ruby Mines have lost much of their romance, since they don't produce rubies, or only very few.

Some years ago, the well-known London jeweller, Mr. Streeter (or rather the then Mr. Streeter's son, who is now, I think, Mr. Streeter himself), was with me on the Irrawaddy on his way to the Ruby Mines, before they were rented from the Government of India by a syndicate, of which the Streeters were the principal partners. Our ship, called the 'Amherst,' went on a sandbank and stuck there three days, possibly in order to prevent Mr. Streeter from taking over such a ticklish concern. Mr. Streeter, however, did not read the warning in the proper light, and a little later on he and I were taken off the 'Amherst,' and were landed at Khanyāt, whence Mr. Streeter proceeded to the Ruby Mines. The consequence was that the said syndicate rented the Ruby Mines from the Government at a yearly rental of four lakhs of rupees, a sum that at that time represented 30,000*l.* a year! Hitherto, however, the undertaking has proved a disastrous failure, though some cheery prophets say that there are better times coming.

But whether the traveller visits Bhamó and the Ruby Mines or not, he should invariably come down the river from Mandalay in one of the Irrawaddy Flotilla Company's steamers, all the way to Rangoon, or at any rate to Prome, as the Irrawaddy is a particularly beautiful river, more especially along some of its higher reaches; though, unfortunately, in the tourist season the river is at its lowest mark, with its banks sometimes so high above the level of the water as to interfere with the general view of the surrounding country. Burmah of course is particularly the land of pagodas, for wherever you go you come across them, and to the stranger their white-sepulchre appearance looks quaint and pleasing, while the inhabitants of the country are a most genial kind of people, if one could only understand them.

CHAPTER XXVIII

> I travel and travel for evermore,
> I travel on sea and I travel on shore,
> I clamber the mountain and scamper the glen
> And visit the wilds and the haunts of men;
> Yet, somehow or other, wherever I stray,
> My heart's in the Highlands—for ever and aye.
> Heather Bells.

Benefits of travel—Bacon's opinion—Advice of the Author—Reading compared with observation—The Indo-Chinese race—Original divisions of mankind—Presumable origin of the Indo-Chinese—Religious tenets—The Mohammedan Malays—Habits of the Indo-Chinese—Their social system—Minor differences among themselves—The barber in Eastern nations—'The Maid of Mandalay'—First fiddle to *Mandalay Herald*.

THERE are various kinds of travel—travel for health, travel for pleasure, travel for knowledge, and travel for adventure. The benefit of travel, no doubt, depends not more on the travel than on the traveller himself; for true it is that a wink is as good as a nod to a blind horse, and equally true it is that on an entirely ignorant traveller travel is mostly thrown away. To such a one the Pass of Thermopylæ or the Plain of Marathon would be only a pass or a plain, and nothing more. And so he travels through land and sea with his eyes open outside and his mind shut within, often caring little and learning less of the interesting objects around, excepting for the sheer sake of 'doing' them. Such people are occasionally met with, but only very occasionally, and by no means represent the great bulk of travellers, who are, as a rule, as well educated and informed as any of their class, or any class of the community, so far as that is concerned.

'Travel,' says the universal Bacon, 'in the younger sort is a part of education; in the elder, a part of experience.

He that travelleth into a country before he hath some entrance into the language, goeth to school and not to travel.' Bacon ought rather to have said that mankind should be always in school, from the first dawn of intelligence till the *hic-jacet* of the grave. Bacon himself, though perhaps no great traveller, caught his death when travelling and experimenting on the preservative powers of snow on a common barn-door fowl that he had killed for the purpose. In fact, while travelling he anticipated the freezing chambers of the present-day shambles and slaughter-houses throughout America and Australia.

Be that as it may, travel is probably the best, as it is certainly the most costly, system of education, and at all ages, except the very youngest, on which its benefits are comparatively thrown away, as very young children are more or less in the condition of the blind horse stated above. It is no great good without a certain previous groundwork of information; but, given that, then travel becomes a most effective training school. It adds to one's knowledge in a way that the best book-lore can never do. To read about a thing and see it with one's own eyes are quite two different things; for the effect of reading is vague, often incorrect, and generally transitory, while that of seeing is clear, more lasting in character, and if not always correct, the fault is not in the stars of the observer, but in the observer himself. Ideas pour in through the eyes, the ears, and other senses, without as much as announcing their arrival, so silent and subtle is their influence.

Even the doubting Thomas believed when he *saw* with his own eyes and *felt* with his own fingers. Once upon a time, at college, I used to pore a good deal over Roman antiquities, which I did not very well understand. And how I used to bless the Romans, that they ever existed, to give me such an amount of toil and trouble. Only the vaguest ideas remained in my memory about them.

But on my way home, quite lately, I at last decided to visit in person this ancient empress of the world, about which I had read so much and remembered so little. So I spent my last Christmas there, the best ten days I have spent for a long time. By attending some of Dr. Forbes' peripatetic lectures, and by engaging an intelligent demonstrator for myself on certain occasions, I came to learn more about Rome in these ten days than I had previously done in twice as many months. For some of the things that used to puzzle me before were now plain enough before my very eyes. And I now quite believe that there was such a person as Julius Cæsar, or somebody else of the same name. And at the present moment I can easily recall to memory, not only Rome itself, but also my frail old guide, wrapped up in a mantle that might well serve for a Roman *toga*, lounging back in his seat as we drove along, and complacently repeating to himself the words of St. Paul, ' I am a Roman citizen.'

The general tendency of books is to exaggerate, that of travel to correct the imagination, and impress the mind more deeply and thoroughly, being the result of experience as distinguished from vague and vapoury opinion only. Hence it is that the conceptions of natural objects by the student in his study are seldom true to the facts and realities. You cannot impart a true conception of a mountain to one who has never seen one. He must *see* it first. You may bring him daily to gaze in picture galleries, where images of mountains may be displayed, yet he cannot recognise a real mountain when he sees one. The best of art is but a poor, flimsy thing in comparison to Mother Nature.

While quitting the shores of Burmah, probably for ever, it may not be out of place to make a few general remarks upon the Indo-Chinese race, among whom I had lately been sojourning, and among a portion of whom I had lived for some considerable time previously. Doctors are known to differ, and so do ethnologists, about the varieties of the human race. For while some of them divide the race into five or six, or even more varieties, others restrict it to only three, on purely scientific grounds alone, and apart altogether from the Biblical authority of Shem, Ham, and Japhet. These three main types are of course the Circassian, the Negro, and the Mongolian. The last classification is as likely to be true as any of the others.

As regards colour alone, it is certainly a most plausible theory. For black is the opposite of white, while yellow is a kind of half-way house between. Yellow seems as necessary a point to start from as either black or white; for the mere mingling of black and white blood would not produce the true yellow colour of the Mongolian, but some-

LÁÖS TRIBESMAN.
Profile view exhibiting moderately protruding jaws, and entire want of—*occipital protuberance!*

thing entirely different. Yet all the colours that we come across may be derived from a mingling in certain proportions of these three principal colours.

The many more or less pronounced local varieties, scattered here and there, are mostly the results of conformity to surroundings and other minor causes. It is found, for instance, that though cold climates are favourable to the maximum vigour of both body and mind, yet a too rigorous climate stunts the development of both mind and body alike. Hence, therefore, the existence of the small squat Laplanders not so very far away from the Scandinavians, one of the most vigorous of races.

There are certain races, however, that are such great anomalies, that some naturalists would ascribe to them a primary place for themselves among the varieties of the human family. The Papuans (the natives of New Guinea) are nearly as black as the true typical negro of Africa, and they resemble them also in their curly hair and their light-hearted disposition. But while agreeing with them in these respects, they differ widely from them in form and feature. For instead of the stout build, the thick lips, the flat nose, the protruding jaws, and the receding chin of the typical negro, they are of a light and lithe frame of body, and with decidedly Circassian or even Roman-nosey features. In their geographical distribution they are far away alike from the Circassians of Europe and the negroes of Africa, and are much more in proximity with the Mongolians of Asia, with whom they have but little physical affinity. And how they got to New Guinea is a conundrum that can only be answered by supposing that they had a boat of their own at the Deluge, or that there must have been some tremendous terrestrial disturbance since the first appearance of man on the face of the earth.

Various other anomalies might be quoted, like the hairy Ainos of Japan, the Negrettoes or natives of the Andaman and Philippine Islands, &c.; but a few are enough at a time. Ethnologists, not many decades ago, conjectured that the various families of the human race could best be classified according to the measurements of their skulls, and this new science they call Craniology. There was naturally quite a rage for human skulls among scientific people. If they did not manage to get them otherwise, they would be in danger of chopping them off the shoulders of innocent people, like the Dyaks of Borneo when in search of a wife, while they (the hypocrites) said that they were all the time in search of Mother Wisdom, quite a demure but essentially lovable old woman withal.

And so they gathered skulls, skulls, skulls, in pots, in pans, in bags, and in baskets, from all parts of the world. And when they had gathered these skulls together in quite gruesome Golgothas, then they, the scientists, began to put their own heads together also, in order to arrange and classify the other skulls. And when the wise people had put their own heads together, they found that after gathering all these heaps of skulls from all parts of the globe, yes, they found that the skull classification came to nothing at all. Thus Craniology, as a prime factor for the scientific classification of the human race, fell to the ground, and broke like a rotten egg—and there let it remain for the present.

The terms 'Indo-China' and 'Indo-Chinese' are comparatively modern ones, and have come mostly in vogue since the French occupation of Cambodia and Cochin-China during the latter half of the present century. They have no further meaning, so far, than merely the country and the people between India and China, and more especially those east of Burmah, between it and the China Sea. There are good scientific reasons, however, for including both Burmah and Siam, not only as comprising that portion of the world between India and China, but as also including a people more or less homogeneous in their physical characteristics.

These people, the Indo-Chinese, are probably no primary or original division of the human race, but they have certainly as much right to be considered such as some other divisions adopted by ethnologists. They are probably a comparatively modern race, and inhabit, in part at least, a geologically modern country. As a race they are likely less ancient than the Aryans of India (the mild Hindoos), on the one hand, and the true Mongolians (or heathen Chinese) on the other. And, moreover, they have in all probability sprung from a blending of these two races, which are now separated from one another by these new children of their own production.

To speak in general terms, throughout the whole vast

stretch of this country, from China in the north to Cape Cambodia in the south, and from India in the west to the China Sea in the east, the inhabitants are essentially the same stock, and only distinguished among themselves by merely local peculiarities, arising in the progress of ages. It is the same race also that inhabits Java and the Malayan Peninsula, and the very head-hunting Dyaks of Borneo themselves belong to this great Indo-Chinese family.

The race, as a race, is distinguished by a brown colour of skin, varying considerably in shade, but seldom so fair as that of the typical Mongolian, and seldom so dark as that of the typical mild Hindoo, from whom I presume the race to have originally started. In stature the Indo-Chinese are shorter than the Mongolians, and even than the Aryans of India. But they are much better built than the latter, and have actually well-developed *calves* to their legs, which Indians scarcely ever have. Their stature is also very uniform, seldom varying among themselves more than an inch or two, and few of them ever attain to the average height of the Europeans.

They have broader and less regular features than the Indians, and have a slight obliquity of the eyes, but never amounting to the true Mongolian type, and frequently it is scarcely discernible at all. They are also perceptibly *prognathous*, with the front of the two jaws meeting one another at an angle, and protruding somewhat; and I have seen some in which this protrusion of the jaws was very marked indeed.

The men of the race are generally quite innocent of a beard, though occasionally some of them produce a few straggling hairs which they cultivate with great assiduity, and still more occasionally they are able to produce a moustache, though never quite of Lord Dundreary proportions. Their hair is long when they allow it to grow, and of a rich glossy, raven blackness. Their limbs and figures are well proportioned, though not very large, and they have small neat hands and feet, the true imprints of nobility according to some people's silly ideas.

Though their features are perhaps not so regular as those of the Aryans, their expression of countenance is not at all unpleasing, and they are of a frank, genial, and humorous disposition. These are their chief characteristics of form and feature.

They are almost invariably Buddhists by religion, and believe that the happiest consummation to be wished for by the most devout amongst them, is the attainment of Nirvana, which means nothing short of utter annihilation of individuality. Some of the most primitive tribes of this Indo-Chinese race have scarcely any religion at all, while one of its most important branches, the Malays, are all Mohammedans.

More than one ethnologist have given the Malays a distinct place for themselves as a principal family of the human race; but they are really nothing else than Indo-Chinese modified by circumstances. The Malays in past ages were the people who dwelt near the sea; and people who live near the sea-coast are naturally greater rovers than the more bucolic inhabitants of the interior, even when belonging to the same race and country. And thus the Malays, above all other Asiatic tribes, became the greatest rovers and pirates in the East, extending their predatory operations all the way from India to China.

Their love of roaming brought them in contact with other roamers in the Mohammedans from Persia and Arabia, and even from Africa. The consequence was that the Malays adopted the religion of the strangers, and became a widely scattered Mohammedan race, for they practically inhabit the sea-coast of the greatest portion of the Malayan Archipelago as well as of the Malayan Peninsula, both of which derive their name from the Malay race.

Whatever may be the reason, they differ considerably from the rest of the Indo-Chinese in their disposition, for they are a quiet, demure people, who seldom laugh or smile. They have also the reputation of being treacherous and cruel, but modern opinions differ materially on this subject. The opinion has probably spread from people who came across Malay pirates, and of course pirates of all races are more cruel than ordinary people.

Granting the common origin of the Malays and the rest of the Indo-Chinese people, this gravity of their disposition becomes more curious when viewed from the standpoint of their religious faith. The Buddhist religion professed by the great majority of them, cannot on the face of it be a very cheery religion, seeing that final extinction is the great goal it places before its adherents ; for the human soul, wherever it is, must surely shrink back upon itself, and startle at destruction.

On the other hand, the Mohammedan creed, embraced by the Malay portion of the same race, promises ample rewards to the faithful in the way of dark-eyed *houris* and sensual pleasures, which, according to their standard, is the pinnacle of bliss. It might, therefore, be naturally expected that the Mohammedan Malays would be the more buoyant and joyous lot of the two, with such hopes in front of them, while the Buddhist looks forward to nothing more than perhaps a series of transmigrations followed by extinction. Yet, whatever is the reason, it is not so. For the Buddhist acts upon the principle of the ancient text of which he never heard—' Let us eat and drink, for to-morrow we shall die.'

That the Malays belong to the Indo-Chinese race there can be no possible doubt, though they may not be so pure as the rest of their racial brethren, because they must have mingled more with the other races with which they were continually coming in contact.

With this Malay exception, the Indo-Chinese are also noted for their free and easy habits of life, and they have the reputation of being profoundly lazy. The countries which these people inhabit are rich in the mere simple necessaries of life, like rice which constitutes the staple food of most Eastern nations ; and as long as the Indo-Chinese gets enough for to-day, he cares but little for to-morrow. This kind of temperament, though amiable enough in some respects, and exceedingly fortunate to the individual, is yet the curse of a race. And it will eventually lead to the total extinction of this interesting and agreeable people by their elder brothers, the Mongolians of China, with their thrift, their energy, and their power of multiplying wheresoever they may go. It is rather a pity that this genial people should be entirely supplanted by the heathen Chinese, but, as matters stand, this is certainly the outlook of the race in the near future.

Socially, the Indo-Chinese resemble their Mongolian *parti*-ancestors in having no caste of any kind ; and therein they differ widely from their other *parti*-ancestors, the miserable Aryans of India, whom the system of caste has made one of the most contemptible of races, and ever a weak prey to whomsoever chose to conquer and oppress them.

Hereditary rank is also rare among the Indo-Chinese peoples outside the reigning families, though personal distinctions are freely distributed among those who deserve them; as in Siam, for instance, where the grades of distinction from below upwards comprise *Nai, Khum, Luang, Phra, Phya, Chauphya*, and *Khorn*. The last is the highest title of all, and is included in the name of the present ruler of Siam, whose full designation will beat that of the Duke of York's son to fits, and moves as follows—Phra Bat Somdetch Phra Paramindr Maha Chulalongkorn Phra Chula-chom Klao-Chow Yu-Hua! Whether this want of hereditary titles can account altogether for the more open and frank disposition of the Indo-Chinese, it is not easy to say. But it certainly encourages the individual to think himself no better nor worse than his neighbours, and therefore to be less cringing and contemptible in his general behaviour; so that, taken as a race, they may be summarily described as equally poor (as regards mere treasure), equally lazy, and equally cheerful and happy, like the jolly beggars of the ancient legends.

This genial race is also noted for the entire freedom of the women, who indeed are sometimes perhaps a little too free, and who are usually more industrious and energetic in worldly affairs than the men themselves. Marriage among them is a looser knot than even with our American cousins, and morality in their eyes is not considered so great a virtue as among Europeans. But I don't care to tread on this delicate ground; and notwithstanding a few drawbacks of this nature, they are essentially a lively and genial people.

In minor matters of taste and so forth, the different nationalities of which this race is composed vary naturally among themselves. For instance, the Burmans, male and female, universally wear their hair very long, and they are very vain and proud of it, gathering it in great heavy queues on the top of their heads. Their next door neighbours, the Siamese, on the other hand, invariably crop their hair quite close, both male and female.

This close cropping of hair enables the observer, in a measure, to take better stock of the shape of their attic regions; and it often occurred to me that their skulls are rather deficient behind, as the backs of their heads go up almost straight from the napes of their necks, with scarcely any bulging backwards at all. In short, they do not possess much of an 'occipital protuberance,' a term made familiar to the public by the late Ardlamont murder trial. Phrenologists say that the intellectual organs of the brain are mostly placed towards the front of the head, while the baser passions are placed behind, as they ought to be, towards the 'occipital protuberance' just mentioned. But judging generally of the Siamese and Laós tribes, their heads look as if they had no baser passions at all, and as if they were therefore all intellect. Yet, in spite of all this, I am not at all sure that they have got entirely rid of the old leaven in the blood, while as regards their intellectual qualities, they have never yet done anything wherewith to startle the world.

Again, whereas the Burmese males are invariably and elaborately tattooed from the waist to the middle of the thighs, and the intervening Shans are tattooed still further down the legs, the Siamese and Cambodians do not go in for this kind of adornment at all, or only to a very trifling extent, as Europeans themselves occasionally do. The Burmese women, as I said, wear their hair long and generally have beautiful and abundant tresses, of which they are immensely vain, while their Siamese sisters always crop their hair very short indeed, in spite of the exhortation of St. Paul to the women in Corinth, but of which, however, the poor women of Siam have never heard.

So that as the masculine gender in Siam are mostly beardless, it is sometimes not altogether easy for the stranger to distinguish the men from the women, especially when they are young folk. I was struck with this resemblance more than once, and made one time a remark to that effect to the philosophic interpreter; when he replied that the Siamese women have the corners of their foreheads shaved; and, says he in addition, 'Can't you know them by the way they walk?' Perhaps I should, but I didn't. I have already remarked that the barber, instead of the tailor with us, makes the man in Eastern countries, when he cuts off the *Kohn-chúk* or top-knob at a certain age. But why, I then found that the barber makes the *women* also, by elaborating their graceful foreheads. Indeed, the barber with Eastern nations is a very necessary personage, and no wonder that he so frequently figures among the tales and legends of these very *barberous* countries.

Last of all, the Burmese, male and female, smoke, smoke, smoke from mere infancy, till they get so weak and old that they cannot suck any longer. And the size of the green cheroots that you see in Burmese ladies' pretty mouths quite puts you off, as they distort their ruby lips out of all reckoning. On the other hand, the Siamese and Cambodian women seldom, if ever, smoke. This is certainly a blessing.

But they are such slaves to the constant chewing of that horrid stuff *pansupari* (a mixture of areca nut, betel leaves, lime, garlic, and other horrors), that their mouths are always reeking with it; and, in combination with their somewhat prognathous jaws, it makes them look so slobbery, and their speech so blubbery, that they sometimes do not look at all particularly kissable. There they are for you, then, gentle reader; the Burmese maiden or *Minkalay*, with her long raven tresses, and with her big cheroot in her mouth; and on the other hand the Siamese damsel or *Phuing-sow*, short cropped, and chewing her large quid of *pansupari*. And so you may take your choice.

On first going up to Upper Burmah in 1885 people were much struck with this inveterate habit of smoking, even among women and children. Some time afterwards a newspaper, called the *Mandalay Herald*, was started up there, and, for the sake of amusement I made an effort in its pages to sing the praises of 'The Maid of Mandalay,' hoping thereby to wean her from her smoking habits! And as the reader may feel curious to know what sort of a girl she was, I may as well trot her out here again for his personal inspection, premising that the words *Nam le voo* mean 'I don't understand you,' and that they are the very first words the stranger learns after landing in the country.

THE MAID OF MANDALAY; OR, *NAM LE VOO.*

To the Editor of the MANDALAY HERALD.

SIR,—In your praiseworthy efforts to establish the first English newspaper in Mandalay, let me offer you what will probably be your first contribution from the Muses, and wish good luck to the 'Mandalay Herald' and the 'Mandalay Maid.'

> Oh, darling dear, I wish you would
>   Throw that cheroot far out of view,
> It surely cannot do you good,
>   And ill becomes your beauty too;
>   But all she said was: *Nam le voo.*
>
> Must I behold your ruby lip,
>   Created for caresses due,
> Which Mercury himself might sip,
>   So grossly marred with garlic hue?
>   But all she said was: *Nam le voo.*
>
> I rather like a pouting maid,
>   For maids were made to pout and pooh,
> But you your bonnie mouth degrade
>   By sucking of tobacco stew;
>   But all she said was: *Nam le voo.*
>
> Your slender fingers might entwine
>   Some fairer ware than what they do,
> Or might be even clasped in mine,
>   If that cigar afar you threw;
>   But all she said was: *Nam le voo.*
>
> I'd cease to puff that horrid fume,
>   If you were I and I were you,
> Nor ever more the weed consume,
>   But all my days the bane eschew
>   But all she said was: *Nam le voo.*
>
> As merry as the month of May,
>   And gentle in your manners too,
> A pity 'tis your winning way
>   Your hateful habit should undo;
>   But all she said was: *Nam le voo.*
>
> Oh, maiden mine, so fresh and fair,
>   With laughing eyes so bright and blue,
> And lovely locks of raven hair,
>   Your mouth is like a chimney flue;
>   But all she said was: *Nam le voo.*

I like to see your jaunty air,
   And kirtle shades of varied hue,
That whiles reveal the neatest pair
   Of ankles bare that e'er I knew;
   But all she said was: *Nam le voo.*

A pity that your fragrant breath,
   And lips designed to bill and coo,
You hopelessly should do to death,
   And spoil your favours how to woo;
   But all she said was: *Nam le voo.*

You are so *illigantly* bound,
   That from your neatly rounded queue,
A single fault can not be found,
   Down to your dainty sandal shoe;
   But all she said was: *Nam le voo.*

Oh, pray do not a bellows make
   Of that which was intended to
Be sweeter than the sweetest cake,
   Though even baked with fragrant dew;
   But all she said was: *Nam le voo.*

I spoke and spoke, and she replied,
   I made my bow and said adieu,
My pretty precepts she defied,
   But whiffed away that maiden true;
   And still she warbled: *Nam le voo.*

And thus the Maid of Mandalay,
   Trip, tripping on toe-tips withdrew,
And I resumed my weary way,
   Still thinking of her een sae blue,
   And her sweet charming *Nam le voo!*

Many years afterwards, when I reached Mandalay on this journey, I met the same paper still growing in wit and wisdom. And as the above song was the first effort of the Muses that ever appeared in its pages, I hope, when it becomes the real and only 'Herald of the Far East,' its proprietors will be pleased to place me on the Civil Pension List, as being their very own original first fiddle.

THE MAID OF MANDALAY.

To face page 282.

CHAPTER XXIX

> There *was* a low thief of Calcutta,
> Who saw a man open and shut a
> Rich cashbox, and said
> To himself, 'I'll be dead,
> If I don't steal the swag from the gudda.' [1]
> *Limerick Rhymes* (Oriental Edition).

Calcutta the mother of thieves—Trip to Darjeeling—A lost cashbox—Predicaments of penury—From blunder to blunder—My last rupee—My own master again—Recovery of cashbox, broken and robbed—Advice to intending travellers—The value of money—Lord Love *versus* Lord Lucre—Mount Everest in clouds—Beauty of Darjeeling scenery—Philosophical conclusions of 'Through the Buffer State.'

BUT I must now let the globe-trotters and the maids of Mandalay fight out their own battles, as I must be sailing from Rangoon, encounter heavy monsoon weather in the Bay of Bengal, and land at last in Calcutta.

O Calcutta, thou City of Palaces and Mother of Thieves! There were still some few days to spare after arrival here, and how could they be better spent than by paying a visit to Darjeeling, reputedly the grandest and most beautiful of hill stations throughout the whole of the Himalayan Range, and therefore probably throughout the whole world. After two or three days' stay at the Great Eastern Hotel, thither therefore I proceeded, but soon wished that I hadn't.

'See Darjeeling and die' is a very old phrase. 'See Naples and die' is another one. But there are so many of these places, the sight of which is said to be worth dying for, that I quite discredit the whole lot of them. I have seen both Darjeeling and Naples, and still hope to live a

---

[1] *Gudda* is Anglo-Indian slang for a gowk. Literally in Hindustani means—a moke.

few years longer, unconsumed by their overpowering splendour. To confess the honest truth, I would much prefer never to see any of them at all, than give up the ghost for such a silly reason. And I fancy that the inventors of these pretty phrases had not themselves died at the time, or they might have a different tale to tell. Now however, that they *have* died, and they *have* seen Darjeeling or Naples, what have they *now* to say on the subject?

I had no servants till I reached Rajputana in the north-west of India, while I was still in the far-away north-east of that extensive country. I was in plenty of time for the train at the Sealdah Station; and my luggage, as I thought, being all put into a certain compartment, I strolled up and down the platform till it was time for the train to start. It was early in June, just the very height of the season at Darjeeling, and so near the end of it that scarcely any people were going up then, as being too late. I was therefore, evidently, to be the only European traveller by this train; or at any rate the only one travelling with a first-class ticket, while there were no less than four different first-class compartments on the train.

Shortly, however, before the train was to start, some natives began to put the luggage of some other passenger into my compartment, and I mildly remonstrated with them, seeing there were so many other compartments empty. But they said they were told to put the luggage into this compartment, probably by the railway servants; and as I had no right to object, I said nothing more on the subject. This luggage got mixed with mine, but that is nothing unusual, and I never suspected any harm.

At last the other passenger and myself went into the train, which started immediately after. Chatting along after leaving Calcutta, I discovered that my companion was a railway engineer, and was one of the engineers of the railway over which we were just passing. He left the train at Naihati, the third or fourth station out of Calcutta, and just after the train had started again, I looked to see if my luggage was all right, and lo, to my horror, my cashbox was missing!

And then the whole affair flashed across me at once. The cashbox had never been put into the train, and while other compartments were empty, this passenger's luggage had been mixed up with mine to put me off the scent before starting. When taking my ticket at Sealdah I found that I was travelling with an excess of luggage, and on remarking that small hand-things like a cashbox were not generally weighed at stations, one of the European railway servants replied officiously that they weighed everything at Sealdah; and it is only to be hoped that these servants were as honest as they were officious.

I therefore took the cashbox off the scales, opened it in their presence, took out the rupee notes I wanted, and closed it again, never dreaming that it would not be placed in the compartment with the rest of the luggage. After missing the box I telegraphed from the next station to the station-master at Sealdah, asking him to send the box on to Darjeeling, and to wire to me to a certain station we would be reaching before crossing the Ganges. For I still hoped that the box had been left behind by mistake, and at any rate, though we had not gone far from Calcutta, I could not get a train back there for several hours. And so I thought that if the cashbox was stolen, it *was* stolen, and that nothing I could then do could prevent it. When the train reached the station where I expected a reply to my telegram, there was none, and this puzzled me still more.

There was no help for it but to keep on to Darjeeling, where I duly arrived with only a few rupees in the world, and without a soul there that I knew, while even the papers by which I could prove my identity were in that unfortunate box. When I realised the situation I telegraphed to my agents in Bombay not to cash any cheques in my name, as the cheque-book was in the box and might be used for evil purposes by the fraudulent thief. And yet when I reached Darjeeling, I again telegraphed to send myself some money, to relieve me from my unpleasant predicament.

I went to the principal hotel, but it was full till next day, when some visitor was leaving, and I would get his room. The manager perhaps might not have so readily promised if he knew that I was penniless. I therefore went into a boarding-house, and after I had got my luggage into my room, I told the landlord what had happened, as I knew it was different turning a man out of doors, and keeping him there when there already. But the landlord, who was a bluff German, good-naturedly took me on trust and made no objection whatever.

I telegraphed about my box again and again, till I was now left with the magnificent sum of two rupees to bring me to my destination, fifteen hundred miles away. For three days I waited for a telegram from my agents, but none came; and I was aware that mercantile firms are reluctant to give money on the authority of mere telegrams; and rightly so too, as anybody can send a telegram to anybody else, in anybody else's name; and had I not myself already warned them?

And so I jingled in my pocket the two rupees still left me with much appreciation. But as a last resource, I eventually used one of them in telegraphing in another direction altogether, in order to get enough cash to bring me back, as my leave was now nearly over. And so I was left with one rupee with which I could not jingle, as rupees prefer to jingle in company with others. 'Go now and be miserable,' I then thought to myself, 'for you are really and truly stranded.'

There are two telegraph offices at Darjeeling, one at the railway station, near where I was staying, and the other one in the Post-office, about three-quarters of a mile up the side of the mountain; and it was from the railway one that I was communicating. Just after sending away this last telegram it occurred to me to go up to the other office, and make further inquiries there. I did so, and found with a confused mixture of anger and pleasure that my agents had promptly replied after all, and that the money was lying there for the previous three days, while I was all the time fretting away for the want of it. The telegraph people did not know where I was living, did not think I had yet arrived, &c. &c.; and sure enough the telegraph clerk at the railway station did not make use of my address, as he said that he knew where I was living. The next day a similar sum arrived from the other quarter to which I had wired, and I was my own master once again.

This was the first time I had ever been stranded by robbery; and, indeed, I had seldom lost anything of value by thieves before this journey. But I had been put in a fix by money matters when travelling on two or three occasions before. Not because I am not a millionaire, nor ever hope to be; but because there is really no safeguarding against accidents like these when wandering about, as they may occur at any unexpected moment.

The reader, sitting cosily in an easy chair, scarcely knows the value of money, for it is only appreciated when it is wanted, and not forthcoming. And the traveller, even when rich, never knows when he and his precious money may be parted by accidents on land and sea, for there is no certain, sure, and safe way for guarding against them.

I once met two fair travellers stranded in far-away New Zealand, and waiting for remittances from home. Later on, on arrival at San Francisco, I found an old shipmate stranded there with his money stolen from him. I did what little I could to help him out of his difficulty; and some time afterwards, having exceeded my previous calculations, I was myself stranded in New York for want of money, and anxiously waiting a reply by cablegram to a letter I had written to London from New Orleans, for that purpose. Such are some of the troubles which the traveller is heir to, and which really give a certain amount of pleasure—when they are over.

So, gentle reader, if you are going to travel, please make up your mind before starting, that you *may* be stranded—any day. But by all means take due precautions, and take good care at any rate (I warn you from experience), to make yourself sure and certain—*that your cashbox is in your carriage before the train starts!*

Fortunately for me, most of the money I had brought with me had been already expended, though the loss of what still remained, as well as of my cheque-book, put me to great inconvenience at the time. But there were several things in the box besides the money, including a rather large collection of silver and copper coins, &c. &c., which I had gathered in various countries through which I had myself personally travelled, and various other nicknacks of no value to anyone whatever but myself. And I may state in passing that the box was afterwards found, broken open and damaged, and thrown into a corner of the Sealdah Station of Calcutta, with everything of value stolen out of it, and thereby proving that :—

> There *was* a low thief of Calcutta,
> Who saw a man open and shut a
> Rich cashbox, and said
> To himself 'I'll be dead,
> If I don't steal the swag from the gudda.'

And the box is now once more in my possession, as an old and valued companion, that has already travelled many a weary step with me on land and sea, and perhaps may do so even yet again.

It would have been a very different and serious matter with me if the box had been stolen in the wilds of Siam or Cambodia, with much of my work in front of me, and no funds to pay. And though one's purse or cashbox is avowedly 'trash,' according to Shakespeare, yet the thief who would have filched me of it then would have made me poor indeed. I had scarcely ever lost anything when travelling before. And this time I had gone through the wilds of Siam, Laös, and Kumēr, among tribes who had seldom or never seen a European before, and who could have easily robbed me of both life and property every time I laid myself down to sleep. But they never touched anything. Yet I was cruelly robbed twice in the so-called countries of law and order. Such, O Mrs. Grundy, are the blessings of thy vaunted civilisation!

It is in a predicament like this, as I said, that one realises the full value of money, and how much the monarch Mammon rules the world; for he is by far the greatest potentate on earth, to whom kings and lords must cringe and cower, and, as a matter of fact, if you watch them carefully, you will find that Lord Lucre pinches Lord Love by the nose, and leadeth him whithersoever he listeth, so earthly we are indeed, and so difficult it is to withstand the fascinating sheen of glittering gold.

Why, it spoils one's appreciation of even scenery itself to be looking at it through empty pockets; and I would much better have enjoyed the beauties of this the grandest portion of the whole Himalayan range, if that thief of Calcutta had not come across my path.

O Gold, how great is thy power! and O Virtue, how weak are thy walls to withstand his batteries! Why, Zeus himself, though the veritable 'boss' of the heathen Greek gods and armed with thunder, was yet quite unable to corrupt the virtuous Danae, till at last the shifty old rascal thought of converting himself into a shower of gold. And then, alas, alas!—there was no further resistance.

The best sight of Mount Everest, the highest mountain in the world (if Mount Hercules in New Guinea is only a myth), is obtained at a place some forty or fifty miles from Darjeeling, but I hadn't the means to go there, for penury represses the noblest rage, whatever philosophers may be pleased to say to the contrary.

When I got the needful at last, my time was nearly up, and I could only stay one more day on the bonnie, bonnie heights of Darjeeling. This I passed in climbing Jellapahar, a mountain top four miles away, where a view may be had of Mount Everest, though not such a good one as the one forty miles off. Some 'casual' living at the boarding-house went up with me, and we started in the very early morning, for on these misty mountain regions you are more likely to get a good view in the mornings than at any other time, as the atmosphere is likely to be less cloudy then. But we had only our labour for our pains, as we were not lucky enough to see the peak of Mount Everest after all, although we sat on our elevated summit for nearly an hour, to see if the clouds would disperse and pass away, but they wouldn't. On the contrary, it commenced to rain heavily, and we both came back drenched to the skin. This ended my wanderings, as on the next morning I was rushing back to duty as fast as the mountain train could carry me, which was only at the very modest rate of seven or eight miles an hour after all.

As a pure mountain scenery, lacking the additional charms of sea, lake, or river, the beauty of Darjeeling is probably unsurpassed by any other locality in the world, with such lofty mountains and deep-sinking valleys. Though our American cousins possess the longest rivers and the largest lakes, and though they have even higher railways than the one at Darjeeling, yet their mountains are beaten hollow by the Himalayan range. For even though I was not able to get a view of Mount Everest itself, yet I got several very good views of Kuchinjunga, the next highest mountain on the globe, only 1,000 feet lower than Mount Everest itself, and which I repeatedly observed from the top of Snow Hill in my days of small means.

There is scarcely anything on earth more calculated to stir the divinity within us than the sight of mighty mountains, covered with eternal snow. Yet when watching them on this occasion, I confess I sometimes found my mind rummaging among the contents of my lost cashbox, and breathing anathemas against the vile thief who had placed me in such an unpleasant position. So earthly in truth we are, that our own puny selves are more important personally to us than all the grandeur and glory of the whole universe; for the universe, without us, to us would be nothing. And with that very wise and philosophical remark, I may as well bring to a close this random narrative of THROUGH THE BUFFER STATE.

PRINTED BY
SPOTTISWOODE AND CO., NEW-STREET SQUARE
LONDON

www.ingramcontent.com/pod-product-compliance
Lightning Source LLC
Chambersburg PA
CBHW030013240426
43672CB00007B/934